HIKING APPALACHIAN TRAIL THROUGH GEORGIA, NORTH CAROLINA, AND TENNESSEE

THE MILE-BY-MILE GUIDE TO 471 MILES OF THE SOUTHERN REGION OF THE APPALACHIAN TRAIL

Joshua Niven and Amber Adams Niven

ESSEX, CONNECTICUT

FALCONGUIDES®

FalconGuides is an imprint of The Globe Pequot Publishing Group, Inc.
64 South Main Street
Essex, CT 06426
www.globepequot.com

Falcon and FalconGuides are registered trademarks and Make Adventure Your Story is a trademark of The Globe Pequot Publishing Group, Inc.

Copyright © 2026 The Globe Pequot Publishing Group, Inc.

Photos by Joshua Niven and Amber Adams Niven unless otherwise noted

Maps by The Globe Pequot Publishing Group, Inc.

All rights reserved. No part of this book may be reproduced in any form or by any electronic or mechanical means, including information storage and retrieval systems, without written permission from the publisher, except by a reviewer who may quote passages in a review.

British Library Cataloguing in Publication Information available

Library of Congress Cataloging-in-Publication Data
Names: Niven, Joshua author | Niven, Amber Adams author
Title: Hiking the Appalachian Trail through Georgia, North Carolina, and Tennessee : the mile-by-mile guide to 471 miles of the southern region the Appalachian Trail / Joshua Niven and Amber Adams Niven.
Other titles: Guide to the trail's greatest hikes
Description: Essex, Connecticut : FalconGuides, an imprint of The Globe Pequot Publishing Group, Inc, [2026] | Distributed by NATIONAL BOOK NETWORK. | Includes bibliographical references. | Summary: "Authors Joshua Niven and Amber Adams guide hikers across the best trails that the Appalachian Trail has to offer"— Provided by publisher.
Identifiers: LCCN 2025012525 (print) | LCCN 2025012526 (ebook) | ISBN 9781493087150 paper : acid-free paper | ISBN 9781493087167 epub
Subjects: LCSH: Hiking—Appalachian Trail—Guidebooks | Hiking—Appalachian Trail—Georgia—Guidebooks | Hiking—Appalachian Trail—North Carolina—Guidebooks | Hiking—Appalachian Trail—Tennessee—Guidebooks
Classification: LCC GV199.42.A68 N595 2026 (print) | LCC GV199.42.A68 (ebook) | DDC 796.510974—dc23/eng/20250801
LC record available at https://lccn.loc.gov/2025012525
LC ebook record available at https://lccn.loc.gov/2025012526

♾™ The paper used in this publication meets the minimum requirements of American National Standard for Information Sciences—Permanence of Paper for Printed Library Materials, ANSI/NISO Z39.48-1992.

The authors and The Globe Pequot Publishing Group, Inc., assume no liability for accidents happening to, or injuries sustained by, readers who engage in the activities described in this book.

CONTENTS

ACKNOWLEDGMENTS	vi
HOW TO USE THIS GUIDE	vii
LAND ACKNOWLEDGMENT	xiii
THE APPALACHIAN TRAIL	1
THE PEOPLE'S PATH	1
BIRTH OF THE APPALACHIAN MOUNTAINS	4
PLANTS OF SOUTHERN APPALACHIA	5
WILDLIFE OF SOUTHERN APPALACHIA	7
WEATHER IN SOUTHERN APPALACHIA: HIKING THROUGH THE SEASONS	9
AT CULTURE	11
HIKERS	12
SHELTERS, LEAN-TOS, AND HUTS	12
TRAIL MARKERS	13
TRAIL CLUBS AND VOLUNTEERS	14
TRAIL MAGIC AND ANGELS	16
TRAIL TOWNS	16
TRAIL TALK	17
BACKPACKING BASICS	18
EQUIPMENT: THE TEN ESSENTIALS	18
WHAT TO WEAR	18
WATER: MANAGEMENT AND TREATMENT	19
FOOD: WHAT TO EAT AND PROPER STORAGE	20
PLANNING AND LOGISTICS	21
OUTDOOR ETHICS	24

HIKES

Georgia   27

1: AT Approach Trail: Amicalola Falls to Springer Mountain   30
2: Springer Mountain to Woody Gap   38
3: Woody Gap to Neels Gap   45
4: Neels Gap to Tesnatee Gap   54
    Trail Town: Blairsville, Georgia   58
5: Tesnatee Gap to Unicoi Gap   59
    Trail Town: Helen, Georgia   64
6: Unicoi Gap to Dicks Creek Gap   65
    Trail Town: Hiawassee, Georgia   72
7: Dicks Creek Gap to Bly Gap   73

North Carolina and Tennessee   78

8: Bly Gap to Deep Gap (USFS 71)   82
9: Deep Gap (USFS 71) to Winding Stair Gap   86
    Trail Town: Franklin, North Carolina   93
10: Winding Stair Gap to Tellico Gap   94
11: Tellico Gap to Nantahala Outdoor Center   102
12: Nantahala Outdoor Center to Fontana Dam Visitor Center   107
    Trail Town: Fontana Dam, North Carolina   113
13: Fontana Dam Visitor Center to Newfound Gap   114
    Trail Town: Gatlinburg, Tennessee   126
14: Newfound Gap to Davenport Gap   127
15: Davenport Gap to Max Patch Road   135
16: Max Patch Road to Hot Springs   140
    Trail Town: Hot Springs, North Carolina   145
17: Hot Springs to Allen Gap   146
18: Allen Gap to Devil Fork Gap   154
19: Devil Fork Gap to Sams Gap   162
20: Sams Gap to Spivey Gap   166
21: Spivey Gap to Indian Grave Gap   172
    Trail Town: Erwin, Tennessee   178

22:	Indian Grave Gap to Iron Mountain Gap	179
23:	Iron Mountain Gap to Hughes Gap	184
24:	Hughes Gap to Carver's Gap	188
25:	Carver's Gap to US 19E	194
	Trail Town: Roan Mountain, Tennessee	203
26:	US 19E to Dennis Cove Road	204
27:	Dennis Cove Road to Wilbur Dam Road	210
28:	Wilbur Dam Road to TN 91	218
29:	TN 91 to Low Gap	224
30:	Low Gap to Damascus	228
	Trail Town: Damascus, Virginia	232

RESOURCES	233
APPALACHIAN TRAIL COMMUNITIES: CONNECTING TRAIL AND TOWN	234
GLOSSARY OF TRAIL TERMS	235
SOURCES	237
ABOUT THE AUTHORS	239

ACKNOWLEDGMENTS

We would like to extend our deepest gratitude to the dedicated individuals who helped make this guidebook as accurate and comprehensive as possible. A heartfelt thank you to Vic Hassler from the Tennessee Eastman Hiking Club, Paul Curtin from the Carolina Mountain Club, and Ashley Luke from the Georgia Mountain Hiking Club for their meticulous fact-checking and commitment to ensuring that all information is current and precise. And thanks to Ann Simonelli from the Appalachian Trail Conservancy for helping procure historical images that add depth and context to this guide. Your expertise and dedication to the hiking community are invaluable, and this guidebook is stronger because of you.

A special thanks to all the volunteers who spend countless hours maintaining the Appalachian Trail. Your hard work and devotion keep the trail safe, accessible, and beautiful for all who journey along it. This guidebook would not be needed without your commitment to preserving these cherished pathways.

A special thanks also to Grace Young for your unwavering support in caring for our kids and helping homeschool them while this project came to life. Your love, patience, and flexibility have made it possible for us to focus on our work, and for that we are forever grateful.

We would also like to express our sincere appreciation to our editor, David Legere, and everyone on the FalconGuides team for their hard work and passion in bringing this series to fruition. Your keen eyes, thoughtful insights, and steadfast dedication have shaped this book into what it is today.

Lastly, we want to extend our deepest gratitude to our parents for instilling in us a profound love for the natural world and for always encouraging our creative pursuits. Your support has been a constant source of inspiration.

To all of you, thank you. This guidebook wouldn't have been possible without your contributions and support.

HOW TO USE THIS GUIDE

This guidebook comprehensively covers every mile of the southern section of the Appalachian Trail (AT), beginning in the south at Amicalola Falls and concluding at Damascus, Virginia. Each of the thirty hikes is described as a south-to-north walk, but hikers are encouraged to explore the trails in the opposite direction as well, as some may be more suitable given the terrain.

RATING SYSTEM

We have rated each hike in this guidebook as easy, moderate, or strenuous to help you choose the right trail for your skill level and experience.

- **Easy:** These trails are mostly level with minimal inclines, making them suitable for anyone who enjoys a leisurely walk in the woods. They are ideal for beginners or those looking for a gentle outdoor experience.
- **Moderate:** These trails are great for novice hikers and typically involve some inclines and steeper sections. Expect a bit more challenge than easy hikes, but nothing too extreme.
- **Strenuous:** These hikes offer a significant challenge and are suited for experienced hikers. They often feature steep elevation gains, long distances, or technical terrain such as rock scrambling or river crossings.

It's important to remember that mileage on hiking trails can be deceptive. A mile on the Appalachian Trail is not the same as a mile on a road, and factors like terrain, weather, and trail conditions can make a trail feel more challenging than its mileage might suggest. We strive to provide detailed explanations for our difficulty ratings to help you better understand what to expect on each hike.

FINDING THE TRAILHEAD

In each hike section, we provide GPS coordinates to assist in locating and navigating to the trailhead. These coordinates can be entered into the search bar of a mapping program such as Google Maps or Gaia GPS to obtain driving directions.

KEY POINTS

The **"Key Points"** chart lists major landmarks along the trail, including shelters, campsites, water sources (denoted in blue), and vistas. Next to each landmark, you'll find the mileage markers for the section you are hiking. Additionally, to the right of each landmark, we have included the elevations and the distances from Springer Mountain, Georgia—the starting point of the southern Appalachian Trail—and from Damascus, Virginia—the endpoint of the southern Appalachian Trail.

A note on directions:
It's important to note that "north" and "south" on the AT are not always literal due to the trail's occasional veering east, west, or even southbound before resuming its general northward direction. For convenience, directions are oriented around the trail: Everything to your left will be referred to as "west" and everything to your right as "east." For example, a water source may be described as "50 yards east" of the trail, despite what your compass indicates. If compass directions are crucial, the guidebook will specify "compass-north," "compass-south," etc.

SIDEBARS

From time to time, we will pause to share and discuss fascinating facts about the Appalachian Trail and other interesting topics like plants, animals, historic towns, and colorful characters that once lived near the trail.

ABBREVIATIONS

Commonly used abbreviations in this book include:

AT: Appalachian Trail

ATC: Appalachian Trail Conservancy

CCC: Civilian Conservation Corps

CMC: Carolina Mountain Club

TEHCC: Tennessee Eastman Hiking & Canoeing Club

USFS: USDA Forest Service

Map Legend

Municipal

20	Interstate Highway
178	US Highway
107	State Road
263	Local/County Road
FR 356	Forest Road
= = = =	Unpaved Road
—+—+—	Railroad
— - - —	State Boundary

Trails

- - - - - -	Featured Trail
- - - - - -	Trail
———	Paved Trail

Water Features

- Body of Water
- Marsh
- River/Creek
- Intermittent Stream
- Waterfall
- Spring

Symbols

- Bench
- Bridge
- ▲ Backcountry Campground
- Boardwalk/Steps
- Boat Launch
- ■ Building/Point of Interest
- ▲ Campground
- Cliff
- Gate
- Lighthouse
- P Parking
- Pass
- ▲ Peak/Elevation
- Picnic Area
- Ranger Station/Park Office
- Restroom
- Scenic View
- Tower
- ○ Town
- 20 Trailhead
- ? Visitor/Information Center

Land Management

- National Park/Forest
- National Monument/Wilderness Area
- State/County Park

HURRICANE HELENE'S IMPACT ON THE SOUTHERN REGION OF THE APPALACHIAN TRAIL

In late September 2024, Hurricane Helene caused widespread destruction across Southern Appalachia, severely impacting parts of the Appalachian Trail and surrounding communities. Recovery efforts are ongoing, and while many sections have reopened, fallen trees and debris may still be present.

Storm-damaged areas are ever-changing. Consider the following when planning your hike:

- **Detours and closures.** Some areas may still have active detours in place. For example, the Chestoa River Bridge in Erwin, Tennessee, is currently being rebuilt after it was washed away in the flood. The detour adds 3.6 miles to the route and includes a ferry crossing over the river. Be aware that sections of trail may reopen and then close again without notice as conditions continue to change.
- **Possible hazards.** Dead trees continue to fall as they rot, and rain may cause landslides in areas lacking root systems. High winds and future storms will have a greater impact.
- **Exposed landscapes.** Significant tree loss has altered the landscape. Some areas lost up to 90 percent of tree coverage. Pack sun protection and extra layers.
- **High fire danger.** Storm debris fuels wildfires.
- **Trail towns.** Be sure to call ahead to check the hours of resupply and lodging establishments. Many trail towns, including Hot Springs, North Carolina, and Erwin, Tennessee, will continue to bear the scars of the storm. Please support these communities by showing patience and understanding during this rebuilding phase.

Damage on the Appalachian Trail in downtown Hot Springs, North Carolina, caused by Hurricane Helene, 2024

Damage on the Appalachian Trail near Hot Springs, North Carolina, caused by Hurricane Helene, 2024

The ATC estimates it will take years for the trail to return to pre-hurricane conditions and for the ecosystem to recover.

For up-to-date information, including closures and detours, visit appalachiantrail.org/helene.

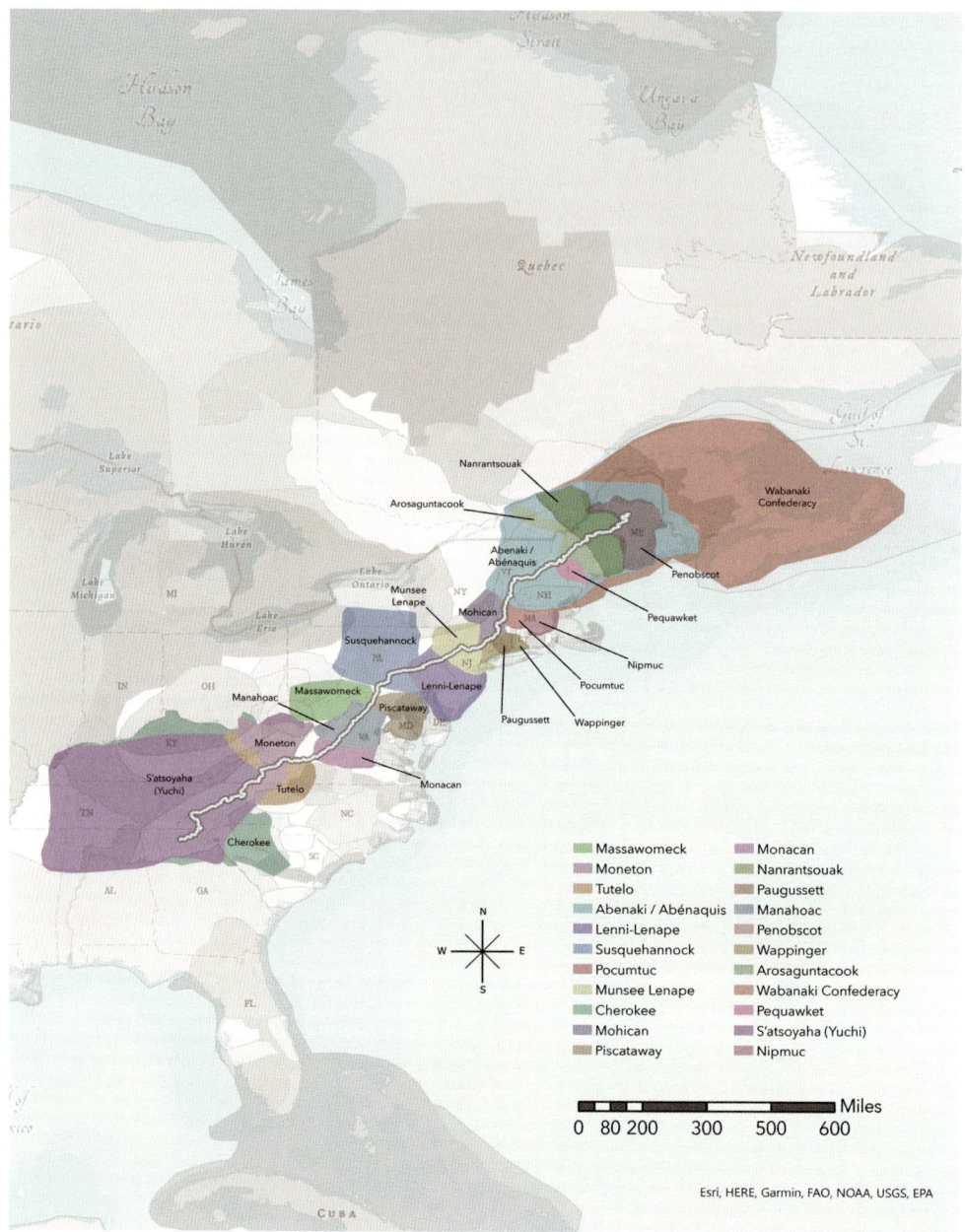

AT Native Lands territory map, originally created exclusively for the Appalachian Trail Conservancy by Mark Hylas

LAND ACKNOWLEDGMENT

When we walk on the Appalachian Trail, we are traversing Native Land—sacred spaces where the ancestors of our nation lived, worshipped, gave birth, built homes, hunted, and foraged. The AT traverses the traditional territories of twenty-two Native Nations, each with a rich history and deep connection to the land.

These indigenous communities were the original stewards of the Appalachian region long before European settlers arrived, and they were forcibly removed from their ancestral lands through brutal policies of displacement and dispossession. This separation from the land, one another, and their cultures was a profound loss, reshaping their histories and identities.

The map opposite illustrates the traditional territories of these Native Nations along the Appalachian Trail, including the current boundary of the Eastern Band of Cherokee Indians in western North Carolina. This map was created by Mark Hylas using spatial data from native-land.ca, a resource provided by the nonprofit organization Native Land Digital.

APPALACHIAN TRAIL OVERVIEW

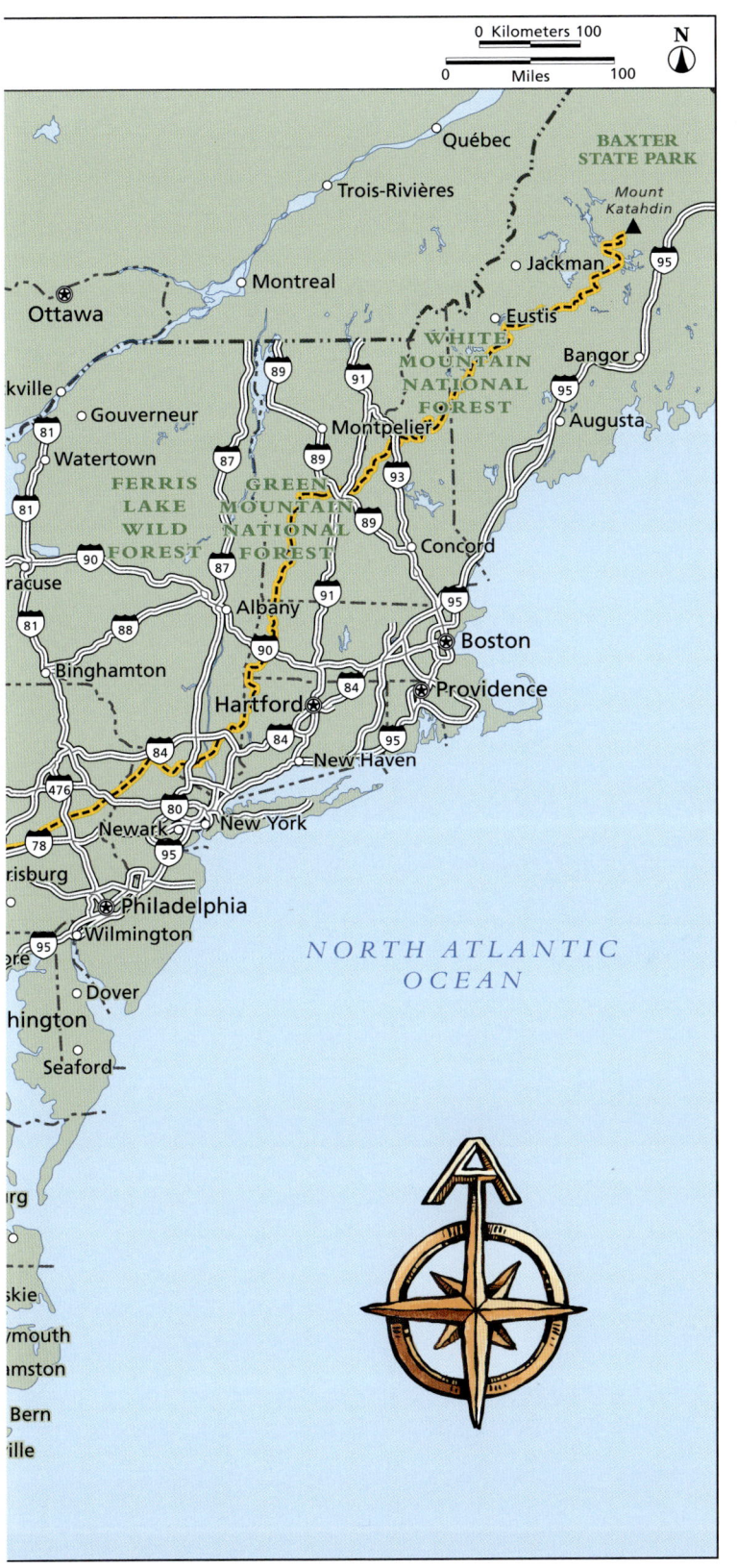

THE APPALACHIAN TRAIL
A FOOTPATH FOR THOSE WHO SEEK FELLOWSHIP WITH THE WILDERNESS

The Appalachian Trail, often called the "AT," is the longest hiking-only footpath in the world, extending more than 2,100 miles from Georgia to Maine. This remarkable trail offers a journey through diverse environments, from dense forests and scenic ridges to open pastures and charming small towns. Along the way it crosses fourteen states, traverses eight national forests, and passes through six other units of the National Park System. Each year, millions of people come to experience the AT, and thousands take on the challenge of hiking its full length. The Appalachian Trail Conservancy (ATC), with the mission to "protect, manage, and advocate for the trail," is responsible for maintaining and preserving this treasured trail in cooperative management with thirty designated trail clubs. The ATC envisions a future where "the Appalachian Trail and its surrounding landscape are protected forever for all to enjoy."

THE PEOPLE'S PATH

A realm and not a trail marks the full aim of our effort. The trail is but the entrance.

—Benton MacKaye

The history of the Appalachian Trail, affectionately known as "the people's path," is a remarkable tale of vision and perseverance. It began in the 1920s with Benton MacKaye's idea, which has endured wars, economic struggles, and political disputes to become the iconic trail we cherish today. Amid the uncertainty of post–World War I America, MacKaye, inspired by a hike in the Green Mountains, envisioned a trail stretching from New England to the South, creating a "forest path" and a series of wilderness camps. His vision, outlined in his 1921 essay "An Appalachian Trail: A Project in Regional Planning," sought to reconnect people with nature and provide a retreat from modern life's demands.

Thanks to the dedication of MacKaye, the crucial support of Myron Avery—who led the Appalachian Trail Conference from 1930 until his death in 1952—and countless volunteers, the AT was completed in 1937.

The establishment of the Appalachian Trail Conservancy in 1925 and the National Trails System Act of 1968 were pivotal for the trail's preservation and protection. Today, thousands of volunteers continue to uphold MacKaye's vision, ensuring the AT's longevity and accessibility.

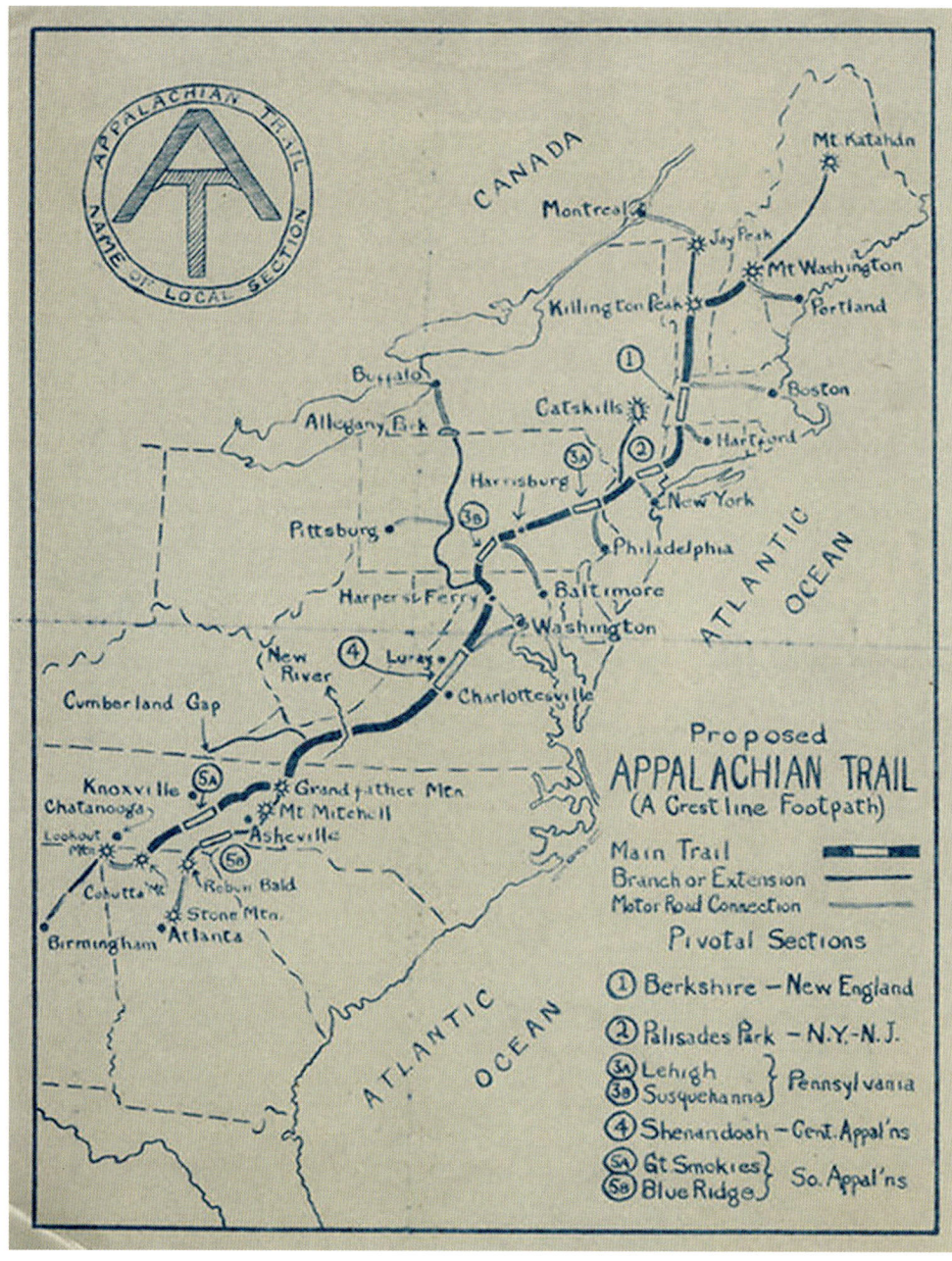

Proposed map of the AT, hand-drawn by Benton MacKaye, 1925; MacKaye Family Papers, Rauner Special Collections Library
COURTESY OF DARTMOUTH COLLEGE LIBRARY

Benton MacKaye and Myron Avery, 1931
COURTESY OF THE APPALACHIAN TRAIL CONSERVANCY ARCHIVES

For a deeper dive into this history, consider reading Thomas R. Johnson's *From Dream to Reality*, visiting the AT Museum at Pine Grove Furnace State Park in Pennsylvania, or exploring the Appalachian Trail Conservancy's website at appalachiantrail.org. For those interested in MacKaye himself, Larry Anderson's *Peculiar Work* offers a fascinating look at the man behind the trail.

DID YOU KNOW?
Myron Avery, a pivotal figure in the completion of the Appalachian Trail, was known for his meticulous attention to detail, especially when measuring the trail itself. He used a measuring wheel to personally survey the path, ensuring its accuracy and alignment. Rarely seen in photos without this iconic prop, his measuring wheel has become synonymous with his legacy. Today it is on display at the Appalachian Trail Museum in Pennsylvania, celebrating Avery's dedication and contributions that helped transform Benton MacKaye's vision into the beloved trail we cherish.

An illustration of Avery's wheel will accompany you throughout the book. Look for it beside the hike specs in each chapter!

A FOOTPATH FOR THOSE WHO SEEK FELLOWSHIP WITH THE WILDERNESS

Myron Avery with his measuring wheel and notebook
COURTESY OF THE APPALACHIAN TRAIL CONSERVANCY ARCHIVES

BIRTH OF THE APPALACHIAN MOUNTAINS
The mountains are the soul of a region. To understand the mountains is to know ourselves.

—Sandra H. B. Clark

Exploring the Appalachian Mountains is like stepping back in time to witness Earth's geological past. The faulted and folded sedimentary, igneous, and metamorphic rocks you see in the cliffs and ridges offer a window into the mountains' 480-million-year history. Starting in the Ordovician period, these rocks were uplifted and folded through a series of epic mountain-building events. Over eons, weathering and streams sculpted the peaks into the beautiful landscape we see today. Ice and water continued to shape the terrain, creating stunning features like gorges, ravines, and caverns. Along the Appalachian Trail, you can marvel at geological wonders like the Dragon's Tooth and Franconia Notch. For those eager to dive deeper into this rich geological history, Scott Weidensaul's *Mountains of the Heart* is a fantastic resource that explores the region's geology, ecology, and climate.

Benton MacKaye at an overlook in Tennessee, May 1934
COURTESY OF THE APPALACHIAN TRAIL CONSERVANCY ARCHIVES

PLANTS OF SOUTHERN APPALACHIA

Known as the "green tunnel," since most of it travels through dense tree coverage, the Appalachian Trail traverses a mountain region that was once covered entirely by forest. Evergreen trees such as pine, cedar, red spruce, and balsam fir grow in the lofty elevation, contrasting beautifully with the winter snowfalls. Common throughout the north are paper birch, sugar maple, and other hardwoods such as red oak, elm, and beech;

Bee balm near Big Firescald Knob, North Carolina

Chicken-of-the-woods mushroom (*Laetiporus sulphureus*)

farther south you will find hickory, poplar, walnut, hemlock, and more. Before they were destroyed by a blight fungus (*Cryphonectria parasitica*), American chestnut trees dominated the Eastern forests. Their towering height and large diameter placed them among northern giants like the redwood and sequoia. However, the American chestnut had far more to offer than its good looks. The trees were stain-resistant, rot-resistant, strong, and lightweight and produced a nut that was once a valuable cash crop for rural communities. People called them the "cradle to grave" trees for their myriad uses.

Redbud, hawthorn, dogwood, locust, and sourwood trees all produce beautiful blooms during different seasons. Adding to the botanical splendor are flowering and fruit-bearing shrubs like mountain laurel, flame azalea, and serviceberry. Mushrooms, ferns, and mosses flourish in moist and shaded areas created by the leafy canopy of the Southern mountains.

Wildflowers

Early spring brings forth bloodroot, trilliums, violets, trailing arbutus, chickweed, dwarf iris, bluets, wild geranium, jack-in-the-pulpit, Solomon's seal, Solomon's plume, lady's slipper, showy orchis, and many others. In summer, vines of fragrant honeysuckle and wild berries cover the hillsides while milkweed, jewelweed, echinacea, Turk's cap lily, and others bloom. Late summer and early fall introduce goldenrod, black-eyed Susan, false foxglove, and more warm splashes of color. The flora of the Appalachian Trail is truly wondrous all year round.

The Appalachian Trail is home to a vast and intricate array of plant life, with thousands of wildflowers and other species flourishing in this diverse ecosystem. To fully appreciate and understand the flora you encounter, we suggest picking up a recently updated field guide for trees, flowers, or fungi. Field guides are wonderful resources to help you learn about the plants you see along the way, as well as identify those to avoid, such as stinging nettle and poison ivy, which can both cause irritating skin rashes.

PLANTS TO AVOID

Stinging nettle is commonly found along the Appalachian Trail in wooded or shady environments. Typically growing 2 to 4 feet tall, it features heart-shaped leaves with jagged edges and tiny, stinging hairs that cover the entire plant. These hairs contain chemicals that cause a painful, stinging sensation and can lead to a red, itchy rash upon contact with the skin. Wear long sleeves and pants when hiking through areas where this plant might be present. If you do come into contact with it, wash the affected area with soap and water and apply a soothing lotion or antihistamine cream to reduce irritation.

Poison ivy is another common plant along the Appalachian Trail. It is recognized by its "leaves of three" arrangement, where each leaf has three leaflets. The plant can appear as a vine, a shrub, or a ground cover and can have shiny green leaves that turn red in the fall. Contact with poison ivy can cause a painful, itchy rash due to an oil called urushiol, which is present in all parts of the plant. Learn to recognize the plant's distinctive leaf pattern and avoid touching it. If you come into contact with poison ivy, wash the area with soap and water as soon as possible and apply over-the-counter treatments to relieve the itching.

WILDLIFE OF SOUTHERN APPALACHIA

The mountains and rivers of Southern Appalachia support a wide variety of animal life. The black bear, white-tailed deer, fox, raccoon, and many other small creatures are common throughout the region. You are likely to see mice in the shelters at night, while spotting squirrels and chipmunks during the day. Some animals you may not see, but you will undoubtedly hear. The barred, eastern screech and great-horned owls will hoot as you drift off in your shelter at night while coyotes howl in the distant woods. Hundreds of birds patrol the trail from the canopy above while filling the air with cheerful melodies. The region is home to numerous species of fish, amphibians, and insects.

Bears

Black bears are common throughout the Appalachian Trail corridor. While they are typically shy creatures, encountering one can be an exciting experience during your hike. Certain circumstances may lead to human-bear conflicts, posing risks to both humans and bears. With much of the AT being prime black bear habitat and bear populations increasing across AT states, bear encounters are on the rise. Proper preparation before hitting the trail not only enhances your hiking experience but also

Black bear on the Appalachian Trail, 2013 thru-hike

> **BE BEAR AWARE**
>
> By following these guidelines and respecting bear habitat, hikers can safely enjoy the wilderness along the Appalachian Trail while minimizing potential conflicts with bears.
>
> - **Research the area.** Learn which areas have had recent bear activity by visiting the ATC's trail update page (appalachiantrail.org/trail-updates). Use extra caution when stopping where there have been recent bear reports. Some trail sections can be closed temporarily to overnight stays due to adverse bear encounters, so be prepared to walk through.
> - **Stay alert.** Be aware of your surroundings while hiking, especially in areas with signs of bear activity such as scat, tracks, clawed trees, or overturned rocks. Make noise periodically to avoid startling bears, particularly in dense vegetation or near streams. Don't become complacent. Just because there have been no reports of bear activity in the area does not mean that bears are not present. All it takes is one improperly hung food bag to change a bear's habits.
> - **Store food properly.** Keep food and scented items securely stored in bear-resistant containers, or hang them at least 10 feet off the ground and 4 feet away from tree trunks. Some shelters and campsites may have bear cables or boxes for protected food storage. (Please take all food and trash with you.)
> - **Keep a clean camp.** Dispose of food scraps, wrappers, and garbage in bear-proof containers or bear-resistant bags. Clean cooking utensils and avoid sleeping in clothes worn while cooking.
> - **Educate yourself on bear behavior.** Learning bear behavior can help you identify threatening bear body language. For more in-depth information, visit BearWise.org.
> - **Respect bear space.** Keep a safe distance if you encounter a bear. Do not approach or feed the animal. Back away slowly if you see cubs—mother bears can be protective.
> - **Know how to react.** If a bear approaches, stand your ground, wave your arms, and make loud noises to intimidate it. Never run or climb trees, actions that may trigger a chase response.
> - **Carry bear spray.** Consider carrying bear spray in areas with high bear activity. Familiarize yourself with its proper use before hitting the trail.

contributes to the safety of hikers and bears alike. See "Be Bear Aware" for essential guidelines on hiking in bear country.

Ticks

Ticks are one creature to be extra mindful of while hiking. Deer tick and many other tick species can be found in every one of the fourteen states the Appalachian Trail passes through, commonly seen in areas under 2,000- to 2,500-foot elevation. Hikers are at risk of contracting tick-borne diseases, especially Lyme disease, carried by the deer tick. Symptoms of Lyme disease can include fever, chills, headache, fatigue, muscle and joint aches, and swollen lymph nodes. One of the hallmark signs is a distinctive "bull's-eye" rash, though not everyone with Lyme disease develops this rash. If you experience any of these symptoms or find a tick bite on you, consult a health-care professional as soon as possible to discuss potential testing and treatment.

According to the ATC, the highest incidence of Lyme disease has been reported on the trail from Virginia to Vermont, May through July. They recommend checking these body parts frequently when hiking in tick-infested areas: under the arms, in and around the ears, inside the belly button, back of the knees, in and around the hair, between the legs, and around the waist. Consider protecting yourself from bites by treating your clothes with permethrin, a pesticide spray that kills ticks on contact.

WEATHER IN SOUTHERN APPALACHIA: HIKING THROUGH THE SEASONS

Daytime temperatures in spring are warm with cool evenings, creating an ideal environment for flowering shrubs and flowing waterfalls. Springs and water sources are most reliable during this season.

Summer in this region can be uncomfortably hot and humid. Even with higher elevations and ample tree cover, hikers may feel overheated and sticky. High humidity, haze, and dense leaf cover can limit long-range vistas. The term "temperate rain forest" becomes more meaningful and appreciated during the summer months.

Fall showcases the vibrant hues of broadleaf deciduous trees, offering a stunning display of autumn colors. The air is cooler and crisper, providing excellent visibility for long-range views. However, waterfalls may not be as impressive, and springs become less reliable.

Winters in the Southern Appalachians vary from cool and damp to cold and severe, often accompanied by deep snow after major storms. Despite the lower elevation and southern latitude of this area, these mountains can bring potentially dangerous weather, emphasizing the unpredictable nature of mountainous terrain.

Hazards and Safety

Backcountry weather conditions change constantly. It's your responsibility to be prepared, especially for the unexpected. Always be aware of weather forecasts, and research trail closures. Some places on the AT require you to ford rivers that can be waist-high. Take extra precaution during lightning events and after heavy rainfall. Trail updates, such as road closures, shelter closures, special regulations, bear activity, and more can be found on the Appalachian Trail Conservancy's website.

Hypothermia

You can get hypothermia in summer. The weather does not have to be extremely cold for a person to be at risk of hypothermia. It can take just one slip into a cold river, pack and all, with no way to get warm for things to turn dangerous. A cold rain and wind can be a lethal combination, causing body temperatures to drop deceptively low. Wear proper clothing, stay hydrated, and hike smart. Don't hike in the rain if you don't have to, use "camp shoes" for river crossings, and listen to your body.

Dehydration

To stay hydrated on the trail, drink water consistently throughout your hike, not just when you're thirsty. Bring enough water and a method for refilling or purifying more as necessary. Avoid dehydrating drinks like alcohol and caffeine, and be mindful of signs of dehydration, such as feeling dizzy or seeing dark urine. Staying well-hydrated is essential for keeping your energy up and ensuring a safe and enjoyable hiking experience!

Wildfires

High fire danger: Wildfire risk is extremely high in areas damaged by Hurricane Helene. Downed trees in the storm's wake create ideal fuel for rapidly spreading fires. The ATC strongly urges hikers to refrain from building campfires between Davenport Gap and the New River at Damascus, Virginia (NOBO mile 239.4 to 471.0), regardless of official burn bans.

It's crucial to plan and prepare accordingly. Stay informed by checking updates from official agencies, parks, and local news services to identify restricted areas or potential closures. Additionally, monitor predictions for future conditions during your hike, as increasing and shifting winds can rapidly alter circumstances within 24 hours or less. Stay updated on closures, burn bans, and other alerts via the Appalachian Trail Conservancy's trail update page (appalachiantrail.org/trail-updates). You can also access current wildfire and air quality maps through the Gaia GPS mobile app or their website (gaiagps.com).

To help prevent wildfires, adhere to these fire-building guidelines:

- Utilize existing fire rings.
- Only burn dead and down wood no thicker than your wrist.
- Ensure that all wood is burned down to ash.
- Completely extinguish and cool down all fires before departing the area.

AT CULTURE

There are proper ways of doing things in the backcountry, and being respectful is one of the most important. Our trail etiquette is centered on this idea. You'll hear it often, find it in trail registers, and may even say it to others: "Hike your own hike" (HYOH). This saying has become an outdoor pledge among backpackers, meaning do what's best for you and avoid telling others how to hike. Your pace, direction, gear, or hiking companions don't matter as long as you're true to your way and kind to others. If safety stands as our paramount value in the outdoors, kindness undoubtedly claims the second spot. While hiking your own hike, remember to extend kindness to your fellow hikers and the trail itself. Simple things like making room for others in shelters, being quiet after dark, and smiling make all the difference.

Bryan Anderson, Jarred Douglas, and Joshua Niven on Big Firescald Knob

> **DID YOU KNOW?**
> Many hikers mistakenly believe that biodegradable soaps or camp suds are safe to use directly in the water. However, these products are designed to break down in the soil before reaching the watershed. The life in mountain streams is often very delicate, and even small changes in water quality can have significant impacts. The best Leave No Trace practice is to gather water and wash dishes, clothes, and yourself away from the water source. Learn more about how to recreate responsibly in our Outdoor Ethics section.

HIKERS

The term "thru-hiker" describes anyone who has hiked (or is attempting to hike) the entire Appalachian Trail in a continuous journey or within a single year. Thru-hikers represent a large portion of hikers who set out to experience the AT. Each year, more than 3,000 thru-hikers register with the ATC, but only a quarter finishes. "Section-hikers" take their time and piece together the entire trail over the years. "Flip-floppers" are hikers who walk the trail in discontinuous sections. Many choose this approach to avoid crowds or extreme weather and, in some cases, for logistical planning purposes. "Day hikers" are anyone who goes out for a single day, usually with a small pack for food, water, and rain gear.

Each hike description will begin with the hiker symbol you see above.

SHELTERS, LEAN-TOS, AND HUTS

There are more than 270 strategically placed backcountry shelters along the trail, with an average distance of about 8 miles between them. The range varies from 5 to 15 miles and can be up to 30 miles when there's a town with lodging in between. Most shelters, sometimes called "lean-tos," feature an overhanging roof and three walls, accommodating six to eight hikers. However, each shelter is unique, varying in construction materials, design, and location. Some are built of wood, others of stone, and they may have lofts, bunks, or a single wooden floor. Some sit directly on the AT, while others are down a spur trail.

Shelters operate on a first-come, first-served basis for backpackers, with the exception of shelters in Great Smoky Mountains National Park, where reservations are required. Visit https://smokiespermits.nps.gov to reserve a site up to a month in advance. While many shelters are near a creek or spring, not all are, emphasizing the importance of planning ahead. Some have food storage systems for bear protection, but it's advised to always bring a personal food storage container and rope for safe hanging. Be sure you know how to properly hang a food bag (see page 20).

These structures offer more than just shelter from weather; they also act as meeting points for hikers, contributing to the unique experience of the AT while minimizing environmental impact. They have become a crucial aspect of trail life. However, it's essential to note that shelters may become crowded, have mice, and pose a risk of exposing hikers to viruses, particularly in high-use areas. Most shelters along the trail are free to use, but a few require a small fee. This is particularly true for shelters in the Smokies and some farther north, where an on-site caretaker may be present to collect the fee.

Jarred Douglas at Roan High Knob Shelter, 2013 thru-hike

TRAIL MARKERS

The Appalachian Trail is marked with white paint strips 2 inches wide and 6 inches long, referred to as "blazes," or "the white blaze." Most commonly painted on trees, rocks, and posts, they're also found on guardrails, street lights—and the bottom of the ferry canoe in Maine. Blue blazes mark side trails that lead to water sources, shelters, camping, and views. According to the National Park Service, there are approximately 165,000 such blazes along the Appalachian Trail.

Double blazes serve as signals for a change in direction or an upcoming obscure turn. In some instances, the upper blaze may be offset, indicating the change in direction. Keep an eye out for a turn in the direction of the upper blaze whenever you encounter these "kick-over" blazes.

AT blaze, Max Patch, North Carolina, 2023

AT CULTURE 13

Double blaze on the AT near Firescald Knob, 2021

When the trail is above tree line, posts with painted blazes or piles of rocks called cairns are used to identify the route.

If you have gone a few hundred yards without seeing a trail marker, stop and retrace your steps until you locate one. Distance between blazes varies, so be sure you haven't missed a turn. When your map or guidebook indicates one route and the blazes show another, the ATC recommends that you follow the blazes.

TRAIL CLUBS AND VOLUNTEERS

As we look back on a century of progress since MacKaye's original proposal in 1921, we can appreciate the collective effort that has maintained and expanded the Appalachian Trail. Today, thousands of volunteers contribute countless hours to keep the AT safe and accessible. They manage everything from clearing obstructions and refreshing the white blazes to maintaining shelters and addressing erosion.

If you're passionate about hiking and the great outdoors, there's no better way to give back than by getting involved with your local Appalachian Trail club. Each of these dedicated organizations relies heavily on volunteers to help with the myriad tasks necessary for trail upkeep and environmental conservation. Whether you're interested in trail maintenance, building and repairing shelters, or participating in conservation projects, your local club offers numerous ways for you to contribute. Volunteering not only helps

Hard hat and hazel hoe at Carolina Mountain Club workday, June 1, 2024

Volunteers working at a Carolina Mountain Club workday, June 1, 2024

keep the trail in excellent condition but also connects you with a community of like-minded outdoor enthusiasts. By joining a trail club like the Georgia Appalachian Trail Club, Carolina Mountain Club, Nantahala Hiking Club, Smoky Mountains Hiking Club, or Tennessee Eastman Hiking & Canoeing Club, you can participate in trail "work days," educational programs, and special events that support the Appalachian Trail's preservation. Every hour you volunteer makes a tangible difference, helping maintain the trail's beauty and accessibility for hikers and preserving its natural environment for future generations. Reach out to these clubs to learn about upcoming opportunities and to find out how you can make a meaningful impact on this beloved national treasure. See page 233 for trail club contact info.

Paul Curtin, CMC AT supervisor, at a Carolina Mountain Club workday, June 1, 2024

Trail angel and creator of the AT yearbook, Mathew Odie Norman, giving his annual speech after the Appalachian Trail Days parade in Damascus, Virginia, 2024

TRAIL MAGIC AND ANGELS

Trail magic refers to the unexpected acts of kindness, including food, drinks, and services, that AT hikers often experience on the trail. This magic tends to happen at just the right time, like finding a cooler of ice-cold beverages on a scorching day when water is scarce. Trail magic sometimes takes the form of a ride into town or the opportunity to camp on a welcoming lawn. Those who perform these random acts of kindness are known as trail angels. Every AT hiker has a trail magic story and an angel to thank. The generosity surrounding the Appalachian Trail is a testament to the goodness of humanity.

TRAIL TOWNS

The AT is designed to offer long-distance hikers periodic access to towns for resupply, rest, and mail pickups. Some of the finest examples include Hot Springs, North Carolina, and Damascus, Virginia, as well as Hanover, New Hampshire, and Monson, Maine, farther up the trail. In these towns, hikers are warmly welcomed, with local businesses and residents catering to their needs and offering affordable lodging options. These trail towns not only serve as hospitable waysides but also provide hikers contact with the culture of the place, deepening their hiking experience.

Hikers will find numerous access points for resupply and other services along the Appalachian Trail. However, it's worth noting that there are currently more than fifty-five towns along the trail corridor that hold special recognition in the A.T. Community program, led by the ATC. These designated towns and cities serve as invaluable resources for all trail users, offering food, supplies, shuttle services, medical facilities, laundry facilities, recreational opportunities, historical sites, volunteer programs, and much more. Hikers can engage in special events, plan their AT adventures, and explore the diverse offerings of these communities, all while contributing to their economies and supporting trail preservation efforts.

We've featured several well-loved trail towns in this guide. For a complete list of designated towns and counties, see "Appalachian Trail Communities: Connecting Trail and Town."

TRAIL TALK

Some terms used by long-distance hikers might be confusing to non-hikers. Common sayings like "Hike your own hike" or "The trail provides" are easy to understand, but when you hear words like "aqua-blazing," "Nero," or "tramily," you might wonder what these hikers are talking about. Don't worry, though, learning the creative trail lingo doesn't take long once you're in the woods. In the meantime, you can check the glossary at the back of the book for commonly used terms and phrases. Next time you're gathered around the campfire with fellow hikers, pay attention to new words and phrases—it's an ever-evolving language.

Appalachian Trail Days parade in Damascus, Virginia, 2024

BACKPACKING BASICS

EQUIPMENT: THE TEN ESSENTIALS

Joshua Niven's pack during 2013 thru-hike

Proper equipment is paramount in the outdoors. You never know what could happen, so it's always best to be prepared. Get in the habit of packing these essentials to ensure that you are prepared for the unexpected. Of course the longer your hike is, the more equipment you will need. Seasonality also plays a role in determining what kind of gear and how much is necessary. For example, if you are hiking in winter, microspikes might be an essential piece of gear. If you are hiking somewhere buggy in summer, you might consider a bug net. If you are new to hiking, talk with your local outfitters to find out more about gear that will fit your personal needs.

Here are the essentials we recommend for overnighting in the backcountry:

1. Food and water
2. Appropriate clothing
3. First-aid kit
4. Knife
5. Fire-making supplies—matches, lighter, tinder
6. Headlamp or flashlight
7. Navigation equipment—map, compass or GPS unit
8. Tent, tarp, or other form of shelter
9. Sleeping bag
10. Cooking system

WHAT TO WEAR

What you wear outdoors significantly impacts your experience. Your clothing should be breathable, moisture-wicking, non-bulky, and warm when necessary. Pay close attention to the materials, fit, and comfort. Even if you're just heading out for a day, unforeseen events can occur in the wilderness; it's wise to be prepared with extra items.

Shirts, pants, and base layers. Popular fabric choices among hikers include wool, fleece, polyester, nylon, and silk. The time of year you are hiking will determine what material will best fit your needs. Typically, when hiking the AT you will want lightweight base layers that have wicking capabilities and fit so that they don't cause chafing. Mid layers need to be insulating, and your outermost layer needs to be both windproof and waterproof or water resistant at the very least. Pants should be durable enough to sustain bramble snags but allow for good range of motion.

Rain gear. Get yourself a good jacket and rain pants; and while we're at it, don't forget about a pack cover. Think water resistant or waterproof but breathable! There's nothing more unpleasant than hiking in the middle of a summer thunderstorm with a jacket that doesn't let the sweat out! Trust us; we've been there.

Warm jacket. We recommend a puffy insulated jacket that is filled with down or a synthetic blend. A fleece jacket works great too. Just make sure you have some type of mid layer option every time you go into the woods.

Socks and shoes. Pay special attention to what you put on your feet. You want to be sure you have the right support, protection, and traction. It doesn't really matter if you opt for traditional boots or trail runners; just be sure your feet are comfortable and there is enough room to allow for mild swelling. Socks can be thick, thin, low, or tall depending on the weather. Just be sure they are breathable and able to wick moisture away from your skin. Also make certain they are high enough to avoid blisters on your heel. Always bring extra socks! Always!

Accessories. Other things you might need to complete your hiker ensemble include a bug net, gaiters, gloves, a large brimmed hat, sunglasses, and a bandana or buff.

WATER: MANAGEMENT AND TREATMENT

Water management is paramount for thru-hikers on the Appalachian Trail. Thankfully, water sources like springs, streams, ponds, and lakes are abundant along the trail, often encountered daily. Shelters and campsites are typically situated near water sources. However, it's essential to remain vigilant, as sources may dry up during droughts. Keep an eye out for alerts from local rangers and trail clubs regarding low water levels. You can check droughtmonitor.unl.edu for current drought conditions, but always be prepared for potential shortages and avoid relying solely on external updates.

The amount of water hikers carry depends on the availability of water sources. Typically, hikers carry between 1 and 2 liters. New hikers may need more water initially until they adjust. Thru-hikers often experience dehydration due to strenuous activity, so it's vital to drink regularly, even if you're not thirsty. Aim to drink 12 to 16 ounces at each water stop to stay hydrated and avoid overburdening yourself with excess weight from carrying too much water.

There's always a risk of contamination with backcountry water sources. While the water on the AT usually isn't teeming with parasites, viruses and microscopic organisms can still be present. Giardia is a common concern, causing severe nausea and diarrhea. It's strongly advised that all hikers carry a water treatment method, such as a filter or chemical treatment, to stay safe. These methods are effective and more convenient than boiling water. It's better to draw water from a flowing source than from still water. Still water is more prone to stagnation and thus likely to harbor parasites that cause waterborne illnesses.

Water sources are denoted in blue on the Key Points chart included with each hike.

Tucker Adams enjoying lunch on top of Moxie Bald Mountain, 2014

FOOD: WHAT TO EAT AND PROPER STORAGE

Make sure to pack enough food to replenish your energy during and after hiking. Prioritize packable, nutrient-dense, ready-to-eat, and lightweight options. Popular choices include instant rice and beans, lentils, instant pasta, instant mashed potatoes, nuts, nut butter, hard cheeses, dried fruit, tortillas, jerky, tuna, energy bars, oatmeal, and freeze-dried meals. Salt, pepper, and other spices can make all the difference.

Food Storage Requirements

AT visitors must store food and scented items properly. This includes using solid, non-pliable bear-resistant canisters or USFS-provided storage devices (lockers, cables, or poles) or properly hanging your food. Food storage in tents and shelters is not permitted.

- **Bear canisters:** Canisters must be stored at least 70 adult paces (about 200 feet) from campsites. The ATC recommends bear canisters as the most effective and flexible storage method along the trail.
- **Soft-sided bags:** If using bags like Ursacks, they must be hung at least 70 adult paces (about 200 feet) from campsites. Hang them 6 feet from the tree trunk, 6 feet below the branch, and 12 feet above the ground.

Special Regulations

- **Georgia:** Hard-sided bear canisters are required between Jarrard Gap and Neels Gap from March 1 to June 1.
- **Great Smoky Mountains National Park:** Use food storage cables for food, trash, and scented items. Bear canisters can be hung on these cables, but do not tie ropes directly to the canisters.

For more details on US Forest Service regulations for storing food on the AT, visit Appalachian Trail Food Storage Order: nps.gov/grsm/learn/nature/black-bears.htm. For Great Smoky Mountains guidelines, visit nps.gov/grsm/learn/nature/black-bears.htm.

PLANNING AND LOGISTICS

Wilderness Permits

The Appalachian Trail is free for everyone to enjoy. No fees or permits are required to simply walk the trail. However, a few places along the AT require permits to stay overnight in shelters or campsites, including the Great Smoky Mountains and Shenandoah National Parks. You can obtain any necessary permits or learn more about where you need to register by visiting NPS.org.

To help prevent overcrowding on the trail and at shelters, consider registering your hike with the ATC at https://atcamp.org. Keep in mind that this is not a reservation but simply a system to improve everyone's experience on the AT.

Trail Conditions

Always stay up to date on current trail conditions. Trail closures, fire bans, camping regulations, and other updates may impact your hike. Be sure to check for advisories and updates in the area you plan on hiking before heading out on your trip. Visit appalachiantrail.org/home/explore-the-trail/trail-updates for the latest information. Also watch for posted notices at the trailhead.

Transportation

There are many shuttle and taxi services available along the Appalachian Trail. We've provided a few options throughout the book, but for the most accurate and up-to-date transportation information, contact a local outfitter. You can also check out the forums on whiteblaze.net or Appalachian Trail Facebook Groups for ride-sharing opportunities and to connect with other hikers.

Mail Drops

If you'll be out on the Appalachian Trail for an extended period, you might choose to manage food, gear, and personal items through "mail drops"—prepacked resupply packages that you mail to yourself at designated locations along the trail. You can send these packages to a post office or to a trail-friendly business such as an outfitter, hotel, or hostel. Many of these businesses offer package-receiving services for free, with a purchase, or for a small fee, and they often have longer hours than post offices, which is useful for planning your drop. When labeling your package, be sure to use your real name (not your trail name) and bring a photo ID to retrieve it. Follow these guidelines for labeling your package:

Addressing a post office:

Jane Doe
C/O General Delivery
Post Office Address
[City, State, Zip code]

Please hold for AT hiker. ETA May 16, 2025.

Addressing a business:

John Doe
C/O Business Name
Business Address
[City, State, Zip code]

Please hold for AT hiker. ETA May 16, 2025.

Technology

Many hikers today are using apps such as FarOut and Gaia GPS for backcountry navigation. While these apps and other forms of tech can be convenient, it's best to have a backup plan such as a reliable guidebook or map and compass, as glitches are always to be expected with technology. You could lose cell service, the app could crash, or your phone could die. Don't become overly reliant on technology. While the Appalachian Trail is well marked, it's always best to be prepared. You don't want to be stuck guessing where the next water source is.

Hiking with Dogs

You can bring your canine companion with you as you hike the southern Appalachian Trail except for the section through Great Smoky Mountains National Park, where dogs are prohibited. Be sure to keep them on a leash, and don't forget to bring them water.

Mundo in Grayson Highlands State Park

Hiking with Kids

Including young hikers in your adventure can be highly rewarding and create valuable bonding experiences. When planning, consider the child's age, fitness level, and interests. Choose a time when they have the most energy; morning is typically best for children. Start small and gradually progress to longer hikes.

Be sure to pack extra snacks, water, sun protection, and first-aid materials and dress them properly. Prepare yourself mentally for taking many breaks along the way. Make the journey fun by incorporating storytelling and games such as scavenger hunts and identifying plants, animals, and rocks together. Most important, teach them about safety and trail etiquette. Be extra cautious near cliffs and bodies of water.

Amber, Indie, and River Niven on Max Patch, North Carolina

Some kid-friendly sections in the Southern Appalachians include Amicalola Falls, Kuwohi, Max Patch, Laurel Falls, and Roan Highlands.

Kids hiking on Max Patch, North Carolina

OUTDOOR ETHICS

The seven principles outlined below are part of the Leave No Trace initiative. These simple practices help preserve natural environments like the Appalachian Trail. While the steps are easy to learn, it takes a devoted hiker to adhere to them. However, if we all do our part to minimize our impact, the AT will remain beautiful and protected for future generations to enjoy.

Plan ahead and prepare:

1. Know the regulations and special concerns for the area you'll visit.
2. Prepare for extreme weather, hazards, and emergencies.
3. Schedule your trip to avoid times of high use.
4. Visit in small groups when possible. Consider splitting larger groups into smaller groups.
5. Repackage food to minimize waste.
6. Use a map and compass to eliminate the use of marking paint, rock cairns, or flagging.

Travel and camp on durable surfaces:

1. Durable surfaces include established trails and campsites, rock, gravel, dry grasses, or snow.
2. Protect riparian areas by camping at least 200 feet from lakes and streams.
3. Good campsites are found, not made. Altering a site is not necessary.

Dispose of waste properly:

1. Pack it in, pack it out. Inspect your campsite and rest areas for trash or spilled foods. Pack out all trash, leftover food, and litter.
2. Deposit solid human waste in catholes dug 6 to 8 inches deep at least 200 feet from water, camp, and trails. Cover and disguise the cathole when finished.
3. Pack out toilet paper and hygiene products.
4. To wash yourself or your dishes, carry water 200 feet away from streams or lakes and use small amounts of biodegradable soap. Scatter strained dishwater.

Leave what you find:

1. Preserve the past: Examine but do not touch cultural or historic structures and artifacts.
2. Leave rocks, plants, and other natural objects as you find them.
3. Avoid introducing or transporting non-native species.
4. Do not build structures, furniture, or dig trenches.

Minimize campfire impacts:

1. Campfires can cause lasting impacts to the backcountry. Use a lightweight stove for cooking and a candle lantern for light.
2. Where fires are permitted, use established fire rings, fire pans, or mound fires.
3. Keep fires small. Use only sticks from the ground that can be broken by hand.
4. Burn all wood and coals to ash, put out campfires completely, then scatter cool ashes.

Respect wildlife:

1. Observe wildlife from a distance. Do not follow or approach them.
2. Never feed animals. Feeding wildlife damages their health, alters natural behaviors, and exposes them to predators and other dangers.
3. Protect wildlife and your food by storing rations and trash securely.
4. Control pets at all times, or leave them at home.
5. Avoid wildlife during sensitive times: mating, nesting, raising young, or winter.

Be considerate of other visitors:

1. Respect other visitors and protect the quality of their experience.
2. Be courteous. Yield to other users on the trail.
3. Step to the downhill side of the trail when encountering pack stock.
4. Take breaks and camp away from trails and other visitors.
5. Let nature's sounds prevail. Avoid loud voices and noises.

Hike Your Own Hike

In the backcountry, respect and proper behavior are crucial. The core of trail etiquette is summed up in the motto "Hike your own hike" (HYOH), which you may hear or see written in trail registers. This principle encourages you to follow your own path while respecting others' choices, whether it's their pace, route, gear, or companions. While hiking your own hike, be considerate of fellow hikers and the trail itself. Small gestures such as making room in shelters, keeping quiet after dark, and offering a smile can make a big difference.

Blood Mountain view from above shelter, Mile 28.9

GEORGIA

The Appalachian Trail in Georgia winds through the beautiful Chattahoochee–Oconee National Forest, covering more than 78 miles along the Blue Ridge Mountains. This part of the AT mainly sticks to ridges between 3,000 and 3,500 feet in elevation, with some climbs reaching more than 4,400 feet, offering hikers both challenges and stunning views from rocky outcrops and wide-open summits.

This section of the trail is a great place for wildlife lovers, with chances to see wild turkeys, white-tailed deer, black bears, and a variety of songbirds. Thanks to high rainfall, the area is lush with a mix of wildflowers, rhododendrons, mountain laurel, hardwoods, and tall pines. Spring is especially beautiful as the trail bursts into color from wildflowers like native trilliums.

Amicalola Falls State Park is a popular spot for hikers starting their journey in early March, when it hosts the northbound thru-hiker kickoff event. March and April are peak times on the trail, with lots of thru-hikers, spring breakers, and school groups on the move. Be ready for possible snow and chilly temperatures from November to April, especially at higher elevations.

Some must-see highlights along the trail include Springer Mountain, the southern end of the AT; Blood Mountain, the highest peak in Georgia; and Mountain Crossings at Walasi-Yi, a historic building from 1937 built by the Civilian Conservation Corps (CCC). More than half this section of the trail is in designated wilderness areas, offering a peaceful escape from the bustle of roads and campsites. Plus, there are more than 50 miles of side trails for exploring amazing views, diverse wildlife, and historical sites. At Bly Gap, the trail crosses into North Carolina and continues into the Nantahala National Forest.

GEORGIA OVERVIEW

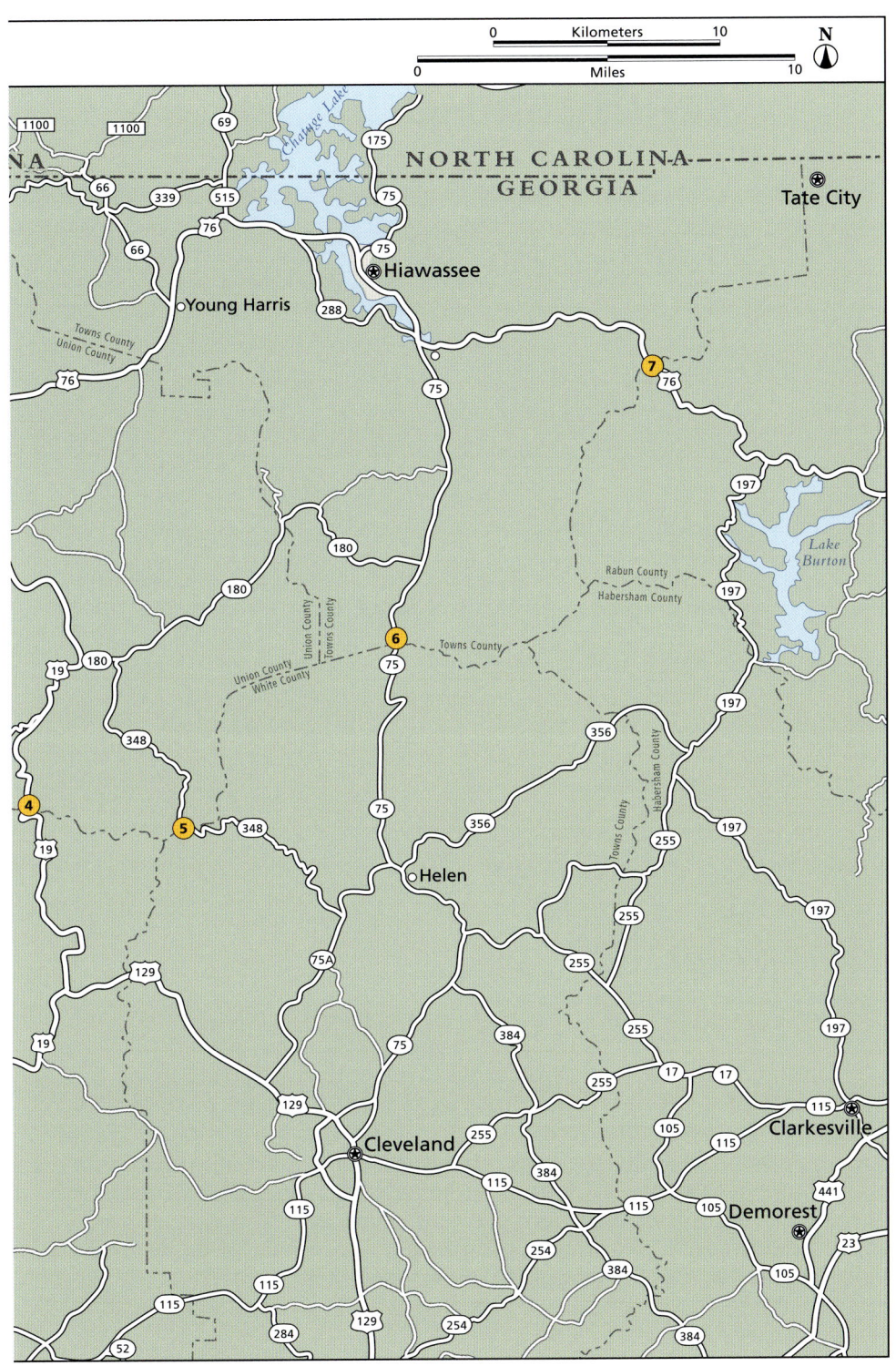

1 AT APPROACH TRAIL: AMICALOLA FALLS TO SPRINGER MOUNTAIN

Amicalola Arch, start of the AT Approach Trail

Start your journey at the **Amicalola Arch**, often referred to as the "gateway to the Appalachian Trail," and trek 8.8 miles to reach the summit of **Springer Mountain**. A short walk from the trailhead leads you to **Amicalola Falls**, a major attraction for waterfall enthusiasts, boasting a height of 729 feet with seven cascades. Upon reaching the summit of Springer Mountain, you encounter the first (or last, depending on your direction) white blaze, two iconic plaques, and a trail register—and enjoy delightful views on clear days.

Distance: 8.8 miles
Difficulty: Moderate due to elevation gain and *a lot* of steps
Nearest town: Dahlonega, Georgia (22 miles south of trailhead)

Water availability: Plan accordingly. The springs in this stretch are known to be unreliable.
Trailhead GPS: 34.5576892 / -84.2489898

FINDING THE TRAILHEAD

Park your car or arrange a shuttle to Amicalola Falls State Park (418 Amicalola Falls Lodge Rd., Dawsonville, GA 30534). Walk behind the visitor center to locate the trailhead at the stone archway.

Good to know:
- Amicalola Falls State Park charges a nominal parking fee. Hikers may use designated long-term parking for two weeks or more, even for the duration of a thru-hike if space is available (fee). Register at the visitor center.
- Springer Mountain is well-known and well-loved, so be prepared to pass plenty of fellow hikers. If you are staying overnight, bring a tent in case the shelter is full.
- Springer Mountain shelter is located just under 0.5 mile north of Springer Mountain.
- West Ridge Falls Access Trail (0.3 mile) is a wheelchair-accessible trail to the bottom of Amicalola Falls. Great views.
- This trail is pet friendly. Just make sure pets are on a leash.

Nearby accommodations:

Amicalola Falls Lodge is located inside Amicalola Falls State Park and offers luxury rooms as well as private cabins and campsites. The park's Maple Restaurant is known for its spectacular views and Sunday brunch buffet. For reservations visit www.amicalolafallslodge.com or call (706) 344-1500.

Len Foote Hike Inn is open year-round and only accessible by foot. The inn offers 20 private rooms and includes a hearty family-style breakfast and dinner. Guests are encouraged to check in at the Amicalola Falls Visitor Center by 2 p.m. in order to arrive early enough for 5 p.m. orientation and 6 p.m. dinner. Call (800) 581-8032 or visit hike-inn.com to make a reservation.

THE HIKE

The AT Approach Trail is marked with blue blazes and starts at the Amicalola Falls State Park Visitor Center under the iconic stone archway. Even though these 8.8 miles are not officially part of the Appalachian Trail, we find them valuable to include in this guidebook. The picturesque approach trail is popular among the AT community and is the ATC's recommended route to begin a northbound thru-hike. It's an excellent choice for a moderately challenging day hike or a perfect overnight trip for beginners who prefer shorter distances.

Max Epperson Shelter, behind the visitor center

Midway Amicalola Falls view

Upper section, Amicalola Falls

> **DID YOU KNOW?**
> According to the Georgia Appalachian Trail Club, 25–30 percent of those who start their thru-hike in Georgia do not complete the first 30 miles of the trail. This failure is typically attributed to insufficient preparation or a lack of awareness about the rigorous demands of a 2,190+-mile trek.

Departing from the stone archway, walk about 0.5 mile to a serene reflection pond where you might encounter people fishing or children playing, especially in warmer months. After circling the pond, the trail steadily ascends towards the base of Amicalola Falls, showcasing a vibrant display of spring wildflowers like trillium, wild geranium, and bloodroot. Along the way, a majestic poplar tree stands tall on your left before you reach the falls. Take a moment to capture a photo and catch your breath before facing the challenge of climbing the 604-step staircase. Reaching the summit of the impressive waterfall will leave your heart racing, but the breathtaking views make it all worthwhile.

Following the white blaze, you'll pass a trail to Len Foote Hike Inn, marked with lime-green blazes, at 1.3 miles. The terrain then continues to roll through dense forest for approximately 7 miles until you reach the iconic, if somewhat understated, 3,782-foot peak of Springer Mountain. At 5.4 miles, just south of Woody Knob, you'll reach

Springer Mountain plaque, Mile 0. The plaque reads: "Appalachian Trail, Maine to Georgia, a footpath for those who seek fellowship with the wilderness."

Appalachian Trail Southern Terminus plaque, Mile 0

another side trail to Len Foote Hike Inn. Continue to Nimblewill Gap, at 6 miles. From there, Black Gap Shelter is about 1.5 miles away. The shelter is equipped with a privy, bear box, bear cables, a water source, and plenty of flat ground for tenting, making it an ideal starting point for a longer hike. For slower hikers, summiting Springer Mountain, less than 2 miles farther, can be a great way to kick off an AT adventure.

From Black Gap Shelter, hike uphill for 1.5 miles to reach Springer Mountain. On clear days you can catch a glimpse of the Blue Ridge Mountains, yet it's not the view that makes Springer Mountain significant. Rather, it's the official starting (or ending) point of the Appalachian Trail. At the peak, two plaques and a trail register located inside a small vault await hikers, inviting you to sign your name and become part of the Appalachian Trail community. The area offers numerous campsites and a shelter near the summit. For your return journey, either retrace your steps to Amicalola or continue northbound to explore more of the Appalachian Trail.

DID YOU KNOW?

Each year, the Georgia Appalachian Trail Club (GATC), in partnership with Amicalola Falls State Park, hosts A.T. Gateways, formerly known as the Appalachian Trail Kick Off (ATKO), the first weekend in March. Activities, programs, and demonstrations are held at both the lodge and the visitor center throughout the weekend. Many hikers register and start their thru-hike this weekend.

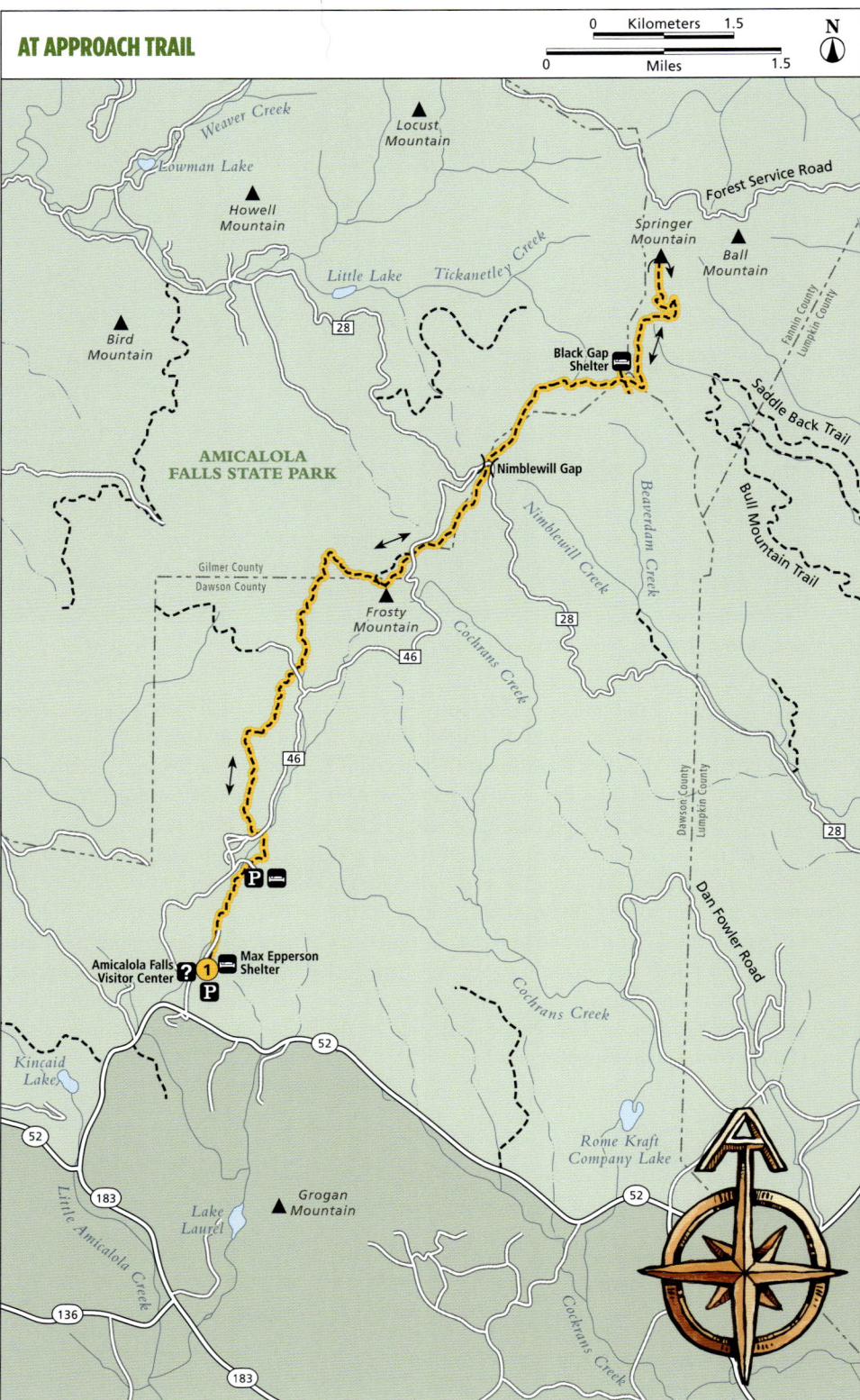

KEY POINTS

SECTION	LANDMARK	ELEVATION (FEET)	MILES FROM SPRINGER MOUNTAIN
0.0	Amicalola Falls State Park Visitor Center (archway behind visitor center), water	1,800	8.8
0.1	Max Epperson Shelter (thru-hiker use only), water	1,858	8.7
0.4	Reflection pond at base of falls	2,003	8.4
0.7	Staircase—604 stairs to top of falls	2,216	8.1
1.1	Parking, side trail to lodge	2,639	7.6
1.3	Trail to Len Foote Hike Inn (5.0 miles east), blazed lime green	2,656	7.5
1.5	USFS 46	2,584	7.3
4.0	Frosty Mountain, unreliable spring 0.2 mile east	3,384	4.8
5.7	Woody Knob	3,406	3.1
6.0	Nimblewill Gap, USFS 28	3,100	2.8
7.3	Black Gap Shelter 0.1 mile west; spring on opposite side of AT, 0.1 mile east	3,300	1.5
8.8	Springer Mountain	3,782	0.0

2 SPRINGER MOUNTAIN TO WOODY GAP

Foggy view from the summit of Springer Mountain, Mile 0

Embark from Springer Mountain, the southern terminus of the Appalachian Trail, and trek 20 miles beneath a lush canopy, crossing streams and passing four shelters. Enjoy amazing views at **Ramrock Mountain** before descending into **Woody Gap**.

Distance: 20.5 miles
Difficulty: Moderate due to steep ascents and descents
Nearest town: Dahlonega and Suches, Georgia

Water Availability: There are plentiful good water sources throughout this stretch.
Trailhead GPS: 34.637467 / -84.195317 (Springer Mountain parking area)

FINDING THE TRAILHEAD

 Head west from Amicalola Falls State Park on GA 52 for 13.6 miles to Roy Road. Turn right and continue 9.5 miles to the second stop sign; bear right and head 2.3 miles to Mount Pleasant Church on the left. Turn right across from the church on unpaved USFS 42, which crosses the AT in 6.6 miles. Walk 0.9 mile south to the Springer summit plaque.

Good to know: As the southern terminus of the Appalachian Trail is accessible solely on foot, hikers need to walk south 0.9 mile from the Springer Mountain parking lot to reach the summit before retracing their steps to continue trekking north.

Special considerations: It's important to be aware that both the eastern and western routes to the USFS 42 parking lot pose hazards in winter, and conditions can worsen during the spring freeze-thaw cycle, especially in wet years. Deep ruts may develop on both routes, creating risky conditions, particularly for passenger cars.

Alternatively, hikers have the option of taking the 8.8-mile Approach Trail, starting at Amicalola Falls State Park. The Appalachian Trail Conservancy (ATC) encourages all thru-hikers to choose the Approach Trail to reduce car traffic on the dirt road and avoid congestion in the parking lot. Many Appalachian Trail enthusiasts consider the Approach Trail a meaningful initiation into their journey, embracing the additional challenge.

Trail register box and the AT's first (or last) blaze, Mile 0

THE HIKE

Once you arrive at the southern terminus of the Appalachian Trail, whether you hiked the short distance from the USFS 42 parking lot or took the AT Approach Trail, you will find the first white blaze (or the last depending on your point of view), two iconic plaques and a trail register. On clear days you can catch a view of the Blue Ridge Mountains from Springer's peak.

Departing Springer Mountain, you officially begin your Appalachian Trail hike. The AT follows its iconic, white blaze through the southern Appalachian Mountains, meandering through north Georgia's rolling Blue Ridge Mountains and exploring some of this state's most beautiful terrain. Wildlife frequents the trail, including wild turkey, black bear, white-tailed deer, wild hog, and songbirds. Throughout the state, wildflowers, rhododendron, mountain laurel, leafy hardwoods, and towering pines line the trail in an ever-changing mix of plant and tree life. In springtime the trail explodes in an array of wildflowers, including beautiful native trilliums.

At 0.2 mile a side trail to the east leads to Springer Mountain Shelter, situated at 3,700 feet in elevation. Established tent sites are located nearby. The trail descends into Big Stamp Gap, where parking is available along USFS 42.

Benton MacKaye Trail sign, Mile 2.0

Long Creek Falls in the snow, Mile 5.2

At 2.8 miles, reach the turnoff for Stover Creek Shelter, located near a stream and equipped with a bear box and bear cables. Continuing to Three Forks, where three streams merge to form Noontootla Creek, the trail begins a gradual ascent. Although Three Forks was once a popular camping spot and some trail guides still reference campsites there, camping is now prohibited due to severe impact on the riparian zone. At 5.2 miles, a few campsites are available along Long Creek; a blue-blazed trail leads to scenic Long Creek Falls.

At 7.4 miles, a spur trail leads west to Hawk Mountain campsites, featuring tent pads, a privy, bear boxes, and water. Hawk Mountain Shelter is a little over 0.5 mile north of the campsite, with a privy and water down the path behind the shelter. Limited camping is available outside the shelter, and bear boxes with bear cables are provided. At 8.6 miles, the AT drops steeply into Hightower Gap, where it intersects with gravel USFS Roads 42 and 69. From there, the trail climbs sharply and undulates for nearly two miles before descending into Horse Gap at 10.5 miles.

From Horse Gap, the hike begins a challenging ascent of Sassafras Mountain in the next mile, passing towering rock outcrops and navigating sharp switchbacks. Sassafras Mountain summit offers resting spots in the densely tree-covered environment, although warm-weather views are scarce in this leafy hardwood forest. Leaving Sassafras, the trail descends 440 feet over the next mile, reaching Cooper Gap at 12.2 miles, where gravel USFS 42 intersects. The AT rolls over Justus Mountain, leading to the Gooch Mountain Shelter junction at 15.7 miles. The shelter's privy is located to the left on a short side trail, accompanied by an excellent spring and nearby tent sites. Bear boxes and cables are also provided.

Parking lot at Woody Gap, Mile 20.6

At 16.9 miles, arrive at Gooch Gap, where USFS 42 leads 2.7 miles west to Suches, Georgia. Water is available north of the road down a marked trail east of the AT.

From Gooch Gap, the trail continues to roll for a mile, passing through Liss Gap before reaching Ramrock Mountain. The actual summit, a brief stroll through a campsite clearing, offers some of the most expansive views in this section of the Appalachian Trail. While the summit itself is wooded, the exposed rock outcrops on Ramrock Mountain provide delightful vistas of the lush green mountains to the south. During spring, blaze-orange azaleas bloom here.

DID YOU KNOW?
Mount Oglethorpe, at the southernmost edge of the Blue Ridge Mountains, was originally designated as the southern terminus of the Appalachian Trail. However, in 1958 increasing development around Mount Oglethorpe prompted the relocation of the trail's southern terminus to Springer Mountain, where it remains today.

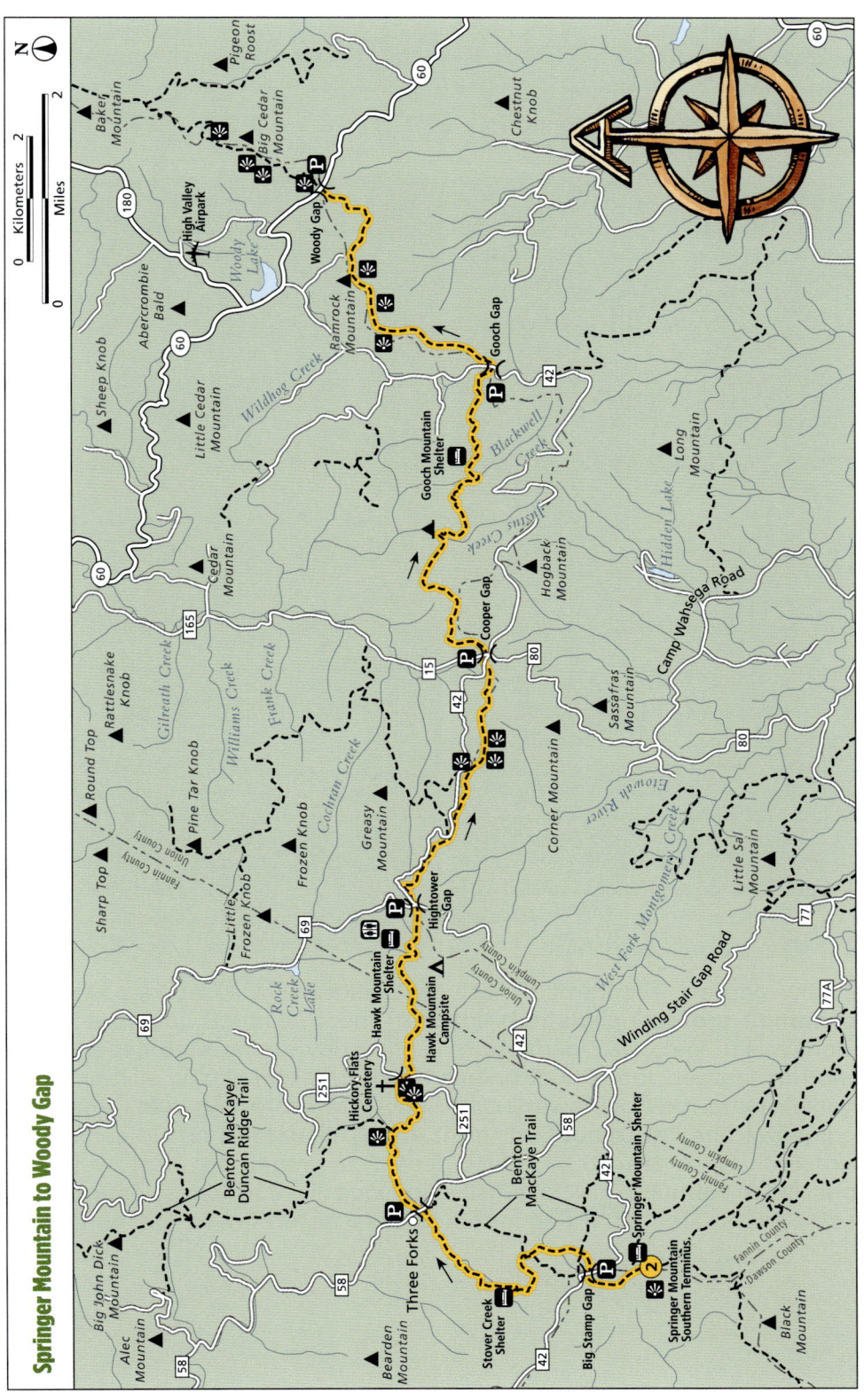

Woody Gap is less than 2 miles from Ramrock Mountain and where this hike concludes. Parking, water, and vault toilets are available at Woody Gap. Suches, Georgia, is 2 miles to the left on GA 60.

KEY POINTS

SECTION	LANDMARK	ELEVATION (FEET)	MILES FROM SPRINGER MOUNTAIN	MILES FROM DAMASCUS
0.0	Springer Mountain (southern terminus). The trail register is located on the back of the rock with the plaque.	3,782	0.0	471.0
0.2	Springer Mountain Shelter, spring	3,720	0.2	470.8
1.0	Big Stamp Gap, USFS 42 (parking)	3,350	1.0	470.0
2.0	Benton MacKaye Trail	3,280	2.0	469.0
2.8	Stover Creek Shelter 0.1 mile east, spring	2,817	2.8	468.2
4.2	Benton MacKaye/Duncan Ridge Trail to east	2,564	4.2	465.8
4.3	Three Forks, USFS 58, footbridge over creek	2,530	4.3	466.7
5.2	Benton MacKaye/Duncan Ridge Trail to west, trail to Long Creek Falls	2,800	5.2	465.8
6.2	Dirt road, 0.2 mile west to Hickory Flats Cemetery	3,070	6.2	457.5
7.4	Hawk Mountain Campsite 0.2 mile west	3,220	7.4	468.8
8.1	Hawk Mountain Shelter 0.2 mile west, water source 0.1 behind shelter	3,193	8.1	462.9
8.6	Hightower Gap, junction USFS 42/69 (parking)	2,854	8.6	462.4
12.2	Cooper Gap, USFS 15, 42, 80 (parking)	2,820	12.2	458.8
13.5	Dirt road	2,750	13.5	457.5
14.2	Justus Creek. Use designated campsites north of creek, to the west.	2,517	14.2	456.8
15.5	Blackwell Creek	2,649	15.5	455.5
15.7	Gooch Mountain Shelter with piped spring 0.1 mile west	2,780	15.7	455.3
16.9	Gooch Gap, USFS 42 (parking), water north of road on east side of AT	3,836	16.9	454.1
18.6	Ramrock Mountain	3,257	18.6	452.4
20.5	Woody Gap, GA 60 (parking), spring north of road 0.2 west	3,202	20.5	450.5

3 WOODY GAP TO NEELS GAP

Blood Mountain Wilderness entrance sign at Woody Gap, Mile 20.6

The highlight of this section is **Blood Mountain**, the highest peak in Georgia, reaching an elevation of 4,461 feet. Its name is thought to have roots in a historic battle between the Creek and Cherokee Indians, resulting in the land being stained red, giving the peak its distinctive name.

While the hike is challenging, the effort is well rewarded with breathtaking views, particularly during the fall, when the vibrant hues of hardwood trees paint a stunning landscape. Spring transforms the rolling terrain into a canvas of abundant wildflowers. Trilliums and other native wildflowers cover the landscape with vibrant blooms as they stretch to reach sunlight from beneath the forest canopy. Other notable landmarks include **Preaching Rock**, which boasts amazing views from rock ledges, and **Blood Mountain Shelter**, the oldest-standing shelter in the state.

Distance: 10.8 miles
Difficulty: Strenuous due to steep ascents and descents
Nearest town: Suches, Georgia (2.0 miles west of Woody Gap)

Water availability: There are numerous good water sources located at the southern end of this hike. The ones toward the north are unreliable. Plan accordingly.
Trailhead GPS: 34.6777 / -84.0000

Good to know: The large parking area offers a restroom and picnic tables. Check for camping and fire restrictions. Increased bear activity has often been reported in this area. Bear canisters are required from March 1 to June 1 at many of the campsites.

View from Preaching Rock, Mile 21.6

THE HIKE

This hike begins in the heart of the Chattahoochee–Oconee National Forest at Woody Gap, located along paved GA 60. Access the trail from the side of the street where the restrooms are situated and begin trekking north. Following the distinctive white blaze, enjoy a gentle incline for the first mile as you make your way to Preaching Rock, which offers incredible views of the surrounding mountains, the town of Suches, and Woody Lake. At 1.4 miles you'll reach Big Cedar Mountain, towering 3,737 feet. On your right, an unmarked spur trail awaits, leading to a serene grassy area with rock ledges, offering yet another tranquil vista.

The trail descends roughly 2 miles until Lance Creek, passing the Dockery Lake Trail junction, where a blue-blazed trail heads southeast for 3.5 miles to Dockery Lake Recreation Area. Just 100 yards north of the creek you'll find four designated tent pads equipped with cables for securely hanging food. As you proceed, the trail gradually begins to ascend to Henry Gap.

At 5.8 miles, Jarrard Gap features a blue-blazed trail to the left, leading 1 mile to Lake Winfield Scott Recreation Area and GA 180. Gaining in elevation, the trail reaches the

View from Big Cedar Mountain, Mile 21.9

Facade of Blood Mountain Shelter, Mile 28.9

junction for Woods Hole Shelter at 7.2 miles. The shelter is a 0.4-mile hike west on a side trail, with water available at the trail's midpoint.

The Freeman Trail bypasses Blood Mountain summit, leading nearly 2 miles east to rejoin the AT at Flatrock Gap. At 7.6 miles, Slaughter Creek Trail is blue-blazed to the left, leading 2.7 miles to Lake Winfield Scott Recreation Area. The stream at the right turn is the last water source before Neels Gap, providing water for upcoming campsites. Blood Mountain Campsite (formerly Slaughter Creek Campsite) features eight tent pads built on a sidehill; no fires are allowed. The trail continues upward to the Duncan Ridge Trail junction, where the blue-blazed trail to the left connects to the Benton MacKaye Trail, creating the 55-mile Georgia Loop.

Side view of Blood Mountain Shelter, Mile 28.9

Hammer impression from original construction of Blood Mountain Shelter in 1937 by the Civilian Conservation Corps with Georgia State Parks, Mile 28.9

Northeastern view at Blood Mountain Shelter, Mile 28.9

Western view at Blood Mountain Shelter, Mile 28.9

After covering 8.4 miles, you reach Blood Mountain, ascending 795 feet in elevation in slightly over a mile. Blood Mountain is the highest point on the AT in Georgia; Blood Mountain Shelter, the oldest shelter on the Appalachian Trail, is located on the summit. The closest water source is the creek at the Slaughter Creek trail junction. The 4,461-foot peak affords panoramic views of the Chattahoochee–Oconee National Forest. Fires are not allowed.

At 9.8 miles, a trail west from Flatrock Gap leads to the Byron Reece Memorial, where parking is available. After hiking 10.8 miles, you reach Neels Gap, situated along paved US 19/129, with parking at the Byron Reece Memorial north on the highway.

Stop in Mountain Crossings at the Walasi-yi Center, which provides hiker supplies, equipment, and a hostel available on a first-come, first-served basis. While at the Walasi-yi Center, check out the Blood Mountain Historical Marker in front of the hiker hostel. The inscription reads:

> *Blood Mountain, elevation 4,458 ft. Chattahoochee National Forest. In Cherokee mythology the mountain was one of the homes of the Nunnehi, or Immortals, the "People Who Live Anywhere," a race of Spirit People who lived in great townhouses in the highlands of the old Cherokee Country. One of these mythical townhouses stood near Lake Trahlyta. As a friendly people they often brought lost hunters and wanderers to their townhouses for rest and care before guiding them back to their homes. Before the coming of white settlers, the Creeks and Cherokees fought a disastrous and bloody battle in Slaughter Gap between Slaughter and Blood Mountains.*

Mountain Crossings' facade and parking lot with mountains in the background at Neels Gap, Mile 31.3

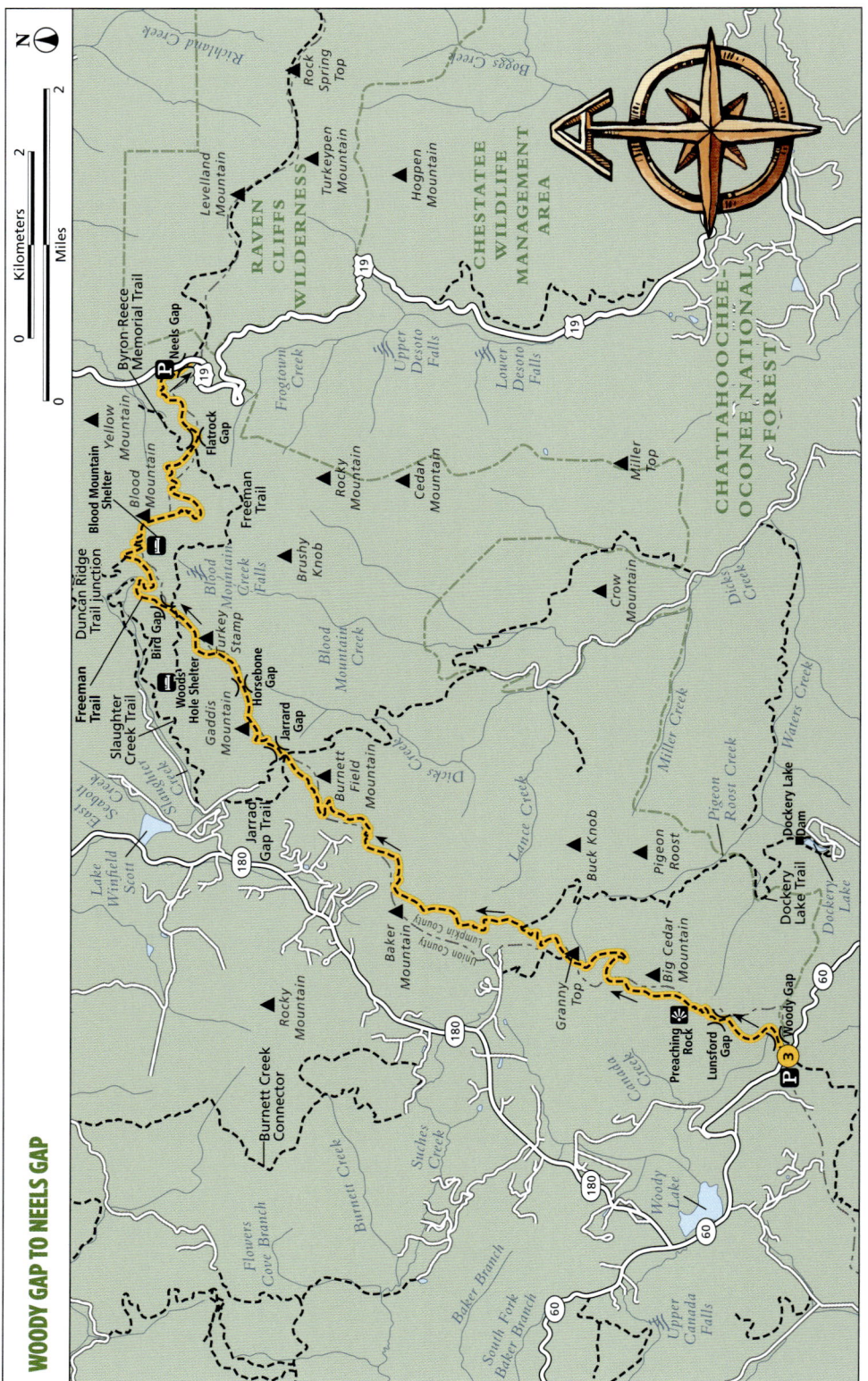

Used hiker shoe tree and AT history plaque at Mountain Crossings, Mile 31.3

KEY POINTS

SECTION		ELEVATION (FEET)	MILES FROM SPRINGER MOUNTAIN	MILES FROM DAMASCUS
0.0	Woody Gap, spring north of road 0.2 mile west	3,173	20.5	450.5
1.1	Preaching Rock	3,593	21.6	449.4
1.4	Big Cedar Mountain	3,737	21.9	449.1
1.6	Spring to the west	3,659	22.1	448.9
2.4	Spring to the west	3,325	22.9	448.1
3.1	Dockery Lake Trail	3,051	23.6	447.4
3.5	Lance Creek, camping, water	2,866	24.0	447.0
5.8	Jarrard Gap, unreliable spring 0.3 mile west	3,250	26.3	444.7
7.2	Bird Gap, Woods Hole Shelter, Freeman Trail to the east	3,663	27.7	443.3
7.6	Slaughter Creek Trail, unreliable spring	3,798	28.1	442.9
7.7	Blood Mountain Campsite	3,798	28.2	442.8
8.0	Duncan Ridge Trail junction	4,164	28.5	442.5
8.4	Blood Mountain, Blood Mountain Shelter (no water)	4,461	28.9	442.1
9.8	Flatrock Gap, Freeman Trail to east, Byron Reece Memorial parking area to the west, unreliable water	3,464	30.3	440.7
10.8	Neels Gap, US 19, water outside hostel via spigot	3,125	31.3	439.7

4 NEELS GAP TO TESNATEE GAP

Back porch view at Mountain Crossings, Mile 31.3

The shortest stretch in Georgia, this section offers numerous scenic views from **Levelland Mountain, Wolf Laurel Top, Cowrock Mountain**, and more. Whether you prefer a day hike or a relaxed backpacking excursion, this hike accommodates both options.

Distance: 6.0 miles
Difficulty: Moderate
Nearest town: Blairsville, Georgia

Water Availability: There are plentiful of good water sources throughout this stretch.
Trailhead GPS: 34.7411 / -83.9206

Neels Gap sign and AT blazes indicating AT north while you pass through the Mountain Crossings building, Mile 31.3

Good to know: Parking is not allowed at Mountain Crossings outfitters. Hikers can park at the Byron Herbert Reece parking lot on US 19/129 and take the blue-blazed Byron Reece Trail, which intersects the AT at Flat Rock Gap after 0.7 mile. Alternatively, you can leave a vehicle at Tesnatee Gap and arrange for a shuttle to take you to Neels Gap.

THE HIKE

Starting at Neels Gap, the trail begins a gradual ascent from the highway, distancing itself from the sounds of civilization while heading east toward Tesnatee Gap and entering the Raven Cliffs Wilderness.

The trail maintains its upward trajectory with a 1.5-mile ascent, scaling almost 1,000 feet in elevation to reach Levelland Mountain, offering picturesque views while winding through switchbacks and passing trailside campsites.

Descending from Levelland Mountain, the trail zigzags toward Swaim Gap. Trailside campsites are scattered on both sides of the trail as it follows a rolling ridgeline under a shaded forest canopy. The AT continues a steady ascent to Wolf Laurel Top, reaching the summit at 3.6 miles. A side trail on the right leads to a picturesque campsite at the mountain's 3,773-foot summit, providing breathtaking views.

Continuing, the trail descends from Wolf Laurel Top to Baggs Creek Gap at 4.2 miles. From the gap, the AT climbs to Cowrock Mountain, which rises to 3,842 feet. A rocky clearing alongside the trail offers captivating views before reaching the Cowrock summit at 5.0 miles.

View from Wolf Laurel Top, Mile 35.0

Jarred Douglas and Bryan Anderson setting up camp near Wolf Laurel Top in 2013, Mile 35.0

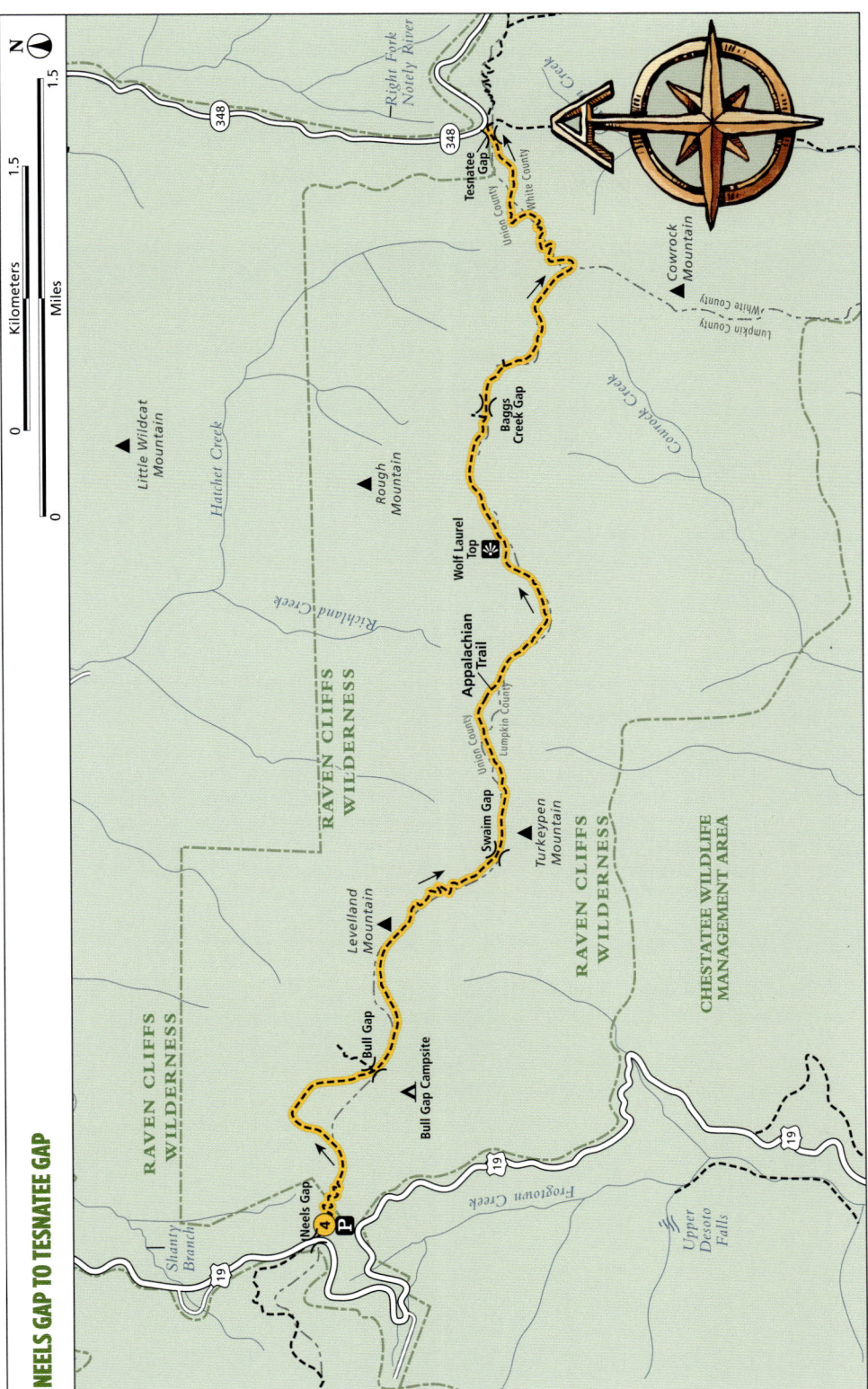

The Cowrock Mountain summit provides stunning panoramic views of the surrounding mountainscape, featuring angular and pronounced peaks in contrast to the rounded, rolling scene from Blood Mountain to the west. Notably, Yonah Mountain is visible on the near horizon, with its sheer walls of nearly bare rock towering skyward. From Cowrock Mountain, the trail gradually drops for 1 mile, leading into Tesnatee Gap.

KEY POINTS

SECTION		ELEVATION (FEET)	MILES FROM SPRINGER MOUNTAIN	MILES FROM DAMASCUS
0.0	Neels Gap, water outside hostel via spigot	3,125	31.3	439.7
1.1	Bull Gap, campsite with water 0.2 mile on side trail to the west	3,662	32.4	438.6
1.7	Levelland Mountain	3,860	33.0	438.0
2.2	Swaim Gap, spring to the west	3,450	33.5	437.5
3.7	Wolf Laurel Top, views to the east in clearing	3,773	35.0	436.0
4.2	Baggs Creek Gap	3,505	35.5	435.5
5.0	Cowrock Mountain	3,842	36.3	434.7
6.0	Tesnatee Gap	3,138	37.3	433.7

TRAIL TOWN: BLAIRSVILLE, GEORGIA

As a designated Appalachian Trail Community, Blairsville, located just 15 miles from the North Carolina border, is a hub for hikers and other outdoor enthusiasts. The AT passes through Neels Gap, where **Mountain Crossings** is located, a premier outfitter with a well-stocked store, hiker hostel, and expert advice for your trail needs. Other hiker-friendly accommodations include campsites at scenic **Vogel State Park**, private rooms at **Misty Mountain Inn & Cottages**, and rustic cabins at **Blood Mountain Cabins**.

Downtown Blairsville has a laundry, post office, grocery stores, medical facilities, and several restaurants to ensure your stay is comfortable and all your hiking needs are met. For shuttle services contact **The Further Shuttle Appalachian** and **The Grateful Hiker** by calling or texting (772) 321-0905.

In spring the **Scottish Festival and Highland Games** showcases traditional music, dance, and games. Other annual events include the **Sorghum Festival**, the **Mountain Heritage Festival**, and **Free Friday Night Concerts** at the **Historic Courthouse**, offering music and community spirit.

5 TESNATEE GAP TO UNICOI GAP

View from Wildcat Mountain, Mile 37.9

This section skirts the headwaters of the **Chattahoochee River** and traverses several rocky areas. Fourteen miles are within the **Mark Trail Wilderness**. Look for interesting plant life such as tall umbrella leaf, a native plant of the Southern Appalachians, which reveals its white blossoms in the spring.

Distance: 15.4 miles
Difficulty: Moderately challenging due to some steep inclines and declines
Nearest town: Helen, Georgia (9 miles east of Unicoi Gap)
Water availability: Plenty of water available via streams and springs throughout this hike
Trailhead GPS: 34.7262 / -83.8476

Rock perch at Wildcat Mountain, Mile 37.9

THE HIKE

The AT briefly traces the highway before embarking on a challenging climb up Wildcat Mountain, where the trail gains nearly 500 feet in elevation over 0.5 mile. Beyond the summit, a spur trail leads to Whitley Gap Shelter; an additional 0.2 mile will take you to Hogpen Gap, at an elevation of 3,453 feet.

Just under a mile from Hogpen Gap, the trail reaches White Oak Stamp on the ridge crest. Along the path, hikers can see Bowman's root, or Indian physic, showcasing its vibrant five-petaled starlike flowers from spring to early summer. The trail then undulates through the woods for approximately 2 miles, continuing along the narrow ridge and reaching the rocky summit of Sheep Rock Top at 3,558 feet before descending steadily into Low Gap, the lowest point in this stretch. A blue-blazed trail guides hikers 190 yards east to Low Gap Shelter, a welcoming spot for a lunch break. The

Tulips bloom in early spring on Wildcat Mountain.

Carved rock monument at Hogpen Gap, Mile 38.2

Mark Trail Wilderness sign, entrance to trail at Hogpen Gap, Mile 38.2

shelter is equipped with a privy, bear cables, and easy access to water, courtesy of a small stream located in front of the shelter.

At 7.1 miles the trail reaches Poplar Stamp, where campsites are available. Water can be sourced from a stream located several hundred feet to the east down an old roadbed.

Traverse numerous small streams and enjoy walking along a historic roadbed constructed by the CCC in 1934, arriving at Cold Springs Gap at 9.6 miles. Contrary to its name, this location does not feature a spring.

At 10.8 miles Chattahoochee Gap invites hikers to explore its spring trail, descending steeply 200 yards east to the headwaters of the Chattahoochee River.

The blue-blazed Jacks Knob Trail guides hikers 2.4 miles west along Hiwassee Ridge to Jacks Gap. Continuing from there, the trail ascends another 2.5 miles to reach the summit of Brasstown Bald, the highest peak in Georgia.

Arrive at Red Clay Gap at 11.4 miles and then traverse numerous rockslides before reaching a spacious flat expanse known as Rocky Knob, the former site of the Rocky Knob Shelter, now repurposed as a campsite. Water is approximately 150 yards downhill west of the AT.

At 13 miles the Blue Mountain Shelter awaits at 3,889 feet about 80 yards west of the AT, with a privy, a nearby spring, and bear cables for added safety. Arrive at the top of Blue Mountain (4,025 feet) and begin a 1.5-mile descent into Unicoi Gap.

AT historical plaque mounted on a giant rock at Unicoi Gap, Mile 52.7

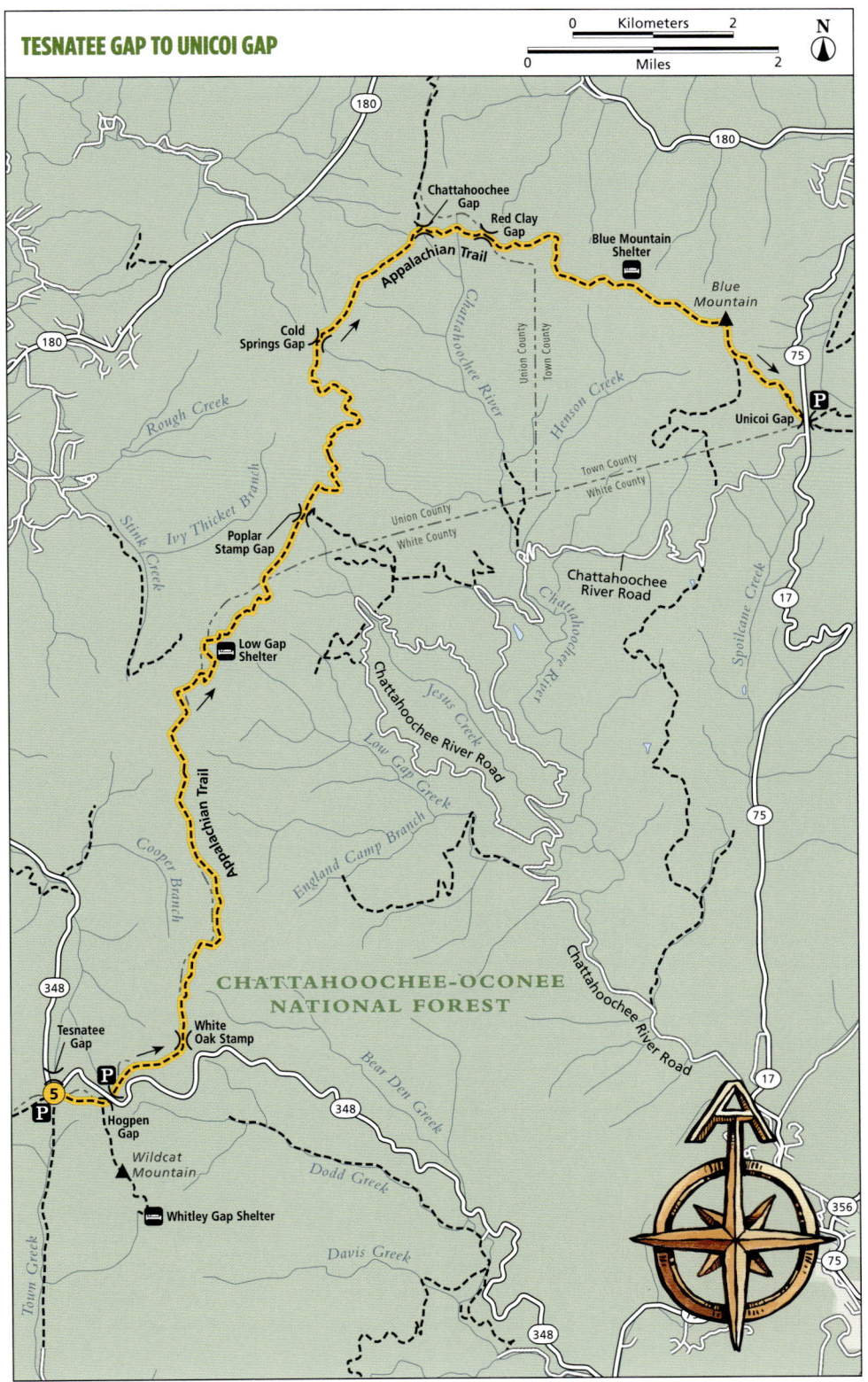

KEY POINTS

SECTION		ELEVATION (FEET)	MILES FROM SPRINGER MOUNTAIN	MILES FROM DAMASCUS
0.0	Tesnatee Gap	3,138	37.3	433.7
0.6	Wildcat Mountain	3,675	37.9	433.1
0.7	Whitley Gap Shelter 1.2 miles east, spring additional 0.3 mile behind shelter	3,627	38.0	433.0
0.9	Hogpen Gap, unreliable spring south of road on east side of AT	3,453	38.2	432.8
1.8	White Oak Stamp	3,470	39.1	431.9
5.7	Low Gap Shelter and spring (0.1 mile east)	3,028	43.0	428.0
7.1	Poplar Stamp Gap, spring 0.1 mile east	3,342	44.4	426.6
9.1	Stream with cascade	3,465	46.4	426.6
9.6	Cold Springs Gap	3,500	46.9	424.1
10.8	Chattahoochee Gap, spring	3,566	48.1	422.9
11.4	Red Clay Gap	3,485	48.7	422.3
12.1	Site of former Rocky Knob Shelter (area still usable as campsite), spring	3,621	49.4	421.6
13.0	Blue Mountain Shelter, spring 0.1 mile south on AT	3,878	50.3	420.7
13.9	Blue Mountain	4,025	51.2	419.8
15.4	Unicoi Gap, GA 75 (parking)	2,949	52.7	418.3

TRAIL TOWN: HELEN, GEORGIA

Just a 5-minute drive from Unicoi Gap, the quaint alpine village of Helen, Georgia, offers an enchanting stop for hikers to rest and resupply while enjoying a taste of local culture. The area once was home to the Cherokee people. Today you can visit historic Native American sites such as the **Sautee Nacoochee Indian Mound** to learn about and honor their rich cultural heritage. By 1912 Helen had become a logging town, but with the decline of the logging industry, the townsfolk decided to reimagine their community. In 1968 local artist John Kollack, inspired by his time in the Bavarian Alps, helped transform Helen into a picturesque Bavarian-style village. From charming chalet storefronts to cobblestone streets and German traditions, Kollack's vision brought the essence of the Alps to the Blue Ridge Mountains of Georgia.

In Helen you can experience the best of both cultural and natural attractions. Savor traditional German cuisine with delicious pretzels, schnitzel, bratwurst, fried cheeses, old-world breads, and pastries. Toast to life with a refreshing pint of German beer at a cozy tavern or pub right on the **Chattahoochee River**. Don't miss **Betty's Country Store**, a beloved local spot offering delicious deli sandwiches, groceries, and unique gifts. For a touch of historical adventure, try your hand at panning for gold nuggets and gems at various gold mining attractions—a nod to the Dahlonega gold rush of the 1820s.

Immerse yourself in Helen's rich cultural heritage at the nearby **Sautee Nacoochee Center**, which features the **Folk Pottery Museum of Northeast Georgia**, a history museum, and an African American heritage site. Nature enthusiasts will appreciate stunning **Anna Ruby Falls**, a breathtaking double waterfall just a short drive from town. With live music, seasonal events, and festivals such as **Helen's Oktoberfest**, there's always something happening in Helen throughout the year.

6 UNICOI GAP TO DICKS CREEK GAP

Parking lot and trail entrance heading north on the AT, Mile 52.7

This stretch boasts some of Georgia's lengthiest climbs and highest peaks on the AT. Noteworthy highlights include expansive views from **Tray Mountain** and the Blue Ridge Swag, offering an extended ridge walk. During the warmer seasons, vibrant wildflowers grace the trail's edges.

Appalachian Trail blaze above Unicoi Gap, heading north on the AT

Distance: 16.7 miles
Difficulty: Strenuous due to numerous climbs
Nearest town: Helen, Georgia (9 miles east of Unicoi Gap); Hiawassee, Georgia (12 miles west of Unicoi Gap)

Water availability: Water is available at Tray Mountain and Deep Gap Shelters. The trail also crosses several streams where water can be treated to drink.
Trailhead GPS: 34.8017 / -83.7428

Good to know: Cell reception is spotty at Dicks Creek Gap. If you need a shuttle, be sure to schedule one ahead of time.

THE HIKE

At the Unicoi Gap trailhead, a large boulder, adorned with a bronze plaque commemorating the Appalachian Trail, marks the starting point. Following the white blaze, the trail ascends wooden stairs, enters a forest filled with boulders, and climbs steadily up the western slope of Rocky Mountain, crossing several small, trickling springs. Through-the-tree views of the surrounding mountains, including the recognizable summit of Yonah Mountain, come into sight. Approaching the summit, the white-blazed Appalachian Trail intersects the blue-blazed Rocky Mountain Trail.

View from Rocky Mountain, Mile 54.2

The hike makes a final ascent to the mountain's rounded peak, traversing lichen-crusted stone as the canopy gradually thins. The summit, 1.4 miles from the trailhead, offers breathtaking views. Along the trail, trailside campsites equipped with stone fire rings provide nice resting spots.

The trail then begins a nearly continuous descent to Indian Grave Gap, winding through a fern-filled forest, descending rustic stone and wood stairs, and passing through gnarly-branched mountain laurel tunnels. Reaching the gravel-paved Indian Grave Gap Road at 2.7 miles, the Appalachian Trail crosses the road, ascending through a tunnel of mountain laurel and continuing toward Tray Mountain.

One mile from the gap, the trail reaches the site of an old cheese factory, now repurposed into a campsite. A steep ledge provides an excellent view of Tray Mountain's peak to the left, offering a preview of the remaining climb to the summit.

Next, the hike arrives at Tray Gap, crossing a gravel road and entering the Tray Mountain Wilderness. The trail begins a notably steeper ascent, meandering through switchbacks on the mountain's lower elevations.

At 5.2 miles the AT reaches the Tray Mountain summit, gaining more than 1,300 feet in elevation from Indian Grave Gap. Windswept trees hugging the mountain's high elevation disperse at the peak, opening up to expansive views of the Blue Ridge Mountains

Views from Tray Mountain, Mile 57.9

and Chattahoochee National Forest. Half a mile from the summit, a short side trail departing to the west leads to Tray Mountain Shelter.

The trail undulates in elevation over the next 2.5 miles, passing through Wolf Pen Gap, Steeltrap Gap, and across Young Lick Knob before descending into the swag of the Blue Ridge.

At 10.4 miles, arrive at Sassafras Gap, where a side trail descends steeply for 0.2 mile to the east to a campsite and water source. The trail continues through Addis Gap and then upward as it skirts the summit of Kelly Knob, climbing more than 800 feet in elevation from Addis Gap.

From Kelly Knob, the AT descends sharply for about a mile until it intersects a short side trail guiding hikers to Deep Gap Shelter. Another campsite is located about a mile north of here, down a blue-blazed trail heading east. By the 14.5-mile mark, the trail arrives at Powell Mountain, initiating another long descent into Moreland Gap. Moreland Gap is just 1 mile from Dicks Creek Gap, where this hike concludes.

View from Kelly Knob, Mile 65

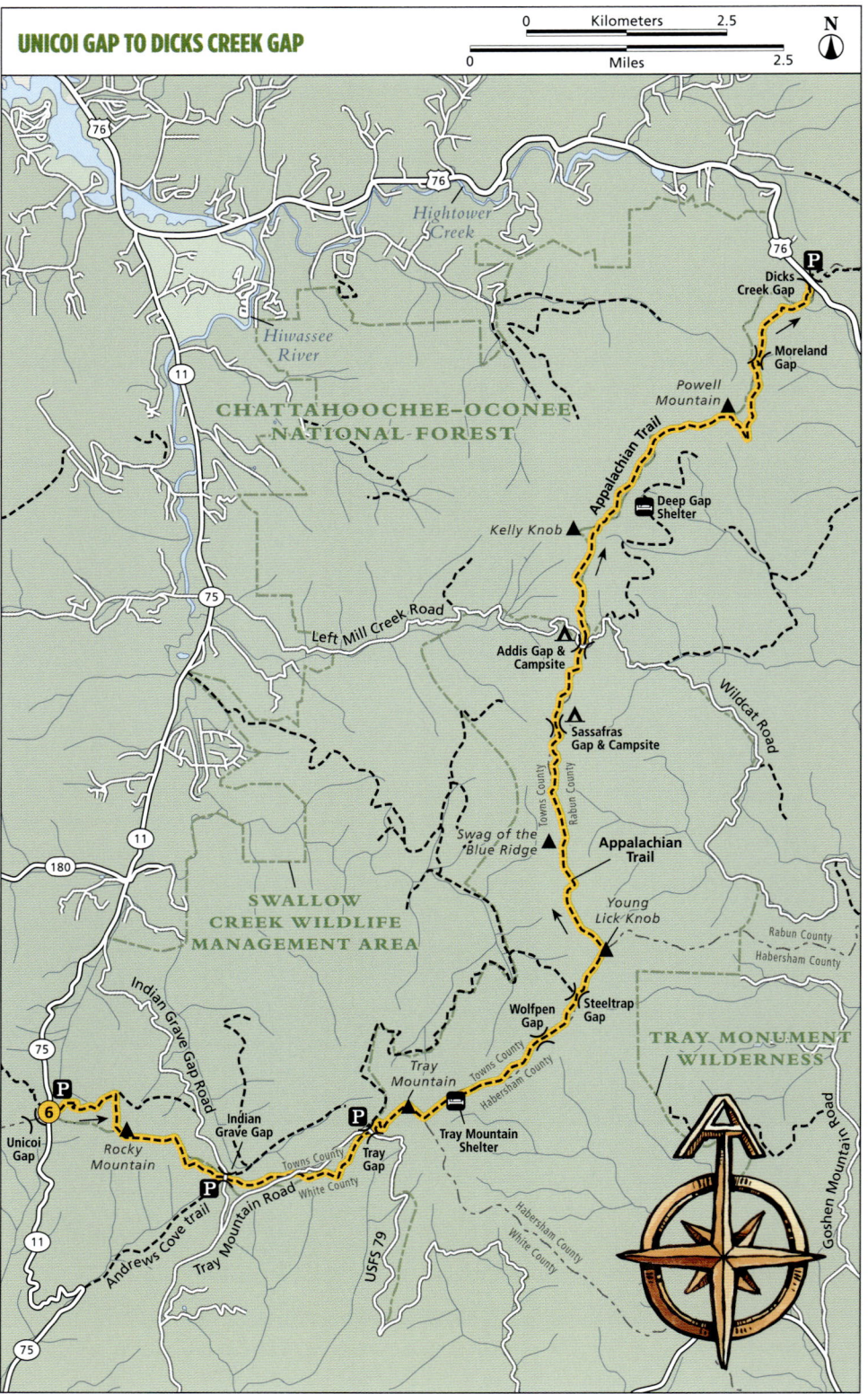

KEY POINTS

SECTION		ELEVATION (FEET)	MILES FROM SPRINGER MOUNTAIN	MILES FROM DAMASCUS
0.0	Unicoi Gap, GA 75 (parking)	2,949	52.7	418.3
0.7	Stream	3,506	53.4	417.6
0.9	Rocky Mountain Trail to west	3,730	53.6	417.4
1.4	Rocky Mountain	4,017	54.1	416.9
2.7	Indian Grave Gap, USFS 283 (parking), Andrews Cove trail to east	3,113	55.4	415.6
3.4	Tray Mountain Road, USFS 79, piped stream to east	3,494	56.1	414.9
3.7	Cheese factory site, water 0.1 mile west on blue-blazed trail	3,576	56.4	414.6
4.4	Tray Gap, Tray Mountain Road/USFS 79 (parking)	3,847	57.1	413.9
5.2	Tray Mountain	4,430	57.9	413.1
5.7	Tray Mountain Shelter and spring 0.2 mile west	4,193	58.4	412.6
6.8	Wolf Pen Gap	3,549	59.5	411.5
7.4	Steeltrap Gap, spring 0.5 mile east	3,450	60.1	410.9
8.0	Young Lick Knob	3,748	60.7	410.3
9.1	Swag of the Blue Ridge	3,447	61.8	409.2
10.4	Sassafras Gap, spring and campsite 0.2 mile east	3,500	63.1	407.9
11.3	Addis Gap, spring and campsite 0.5 mile east down old fire road	3,304	64.0	407.0
12.3	Kelly Knob; trail skirts summit	4,134	65.0	406.0
13.1	Deep Gap Shelter 0.3 mile east, spring	3,572	65.8	405.2
14.2	Vista, blue-blazed trail leading 0.1 mile east to campsite	3,892	66.9	404.1
14.5	Powell Mountain	3,850	67.2	403.8
15.6	Moreland Gap, spring to east	3,017	68.3	402.7
16.7	Dicks Creek Gap, US 76, weak spring	2,675	69.4	401.6

TRAIL TOWN: HIAWASSEE, GEORGIA

Situated along the shores of **Lake Chatuge** and surrounded by the rolling peaks of the Southern Appalachians, Hiawassee, Georgia, is a welcoming Appalachian Trail Community and popular resupply stop for northbound hikers just 12 miles from the trail at **Unicoi Gap**. Known for its stunning mountain views, Hiawassee offers the perfect mix of rest, resources, and recreation.

Hikers will find a full array of amenities, including a large grocery store, full-service outfitter, pharmacies, medical facilities, a laundry, and a post office for mail drops. A variety of restaurants and hiker-friendly businesses—including a local brewery and specialty shops—make Hiawassee an ideal place to linger a little longer. Gear up at **Trailful Outdoor Co.**, or indulge in some Southern comfort food at **Hawg Wild BBQ & Catfish House**.

Lodging options range from budget-friendly motels to cozy cabins and hostels. Around the **Bend Lodge** is a nearby hostel with a warm sense of community tailored to the thru-hiking crowd.

Hiawassee shows its love for hikers as one of Georgia's oldest Appalachian Trail Communities by hosting **Hiker Days** throughout the season. Every Monday in March and April, the town offers a free **"Hiker Feed"** at the Town Square—a local tradition and favorite among thru-hikers for warm meals and good company. During peak hiking season, the town provides a free shuttle to and from Unicoi Gap and **Dicks Creek Gap**, making it one of the most accessible trail towns in the South.

Beyond the trail, the town boasts a wealth of natural and cultural attractions. Hike or drive to **Brasstown Bald**, Georgia's highest peak, for panoramic views of the Blue Ridge Mountains. Explore nearby recreation areas, paddle or swim in Lake Chatuge, and enjoy some of Georgia's finest wineries. Once home to Cherokee communities, the area's rich history adds even more depth to its mountain charm.

For more information visit golakechatuge.com.

7 DICKS CREEK GAP TO BLY GAP

Georgia–North Carolina border sign, Mile 78.3

Enjoy a 9-mile journey through the lush green tunnel where the trail winds its way through dense thickets of mountain laurel, rhododendron, and moss-covered slopes. This stretch features several climbs as it navigates through gaps and knobs. While winter unveils occasional views due to the sparser tree cover, be prepared for the challenging terrain characterized by steep ascents and descents, making this hike potentially demanding for beginners.

Distance: 9.0 miles
Difficulty: Strenuous due to steep ascents and descents
Nearest town: Hiawassee, Georgia (12 miles west of Dicks Creek Gap)

Water availability: There is a small stream at the trailhead and several springs throughout this section.
Trailhead GPS: 34.9121 / -83.6188

Good to know:

- There is no road access to Bly Gap, where this hike concludes. You will need to hike back to your car or continue hiking north 6.8 miles to Deep Gap. You can arrange to be picked up at Blue Ridge Gap, approximately 3 miles south of the Georgia–North Carolina border, but there is no parking on this road.
- Cell reception is spotty at Dicks Creek Gap. If you plan to hike this section southbound and need to arrange a ride, call at Buzzard Knob or schedule ahead of time.

Jarred Douglas in a rhododendron tunnel near Sassafras Gap, North Carolina

THE HIKE

Begin at Dicks Creek Gap, nestled at an elevation of 2,675 feet. Follow the trail through the picnic area and ascend along a small seasonal stream. At 1.1 miles reach a campsite where water is available in the wet seasons. The trail drops steadily into Cowart Gap and begins to climb again for nearly 1 mile to Buzzard Knob.

At 3.2 miles arrive at Buzzard Knob, where views are available during winter, when the tree canopy is less dense. From here the trail continues its roller-coaster pattern, dropping in and out of Bull Gap.

At 4.5 miles arrive at Plumorchard Gap, the midpoint of this section. A blue-blazed trail leads steeply down 0.2 mile east to the shelter and privy. A spring trail can be found to the west near the shelter.

Cross over As Knob (yes, weird name) and down into Blue Ridge Gap, where a dirt road intersects. From here the trail gradually gains in elevation, traversing Rich Cove Gap and Rocky Knob at the 7.0-mile mark.

The terrain levels out for a moment and views of Hightower Bald, Georgia's fourth-highest peak, can be seen in wintertime. At 8.6 miles the trail leads along a narrow ridge crest before crossing into the Nantahala National Forest.

Reach Bly Gap at 3,840 feet, just past the Georgia–North Carolina state line and marked by a gnarled oak tree. Bly Gap offers a good campsite and water source to the right, below the clearing, with fine views to the north.

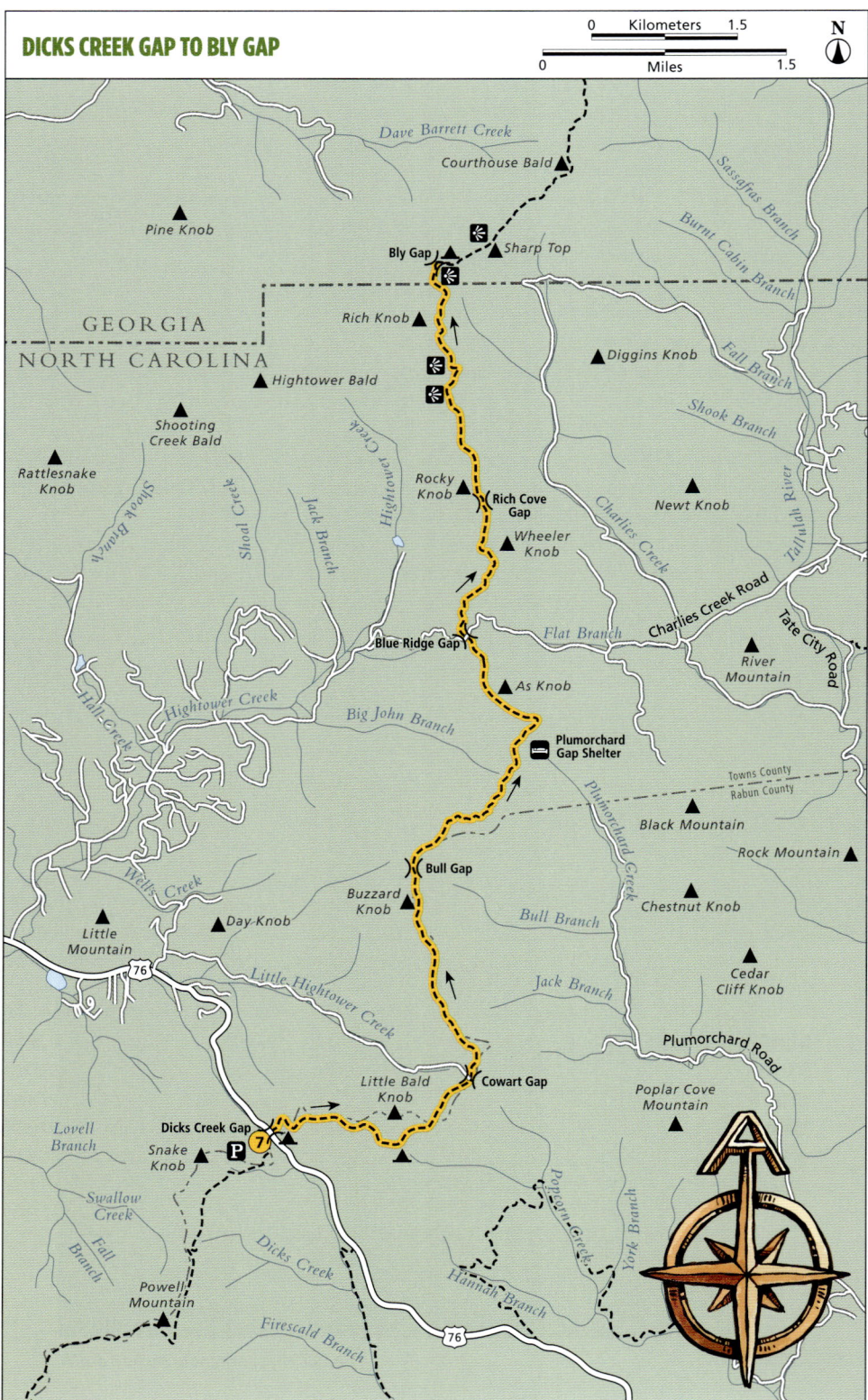

KEY POINTS

SECTION		ELEVATION (FEET)	MILES FROM SPRINGER MOUNTAIN	MILES FROM DAMASCUS
0.0	Dicks Creek Gap, US 76, weak spring	2,675	69.4	401.6
1.1	Campsite, 200 yards to weak spring	3,178	70.5	400.5
1.8	Cowart Gap, spring	2,900	71.2	399.0
3.2	Buzzard Knob	3,656	72.5	398.5
3.3	Bull Gap	3,530	72.7	398.3
3.9	Spring	3,331	73.3	397.7
4.5	Plumorchard Gap Shelter 0.2 mile east, spring	3,153	73.9	397.1
5.2	As Knob	3,460	74.6	396.4
5.8	Blue Ridge Gap	3,050	75.2	395.8
6.8	Campsite and piped spring to west	3,382	76.2	394.8
7.0	Rich Cove Gap	3,460	76.4	394.6
7.6	Rocky Knob	3,569	77.0	394.0
8.9	Georgia–North Carolina border	3,801	78.3	392.7
9.0	Bly Gap, spring 30 feet east	3,840	78.4	392.6

NORTH CAROLINA AND TENNESSEE

It is one of the many blessings of wilderness life that shows us how few things we need in order to be perfectly happy.

—Horace Kephart

The North Carolina and Tennessee sections of the Appalachian Trail span more than 350 miles, meandering along the border between these two states. This challenging route winds through picturesque landscapes that encompass the Pisgah, Cherokee, and Nantahala National Forests, as well as the renowned Great Smoky Mountains National Park, traversing 70 miles within its boundaries. Expect varying weather conditions along this high-elevation trek, which offers cool temperatures even in the summer months.

Rhododendron in bloom (the AT heading south in the distance); the Roan Highlands, with Roan Mountain the furthest peak in the photo

NORTH CAROLINA/TENNESSEE OVERVIEW

Throughout this section, hikers encounter a diverse array of trees, including towering hemlocks, ancient oaks, iconic tulip trees, and sugar maples that define the Appalachian landscape. Spring brings a vibrant display of wildflowers like trilliums, mountain laurel, and galax lining creek sides; the Catawba rhododendron gardens in the Roan Highlands are a notable highlight.

In the rugged terrain of the Nantahala National Forest, hikers navigate steep inclines and descents. A visit to the Nantahala Outdoor Center along the banks of the Nantahala River is a must for outdoor enthusiasts. Fontana Dam, where the trail crosses the impressive structure creating Fontana Lake, provides breathtaking views of the expansive reservoir and surrounding mountains.

As the trail passes through Hot Springs, North Carolina, hikers can enjoy the town's warm hospitality and natural hot mineral springs. Take a moment to unwind and rejuvenate with a relaxing soak in the thermal waters, enjoying a refreshing break along the journey. Scenic vistas abound throughout this section, offering panoramic views of rolling mountains and misty valleys, particularly spectacular from vantage points like Kuwohi, Charlies Bunion, and Max Patch.

> **GOOD TO KNOW**
>
> From Bly Gap at the Georgia–North Carolina border to the Nantahala Outdoor Center on the Nantahala River at Wesser, North Carolina, bear cables or boxes are not provided. Given the history of numerous close and serious bear encounters in this area, it is strongly advised to utilize bear-proof containers for food storage.

Camping in the Great Smoky Mountains National Park attracts more than ten million visitors annually. Northbounders enter the Smokies at the northern side of Fontana Dam; southbounders enter at Davenport Gap. Before entering the park, be sure to obtain a backcountry permit, which requires a per-person per-night fee for overnight stays. Section-hikers can make reservations by calling (865) 436-1231. Thru-hikers need an eight-day permit, available online at www.smokiespermits.nps.gov or by calling (865) 436-1297. Thru-hikers can tent outside AT shelters if shelters are full. Be sure to carry a paper copy of the permit. Fines will be imposed on anyone caught without a permit.

Camping in the Cherokee and Pisgah National Forests is allowed across wide areas of the Appalachian Trail between the Smokies and Damascus, Virginia. These forestlands were acquired by the federal government during the Great Depression after loggers had removed much of the timber. Now, after three-quarters of a century, deep, mature forests cover most mountainsides for miles on both sides of the AT. Unlike some northern sections with strict camping regulations,

> **DID YOU KNOW?**
> *For those who find the steep mountain trails too challenging, the Blue Ridge Parkway provides a beautiful alternative for exploring the Southern mountains. This historic scenic byway extends from Great Smoky Mountains National Park near Cherokee, North Carolina, to the southern terminus of Skyline Drive in Shenandoah National Park, Virginia. Established in 1935 as part of President Franklin D. Roosevelt's New Deal initiatives, the Parkway was designed to connect two national parks and showcase the natural splendor of the Blue Ridge Mountains. Visitors can enjoy stunning views, historical sites, and cultural exhibits along the way.*

hikers in the national forests of Tennessee and North Carolina have the freedom to choose their own campsites away from the main trail.

While this freedom allows for personal choice in camping locations, it comes with the responsibility of adhering to Leave No Trace (LNT) wilderness ethics. Few hikers appreciate seeing trampled areas near water sources or fire rings at every viewpoint, which happens when campers disregard LNT principles. Abusing this freedom may lead to restrictions on camping locations. It's important to use established campsites, leaving surrounding areas undisturbed, or ensure that the chosen campsite looks pristine for the next visitor.

8 BLY GAP TO DEEP GAP (USFS 71)

Famous oak tree at Bly Gap, Mile 78.4

Located just north of the **Georgia–North Carolina border**, this short and sweet hike follows the crest of the **Blue Ridge**, affording outstanding views along the way starting at the open ridge of **Bly Gap**. Muskrat Creek Shelter, in the midst of this section, offers a great place to camp plus a 0.5-mile side trail to amazing views from **Raven Rock Ridge**. Since there is no road approach to Bly Gap, you may consider combining this section with hike 7.

Distance: 6.8 miles
Difficulty: Moderate but still challenging due to a steep ascent and descent of Courthouse Bald
Nearest town: Franklin, North Carolina

Water availability: Water can be found at the trailhead, at Muskrat Creek Shelter, and at Deep Gap, where this hike concludes.
Trailhead GPS: 34.9940 / -83.6002

Campsite near Sassafras Gap, North Carolina

FINDING THE TRAILHEAD

There is no road access to Bly Gap. To reach it, you'll need to hike in from Dicks Creek Gap (page 73). Alternatively, you can trek this section southbound, starting at Deep Gap and concluding at Bly Gap. However, choosing the second option means retracing your steps for 6.8 miles back to your vehicle at Deep Gap. **Note:** The road to Deep Gap (USFS 71) is closed seasonally from December 31 through April 1.

THE HIKE

Starting at Bly Gap just north of the Georgia state line, you'll find yourself on an open ridge boasting breathtaking views to the west of Raven Rock and Boteler Peak. There's an excellent designated campsite at Bly Gap, with a spring located 30 feet east of the trail. Note the famous gnarled oak tree in a clearing.

Continuing along the crest, you'll embark on a steep, 1,000-foot ascent of Sharp Top and Courthouse Bald. This ridge is known for its strong winds, particularly in winter when tree coverage is sparse, so remember to dress in layers or carry a jacket.

The trail descends into Sassafras Gap at 1.9 miles before swiftly climbing again, leading to Muskrat Creek Shelter at 2.8 miles. There's a spring located behind the shelter. As you follow mostly gentle terrain, you'll reach White Oak Stamp at 3.6 miles; water is accessible to the east and camping is available down a blue-blazed trail to the west.

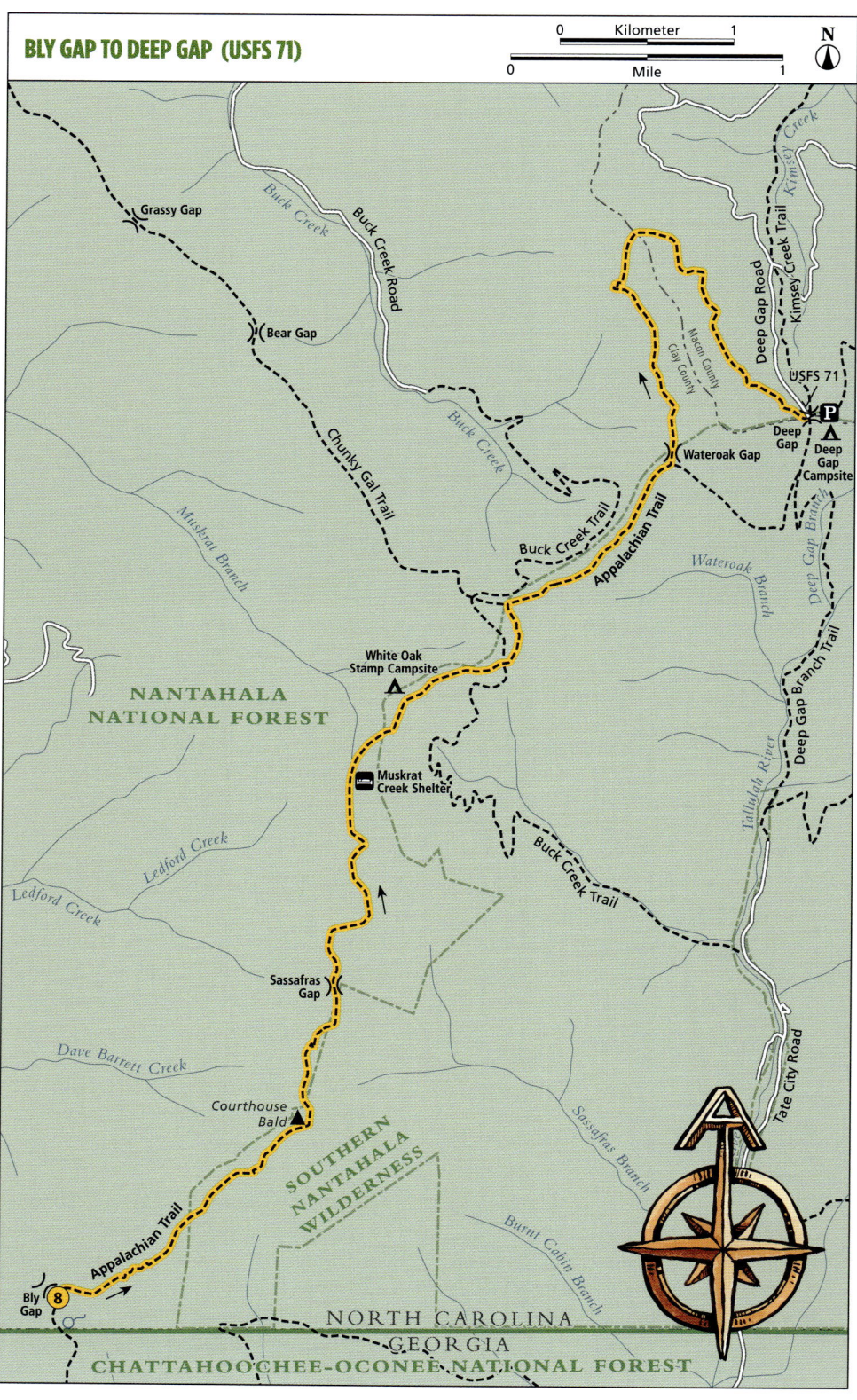

A bit farther north is the intersection with the blue-blazed Chunky Gal Trail, which extends 5.5 miles west to US 64. At 4.7 miles, arrive at a small clearing in Wateroak Gap. The trail then levels out and begins to rise gently, offering glimpses of views through the trees. Finally, at 6.8 miles, you reach the parking area at Deep Gap, where USFS 71 intersects. From here, the blue-blazed Kimsey Creek Trail travels 4.5 miles to Standing Indian Campground.

KEY POINTS

SECTION		ELEVATION (FEET)	MILES FROM SPRINGER MOUNTAIN	MILES FROM DAMASCUS
0.0	Bly Gap, spring 30 feet east	3,840	78.4	392.6
1.3	Courthouse Bald, summit 0.1 mile west	4,708	79.7	391.3
1.9	Sassafras Gap	4,300	80.3	390.7
2.2	Piped spring to the west	4,513	80.6	390.4
2.8	Muskrat Creek Shelter, spring	4,562	81.2	389.8
3.6	Old roadbed, White Oak Stamp Campsite to west, spring	4,620	82.0	389.0
4.7	Wateroak Gap	4,490	83.1	387.9
5.0	Spring	4,568	83.4	387.6
6.2	Spring	4,548	84.6	386.4
6.8	USFS 71, Kimsey Creek Campsite, Deep Gap Campsite on Kimsey Creek Trail, water on blue-blazed trail	4,341	85.2	385.8

9 DEEP GAP (USFS 71) TO WINDING STAIR GAP

View near Timber Ridge Trail

This section offers pleasant hiking with minimal and gradual elevation changes except for a steep ascent up **Albert Mountain**. Venture toward **Standing Indian Mountain**, the highest point south of the Great Smoky Mountains, reaching an elevation of 5,435 feet. From its summit, enjoy magnificent views of the **Georgia Blue Ridge**. Before a lengthy descent into **Winding Stair Gap**, savor the outstanding 360-degree views from the **Albert Mountain fire tower**.

Camping in Betty Creek Gap during a thru-hike, Mile 97.4

Distance: 24.4 miles
Difficulty: Moderate
Nearest town: Franklin, North Carolina (10 miles east of Winding Stair Gap)
Water availability: Seasonal water is available 150 feet west down a blue-blazed trail at the trailhead. Numerous streams and springs are available to source water from on the way to Winding Stair Gap.
Trailhead GPS: 35.0396 / -83.5525

Good to know: Deep Gap Road (USFS 71) is closed seasonally December 31 through April 1.

THE HIKE

From the Deep Gap parking area on USFS 71, begin the long 1,000-foot ascent toward Standing Indian Mountain. Reach a blue-blazed spur trail that leads 250 feet east to Standing Indian Shelter in just under a mile.

As the AT continues its gradual ascent, it reaches the pinnacle of Standing Indian Mountain at 5,435 feet, approximately 2.4 miles from the start. Lower Ridge Trail intersects here, leading 600 feet eastward to the summit, where panoramic views of the Blue Ridge Mountains await. Along the trail

Blue blaze on the Betty Creek Trail, Mile 97.4

to the summit, you'll find popular campsites, but remember that camping is prohibited directly on the summit itself.

From Standing Indian Mountain, begin a long 1,200-foot descent to Coleman Gap. Reach Beech Gap at 5.3 miles. An unreliable spring and campsites are located 100 feet east of the AT. Cross several small streams as the trail continues its gradual descent.

Arrive at Coleman Gap around the 7-mile mark, where you'll navigate through a dense rhododendron thicket. Continue along the gently rising trail for the next mile until you reach Carter Gap Shelter at 8.5 miles. From there the AT carries on to the slope of Ridgepole Mountain, ascending to a height of 4,931 feet. Around the 10.2-mile mark, keep an eye out for an unmarked side trail veering eastward. This trail leads to the Little Ridgepole vista, offering stunning views of Pickens Nose, Little Tennessee Valley, and Rabun Bald.

Arrive at a clearing at Betty Creek Gap, where the blue-blazed Betty Creek Trail intersects to the west. A small spring can be found east, just north of the clearing, and campsites are available on an old roadbed. Continuing past the clearing, the AT leads through a picturesque rhododendron tunnel, eventually arriving at Mooney Gap and USFS 83 at the 13-mile mark.

Continuing, you ascend log steps and traverse the very steep eastern face of Big Butt Mountain, enjoying intermittent views into the Coweeta Valley. Passing gravel USFS 67, follow the level trail toward Albert Mountain. Prepare for a scramble up the side of the steep and rocky slope of Albert Mountain for 0.3 mile. Here, a blue-blazed bad-weather trail branches off to the west.

Views from the Albert Mountain fire tower, Mile 99.9

Jarred Douglas on the Albert Mountain fire tower, Mile 99.9

Arrive at the summit of Albert Mountain at 14.7 miles, where you can take in superb views from the fire tower before embarking on a long, gradual descent. At 14.9 miles you come across a clearing. To the west, a blue-blazed trail marks the Albert Mountain Bypass Trail, offering a bad-weather alternative to the steep and exposed face of Albert Mountain.

At 17.2 miles, a spur trail veers westward to Long Branch Shelter. From this point, continue your hike downhill until you reach Glassmine Gap, where the trail momentarily levels out before gradually ascending again.

At the 20.6-mile mark, you'll encounter a blue-blazed trail intersecting to the west, leading to Rock Gap Shelter. Just north of Rock Gap, a side trail stretches 0.7 mile eastward to the impressive Wasilik Poplar tree, once the second-largest poplar in the East. Even dead, it remains a remarkable sight. On the west side of the AT, a parking area awaits on USFS 67.

Continue to Wallace Gap at 21.3 miles, where you'll cross Old Murphy Road and ascend a narrow path up the road bank. As you hike uphill, you eventually reach a ridge at a gap with eastern views at an elevation of 4,400 feet before descending into Winding Stair Gap, where US 64 intersects.

Hikers descending through a rhododendron tunnel into Winding Stair Gap

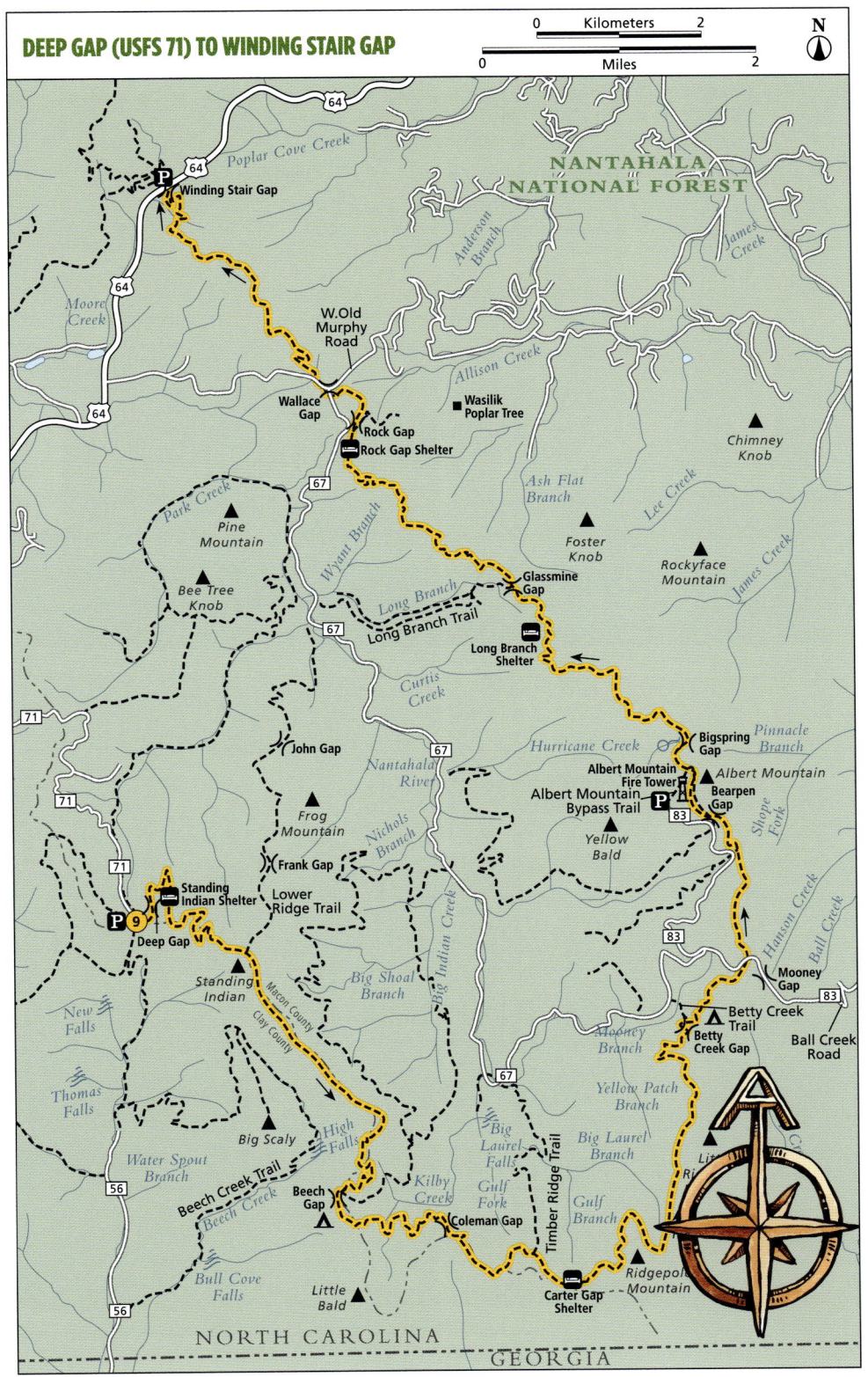

KEY POINTS

SECTION		ELEVATION (FEET)	MILES FROM SPRINGER MOUNTAIN	MILES FROM DAMASCUS
0.0	USFS 71, Kimsey Creek Campsite, Deep Gap Campsite on Kimsey Creek Trail, water on blue-blazed trail	4,341	85.2	385.8
0.4	Spring to west	4,516	85.6	385.4
0.9	Standing Indian Mountain Shelter, stream	4,742	86.1	384.9
1.2	Spring	4,944	86.4	384.6
2.4	Standing Indian Mountain, Lower Ridge Trail, campsites on blue-blazed trail (summit 0.1 mile east)	5,435	87.6	383.4
4.3	Spring	4,944	89.5	381.5
5.3	Beech Gap Campsite, spring	4,460	90.5	380.5
6.4	Stream	4,404	91.6	379.4
7.0	Coleman Gap	4,221	92.2	378.8
8.0	Timber Ridge Trail to west	4,639	93.2	377.8
8.5	Carter Gap Shelter, spring	4,528	93.7	377.3
9.1	Stream	4,738	94.3	376.7
9.6	Spring	4,921	94.8	376.2
12.2	Blue-blazed Betty Creek Trail, Betty Creek Campsite, spring	4,300	97.4	376.0
13.0	Mooney Gap, USFS 83/Ball Creek Road, stream 0.1 mile north	4,498	98.2	372.8
14.4	USFS 67 (Bypass Albert Mountain by taking road 0.2 mile west to parking area, then side trail 0.2 mile from parking area back to AT north of summit.)	4,843	99.6	371.4
14.7	Albert Mountain, fire tower	5,250	99.9	371.1
14.9	Albert Mountain bad-weather trail, 0.2 mile west to parking area on USFS 67	5,052	100.1	370.9
17.2	Long Branch Shelter 0.1 mile west, spring	4,479	102.4	368.6
18.0	Glassmine Gap, Long Branch Trail 2.0 miles west to USFS 67	4,185	103.2	367.8
20.6	Rock Gap Shelter, spring	3,772	105.8	365.2
20.7	Rock Gap, 0.7 mile east to Wasilik Poplar and spring	3,732	105.9	365.1
21.3	Wallace Gap, West Old Murphy Road north to stream	3,738	106.5	364.5
24.4	Winding Stair Gap, US 64, piped spring east of steps	3,690	109.6	361.4

TRAIL TOWN: FRANKLIN, NORTH CAROLINA

Tucked in the heart of the Blue Ridge Mountains, Franklin, North Carolina, is a proud Appalachian Trail Community and beloved rest stop for thru-hikers heading north from Springer Mountain. Known for its mountain hospitality and deep ties to the trail, Franklin welcomes thousands of hikers each year with open arms and a genuine love for the outdoors.

The town offers a range of hiker-friendly accommodations, from locally run hostels like **The Grove Hostel** and **Chica & Sunsets to hotels** and inns. Many lodgings provide laundry access, hiker boxes, and shuttle services to and from the trailhead at Winding Stair Gap. Franklin also provides easy access to essential services, including a post office for mail drops, public library, laundries, pharmacies, and several grocery stores.

Downtown Franklin is a hub for hungry hikers and gearheads alike, offering a variety of local restaurants, resupply spots, and two trusted outfitters. Stop by **Three Eagles Outfitters** or **Outdoor 76** for expert advice and trail-tested gear. Just down the street, **The Lazy Hiker Brewing Company**, located in a former firehouse, is a favorite post-hike hangout where hikers swap stories over local craft beer.

Dive into the town's rich past at the **Macon County Historical Museum** or the **Scottish Tartans Museum**, or explore the area's famed geology at the **Franklin Gem & Mineral Museum**. Known as the "**Gem Capital of the World**," Franklin is a must-visit for rockhounds and history buffs alike.

Each spring the town celebrates its hiking spirit with an Appalachian Trail event featuring gear demos, live music, trail talks, and plenty of trail magic. For more information or to plan your stop in Franklin, visit discoverfranklinnc.com.

10 WINDING STAIR GAP TO TELLICO GAP

Winding Stair Gap sign

A picturesque high-elevation stretch along the main ridge of the Nantahala Mountain range, steeped in Cherokee history. This segment of the AT boasts a combination of historical landmarks, stunning panoramas, water features, and chances to admire wildflowers. With frequent road crossings and trail junctions, there are many opportunities for exploration and excitement. Notable highlights include **Siler Bald** and **Wayah Bald**. Wildflower enthusiasts should keep an eye out for flame azalea, fire pink, evening primrose, bee balm, and more. July and August offer the additional treat of wild blueberries and blackberries, perfect for a trailside snack.

Moore Creek Waterfall and blazes, Mile 109.8

Distance: 19.4 miles
Difficulty: Strenuous due to distance and numerous ascents and descents
Nearest town: Franklin, North Carolina (10 miles east of Winding Stair Gap)

Water availability: Water is available at the trailhead and from numerous sources along the way.
Trailhead GPS: 35.1196 / -83.548

Good to know: Bear cables or boxes are not available throughout his section. Due to numerous close and serious bear encounters, it is strongly recommended using bear-proof containers for food storage.

THE HIKE

From the parking area on the south side of US 64, note the white blazes painted on the guardrails, marking the AT. Cross the road and ascend along a narrow path on the road bank. Once the guardrail ends, the AT enters the woods and continue the gradual climb. As you continue, you'll cross a wooden footbridge suspended over Moore Creek. Enjoy the beautiful cascade waterfall framed by rhododendron before beginning the 660-foot ascent of Rocky Knob.

As the trail gradually climbs beside a meandering creek, look for umbrella leaf, characterized by large pizza-sized leaves atop fleshy stalks with bright blue berries in the fall, flourishing along the water's edge. Trillium, fire pink, evening primrose, and spiderwort

Moore Creek Campsite, Mile 110.4

can be spotted in spring and summer. After ascending and crossing a wide ridge, the trail evens out and reaches Moore Creek Campsite at 0.8 mile.

At around 1.1 miles, the AT leads to Swinging Lick Gap, marked by an aging trail sign. Here the trail turns sharply and ascends toward an east-facing slope offering blackberries in August and winter vistas overlooking the valley toward Franklin.

Descending to Panther Gap, a level area with a nice view in winter, the trail meanders through the woods and begins a long gradual climb to Siler Bald. At the 4.2-mile mark, reach the intersection with the blue-blazed Siler Bald Shelter Loop. Veer left to ascend Siler Bald or right to explore the shelter, accessible via an old road 0.3 mile off the AT. To reach the open summit of Siler Bald, follow the 0.2-mile spur trail leading west for fantastic views of the Southern Appalachians.

From the Siler Bald trail junction, the AT descends 900 feet into Wayah Gap. At 5.8 miles look for trails leading to the Wayah Crest Picnic Area, where road access and parking are available. Just past the picnic area, cross paved NC 1310 at Wayah Gap. From Wayah Gap the trail climbs steadily for the next 2 miles. At 7.1 miles, a short side trail leads west to the historic Wilson Lick Ranger Station, originally constructed in 1913. Displays at the site tell the story of the "Rangers of the Wilson Lick Era."

At 8 miles, the AT joins with the Bartram Trail, a 112+-mile national recreational trail stretching through North Carolina and Georgia. From here the trail is marked with both

Siler Bald Shelter in the fog, Mile 113.8

View from Siler Bald showing the Siler Bald plaque and Nantahala Lake, Mile 114.2

Siler Bald and moon, Mile 114.2

> **DID YOU KNOW?**
> **Wayah**, a Cherokee word that translates to "wolf," is the namesake of Wayah Bald, honoring the red wolves that historically roamed this region. Archaeological evidence reveals indigenous hunting grounds dating back more than 11,000 years, with ancient spearpoints offering a glimpse into their past. "Balds" are treeless expanses that range from shrub-dominated areas to tundra-like grasslands. Botanists like John Bartram have suggested that these balds resulted from a combination of acid soil, toxic roots, and the presence of large herbivores like elk and woolly mammoths. Cherokee lore, however, offers alternative explanations. One story recounts how the Great Spirit used lightning to vanquish a giant hornet that threatened the land. Another legend tells of the Nunnehi, eternal spirit beings who maintained these clearings to aid eagles in hunting for rabbits.

yellow and white blazes until just beyond the Wayah Bald observation tower, about 2.4 miles. Look for a side trail to the Wine Spring Campsite shortly after the two trails coincide.

Reach Wayah Bald and a stone observation tower at 10.1 miles, shortly after crossing a paved path leading to a parking area with latrines. Take in the panoramic views of the surrounding mountains from the tower before a lengthy descent into Licklog Gap. Camping is prohibited on Wayah Bald.

For the next 0.4 mile the Bartram Trail and the AT share the same path until the trail levels out at a small campsite and spring. Here, be mindful to follow the white blaze as the AT veers left and the Bartram Trail heads right.

By the 11-mile point, the AT leads to Wayah Bald Shelter, where a campsite lies to the east. Water can be accessed from Little Laurel Creek, 600 feet west of the AT via a blue-blazed trail. Arrive at a small clearing where several old roads intersect before reaching Burningtown Gap at 14.6 miles.

Traverse a field and ascend a graded trail to reach Cold Spring Shelter at the 15.8-mile mark. Originally constructed by the CCC in 1933, Cold Spring Shelter was restored by the Nantahala Hiking Club in 2012. From this point, continue for just under a mile to Copper Ridge Bald to enjoy a stunning vista of the Little Tennessee River Valley.

At 17.7 miles the AT intersects a short blue-blazed side trail leading to the summit of Rocky Bald, offering breathtaking views. Continue onward, passing Big Branch Campsite, which offers space for four tents and features a nearby water source. From this point, the AT descends sharply for 1.5 miles into Tellico Gap.

> **DID YOU KNOW?**
> During the Revolutionary War in 1776, Colonel Andrew Williamson's troops burned the Cherokee town of Tikaleyasuni near present-day Burningtown Creek (located in a valley east of Burningtown Gap) in North Carolina. This action was part of General Griffith Rutherford's campaign against the Cherokee, aiming to weaken their power before they could join forces with the British against the rebels. Despite fleeing to high ridges, the Cherokee eventually signed peace treaties. However, in 1836 the US Army forced them to leave their lands, once again burning many settlements and leaving lasting devastation.

View from Wayah observation tower, Mile 350.9

Wayah observation tower, Mile 350.9

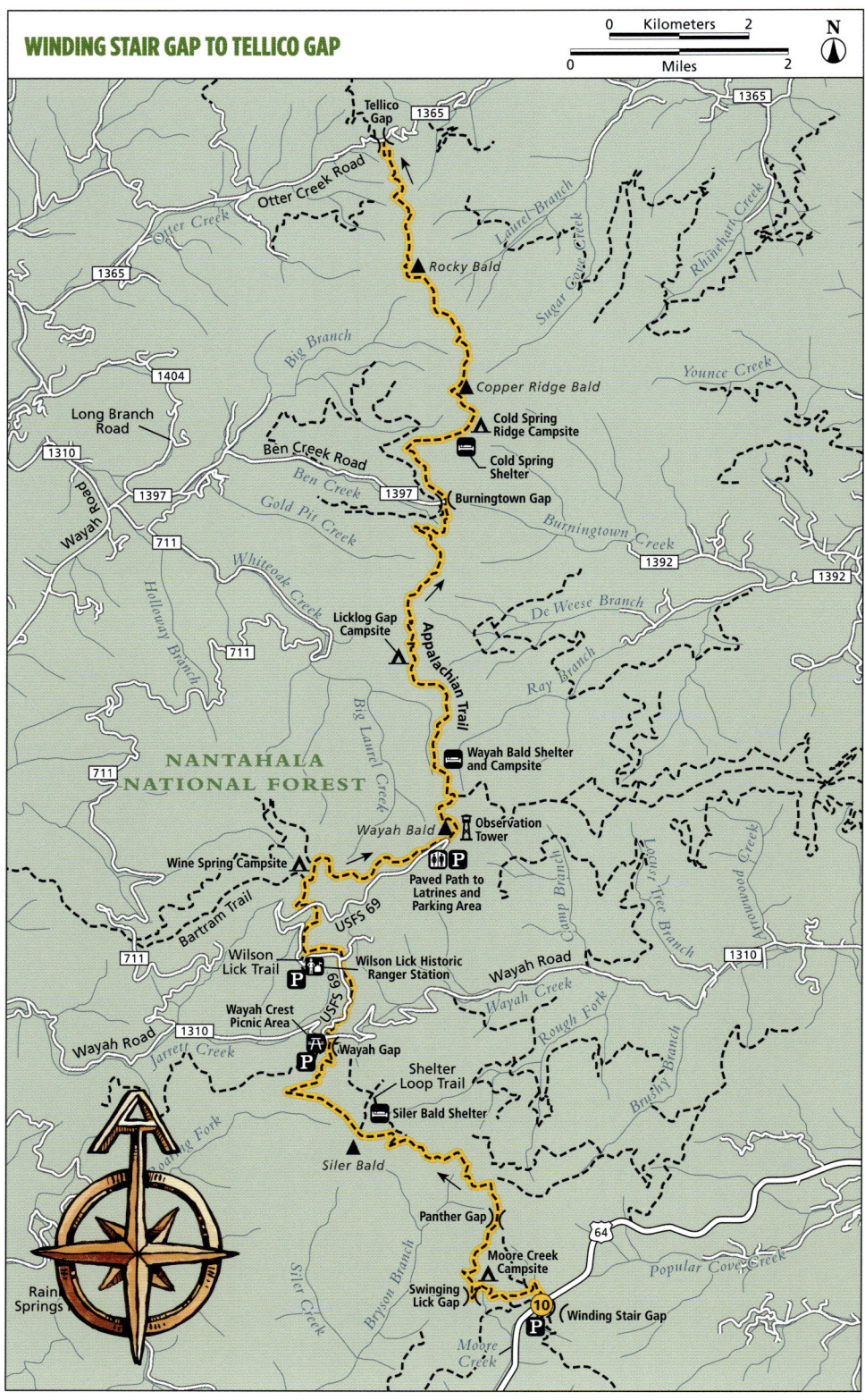

KEY POINTS

SECTION		ELEVATION (FEET)	MILES FROM SPRINGER MOUNTAIN	MILES FROM DAMASCUS
0.0	Winding Stair Gap, US 64, piped spring east of steps	3,690	109.6	361.4
0.2	Forest Service road, Moore Creek Falls	3,727	109.8	361.2
0.6	Logging road	4,026	110.2	360.8
0.8	Moore Creek Campsite, spring	4,011	110.4	360.6
1.1	Swinging Lick Gap	4,100	110.7	360.3
2.0	Panther Gap	4,480	111.6	359.4
4.2	Siler Bald Shelter 0.5 mile east, south end of shelter loop trail, spring	4,769	113.8	357.2
4.6	Siler Bald summit 0.2 mile west, shelter 0.3 mile east, north end of shelter loop trail	4,760	114.2	356.8
5.4	Piped spring	4,481	115.0	356.0
5.8	Wayah Crest Picnic Area 0.1 mile west	4,258	115.4	355.6
5.9	Wayah Gap, Wayah Road	4,180	115.5	355.5
6.7	USFS 69, meadow	4,480	116.3	354.7
7.1	Wilson Lick Trail, 0.2 mile to historic ranger station on blue-blazed trail	4,630	116.7	354.3
7.6	USFS 69, piped spring to the east	4,993	117.2	353.7
8.0	Yellow-blazed Bartram Trail to the west	4,236	117.6	353.4
8.2	Wine Spring Campsite 0.1 mile east, water west of AT	5,290	117.8	353.2
9.7	USFS 69	5,188	119.3	351.7
9.9	Paved path to latrines and parking area	5,298	119.5	351.5
10.1	Wayah Bald and observation tower (no camping on the summit)	5,342	119.7	351.3
11.0	Wayah Bald Shelter and Campsite, 600 feet west to water source	4,712	120.6	350.4
12.3	Licklog Gap Campsite, water	4,440	121.9	349.1
13.7	Intersection with old roadbeds and side trails, AT east	4,515	123.3	347.7
14.6	Burningtown Gap, NC 1397	4,236	124.2	346.8
15.8	Cold Spring Shelter, Cold Spring Ridge Campsite north, spring	4,926	125.4	345.6
16.5	Copper Ridge Bald	5,080	126.1	344.9
17.7	Rocky Bald, 0.1 mile east to views	5,030	127.3	343.7
17.9	Big Branch Campsite, spring	4,978	127.5	343.5
19.4	Tellico Gap, NC 1365/Otter Creek Road	3,850	129.0	342.0

11 TELLICO GAP TO NANTAHALA OUTDOOR CENTER

Wesser Bald tower and tent, Mile 130.4

This section of the trail presents a challenging climb to **Wesser Bald** (elevation 4,627 feet) and a steep descent into the **Nantahala Gorge** (elevation 1,723 feet). Wesser Bald, though now covered in trees, still offers remarkable views from its summit, accessible via a lookout tower and wooden observation deck. The midpoint, known as the "**Jumpoff**," provides expansive views of **Cheoah Bald** to the west, the **Smokies** to the north, and the **Balsam Mountains** to the east.

Distance: 7.9 miles
Difficulty: Strenuous due to steep rocky sections
Nearest town: Franklin and Bryson City, North Carolina
Water availability: Water is limited in this section. There's no water available at the Tellico Gap trailhead. The first water source is 2 miles into the hike near the Wesser Bald Shelter. Multiple water sources can be found toward the north end of the section before reaching the Nantahala Outdoor Center.
Trailhead GPS: 35.2680 / -83.5726

Evening view from Wesser Bald tower, Mile 130.4

THE HIKE

Depart from the gravel parking area on the side of Tellico Road at Tellico Gap, following the white-blazed Appalachian Trail. The trail leads through tree cover, passing a wooden Tellico Gap sign and winding through rhododendron and mountain laurel.

Ascend steeply toward the 4,627-foot summit of Wesser Bald. Young hardwoods dominate the forest, creating a colorful display in autumn against the evergreen backdrop.

Reach the high point near Wesser Bald summit at 1.4 miles. A short side trail leads east to a 30-foot tall tower offering panoramic views of the Nantahala National Forest and the Great Smoky Mountains. Although Wesser Bald is now covered in trees, the tower provides a vantage point for observing surrounding mountain ranges.

Descending sharply from Wesser Bald, the AT veers left, starting on a nearly 3,000-foot descent over 6.5 miles into Nantahala Gorge. As you descend, you'll come to a grassy and dry ridge campsite, followed by a blue-blazed trail leading to a spring, the water source for the upcoming shelter.

Around 2.2 miles in, a short trail branches off to the Wesser Bald Shelter. Just north of the shelter, the Wesser Creek Trail intersects. For the next 2 miles, the AT traces the ridge with brief ups and downs.

Reaching the 4.0-mile mark, arrive at the exposed knob known as the Jumpoff, offering breathtaking vistas of Cheoah Bald and the Nantahala River valley, a highlight of the journey. Continuing onward, the trail descends sharply from the Jumpoff, navigating over rock and wooden steps. At 7.1 miles, reach the A. Rufus Morgan Shelter. The final mile of the trail is well-graded, crossing multiple streams and footbridges.

> **DID YOU KNOW?**
> Rev. Rufus Morgan was born in 1885 in the mountains of western North Carolina. After completing his education in college and seminary, he devoted his life to serving the less fortunate as an Episcopal minister. But alongside his pastoral work, Rev. Morgan nurtured a profound passion for the Appalachian Trail, which was still in its early stages of development. From the 1940s to the 1950s, he dedicated a remarkable forty-three years to the construction and maintenance of the AT, leaving an indelible mark on its history.
>
> Rev. Morgan started by focusing on a stretch of the Appalachian Trail in North Carolina from Bly Gap on the Georgia border to Wesser Bald, a span of 55 miles. His tireless efforts earned him the moniker of "one-man hiking club" as he cleared and maintained his section of the trail almost single-handedly. His passion and dedication went beyond mere maintenance; he was instrumental in supporting the Appalachian Trail Conservancy (ATC) and later founded the Nantahala Hiking Club, a group that continues to steward the trail to this day. He was inducted into the AT Hall of Fame in 2014.
>
> The **Rufus Morgan Shelter**, named in his honor, stands as a testament to his legacy. The shelter provides a welcoming spot for hikers, with accommodations for up to six people; it features a campsite, privy, and nearby water source.
>
> To learn more about Rev. Morgan's remarkable contributions and the history of the Nantahala Hiking Club, visit nantahalahikingclub.org/history-of-the-nhc.

Approaching the Nantahala River, the sounds of cars, buses, and people enjoying the Nantahala Outdoor Center complex may become audible. Use caution as you cross US 19, and then traverse the pedestrian bridge spanning the river. On the other side of the parking lot, the AT continues northbound.

Explore the various restaurants and outfitters in the area, with amenities such as laundry and lodging available for those in need.

> **NANTAHALA OUTDOOR CENTER**
> Nestled along the banks of the river in Bryson City, North Carolina, the Nantahala Outdoor Center (NOC) stands as a premier destination for outdoor enthusiasts seeking adventure amidst the stunning Appalachian landscape. Serving as the gateway to the Nantahala Gorge, NOC offers a plethora of amenities and activities catering to day hikers, section-hikers, and thru-hikers alike.
>
> What started as a whitewater rafting company in 1972 has blossomed into a 500-acre adventure campus with a flagship store in Gatlinburg, Tennessee, and other offices throughout the region, making NOC one of the largest recreation companies in the area. Despite its size, NOC maintains a local, down-home feel, welcoming hikers with open arms.
>
> Stock up on trail essentials at the outfitter's store, offering a wide selection of gear, hiker food, and shakedowns. Refuel with hearty meals at the on-site eateries, and recharge in comfortable lodging accommodations. With shuttle services available, NOC makes it easy for section-hikers to access and depart from the trail at various points along the route. Showers are available year-round, even for nonguests.
>
> Whether you're seeking a whitewater rafting adventure or embarking on a multiday trek along the Appalachian Trail, the Nantahala Outdoor Center offers everything you need for an unforgettable outdoor experience.

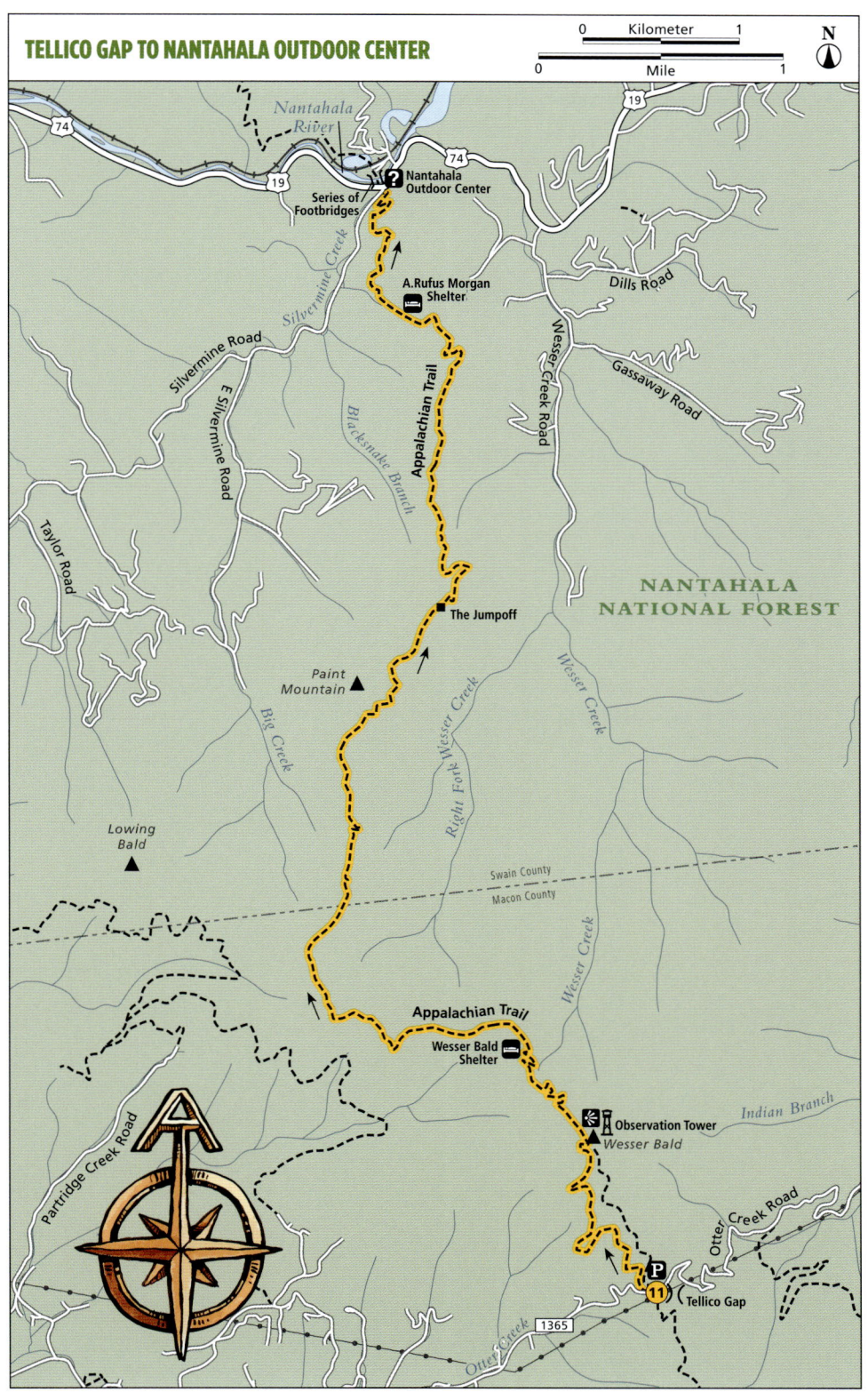

KEY POINTS

SECTION		ELEVATION (FEET)	MILES FROM SPRINGER MOUNTAIN	MILES FROM DAMASCUS
0.0	Tellico Gap, NC 1365/Otter Creek Road	3,850	129.0	342.0
1.4	Wesser Bald, views from observation tower 40 yards east	4,627	130.4	340.6
2.1	Blue-blazed trail to old spring-fed stone cistern, 0.1 mile east	4,208	131.1	339.9
2.2	Wesser Bald Shelter 0.1 mile west (no water)	4,092	131.2	339.8
4.0	The Jumpoff	3,940	133.0	338.0
5.6	Weak spring	3,008	134.6	336.4
7.1	A. Rufus Morgan Shelter, stream	2,184	136.1	334.9
7.5	Series of footbridges and streams	1,997	136.5	334.5
7.9	Nantahala Outdoor Center, US 19/74, Nantahala River	1,732	136.9	334.1

DID YOU KNOW?

The Nantahala National Forest, established in 1920, derives its name from the Cherokee word nondayeli, meaning "noonday sun" or "land of the noonday sun." This name is particularly fitting due to the numerous steep gorges within the forest that only receive sunlight when the sun is directly overhead. Encompassing more than 531,000 acres, the Nantahala National Forest is the largest of North Carolina's four national forests, with elevations ranging from 5,800 feet at Lone Bald in Jackson County to 1,200 feet along the Hiwassee River in Cherokee County.

12 NANTAHALA OUTDOOR CENTER TO FONTANA DAM VISITOR CENTER

View of Rock outcropping during ascent to Cheoah Bald

This section of the Appalachian Trail is strenuous, starting with a challenging 8.1-mile ascent from the **Nantahala Outdoor Center** to **Cheoah Bald**, where you will gain more than 3,300 feet in elevation. The hike culminates with a demanding 2,000-foot descent to **Fontana Lake**. Along the way, you will be rewarded with breathtaking vistas of the **Nantahala Gorge** from the **"Jump-Up"** and sweeping views from the summit of Cheoah Bald at 5,062 feet. As you trek this rugged terrain, you will encounter flame azalea, mountain laurel, and a rich tapestry of other native flora that adorn the trail.

Distance: 29.7 miles
Difficulty: Strenuous due to long climbs and several steep sections
Nearest town: Bryson City, North Carolina

Water availability: Water is available at both the south and north ends of the hike, as well as at several sources scattered along the trail.
Trailhead GPS: 35.3312 / -83.5922

Good to know:

- This section begins with one of the toughest hauls on the Appalachian Trail south of New England. You may want to hike from north to south to avoid the grueling 8.1-mile ascent from the Nantahala Outdoor Center to Cheoah Bald, which involves a demanding elevation gain of over 3,300 feet. Alternatively, you can split this challenging section into more manageable segments by planning early exits at Stecoah Gap (Mile 150.7) or Yellow Creek Road (Mile 158.6). Both of these points offer opportunities to break up the hike or shorten your journey if needed.
- Permits for camping in the Smokies can be printed at the Nantahala Outdoor Center.
- The Bartram Trail, another long-distance trail, intersects the AT and culminates at Cheoah Bald.

Nearby accommodations:

The Hike Inn (3204 Fontana Road), only 3 miles east of Yellow Creek Road (mile marker 158.6), offers comfortable private rooms, laundry facilities, and shuttle services for hikers. Call (828) 479-3677 for reservations.

Creekside Paradise Bed and Breakfast (123 Creekside Lane), about 2 miles west of Yellow Creek Road (mile marker 158.6), offers charming cabins, a full breakfast, hot tubs, laundry facilities, and slackpacking services for hikers. Call (828) 346-1076 for reservations.

Wade Sutton memorial, Mile 139.6

THE HIKE

From the Nantahala Outdoor Center, cross the footbridge and follow the white blaze as it leads across the parking lot to the railroad tracks, marking the beginning of the 8.1-mile ascent to Cheoah Bald, gaining more than 3,300 feet in elevation.

The trail swiftly ascends out of the gorge. After about a mile of climbing, it crosses under power lines below Flint Ridge. Soon you reach Wright Gap, where a dirt road intersects and the trail begins to steeply incline.

At the 2.5-mile mark, the AT comes to a memorial plaque honoring forest ranger Wade Sutton, inscribed: "On December 7, 1968, 783 feet southwest from this point, Wade A. Sutton, North Carolina Forest Service Ranger, gave his life suppressing a forest fire, that you might more fully enjoy your hike along this trail."

As you continue toward Grassy Gap, which sits at about 3,000 feet elevation, enjoy openings along the trail that offer views into the Nantahala Gorge. A reliable spring at 4.3 miles provides the last chance to fill up on water before reaching the upcoming shelter.

At 4.9 miles the trail sharply switches back at the Jump-Up, named for a rocky ridge where hikers would scramble and jump up onto rocks for a view of the Nantahala River valley. The trail now follows graded switchbacks, avoiding the steep section while still offering a nice view.

At 6.2 miles, reach the 4,710-foot Swim Bald and then begin descending about a mile to the Sassafras Gap Shelter, located approximately 120 yards off the trail. Nestled in a ravine, this shelter accommodates fourteen hikers and includes a nearby privy and reliable spring.

View from Cheoah Bald, Mile 145.2

> **DID YOU KNOW?**
>
> The Bartram Trail is a scenic long-distance trail that spans more than 110 miles from north Georgia to the summit of Cheoah Bald, commemorating the legacy of William Bartram. From 1773 to 1777, Bartram embarked on an extensive exploration of the southeastern United States, a region then still under colonial rule. His expeditions were instrumental in documenting and illustrating a wealth of plant and animal species previously unknown to Western science. Beyond his botanical and zoological achievements, Bartram was a perceptive ethnographer whose detailed accounts of Native American villages and their customs provided some of the earliest European perspectives on indigenous life. His comprehensive observations and reflections were later published in 1791 in Travels, a seminal work that remains a key resource for historians and naturalists studying the American South.

As the AT begins its ascent toward Cheoah Bald, keep an eye out for wild blackberries and blueberries in the summer months. Stunning views await atop the grassy slope, which reaches an elevation of 5,062 feet. Take a moment to rest your legs and soak in the scenery before the steep descent into Locust Cove Gap. Just slightly north of the summit, the trail intersects the northern terminus of the Bartram Trail.

Continuing on, the AT arrives at Locust Cove Gap, where a campsite awaits nearby. At 11.8 miles the trail passes through Simp Gap and ascends to a high point on the ridge before beginning its final descent. A series of gradual switchbacks leads to Stecoah Gap, where the trail meets NC 143 at the 13.8-mile mark.

From Stecoah Gap, the trail climbs gently for nearly a mile before descending briefly into Sweetwater Gap, where a steep ascent known as Jacob's Ladder begins. This

Jarred Douglas arriving at Fontana Dam, Mile 166.5

NANTAHALA OUTDOOR CENTER TO FONTANA DAM VISITOR CENTER

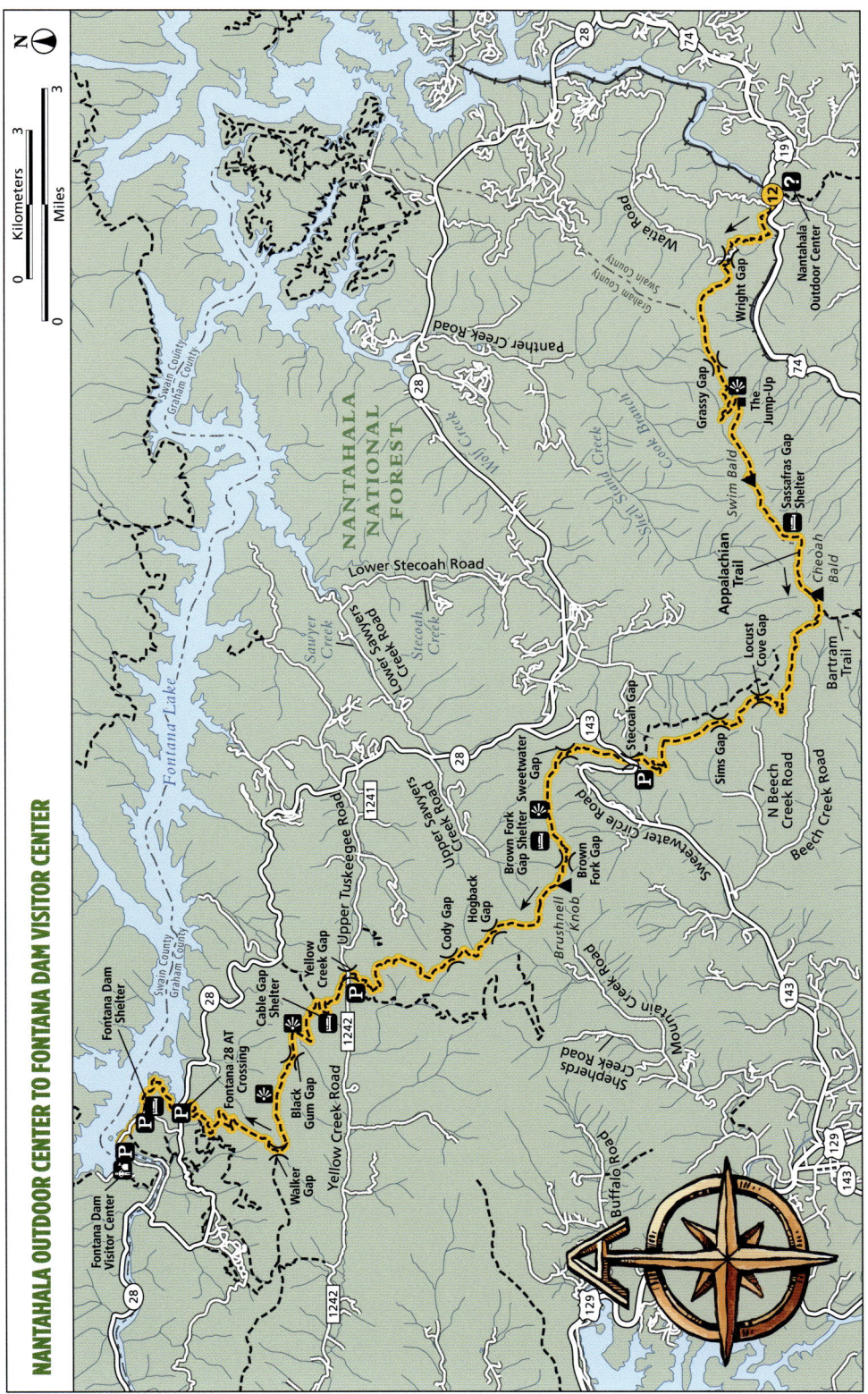

challenging stretch leads hikers up a sharp incline toward a series of cliffs. About 15 yards west of the Appalachian Trail, the cliffs offer fine views of the surrounding forest.

At 16.2 miles, you'll reach the Brown Fork Gap Shelter, with a reliable spring located to the right of the shelter. The trail then undulates through Brown Fork Gap, climbs over Brushnell Knob, and dips through Hogback Gap.

From Hogback Gap, elevation changes are minimal as the trail follows the ridgecrest to Cody Gap. Just beyond Cody Gap, the trail begins a gradual descent.

At 21.3 miles, cross a small cascade before arriving at Yellow Creek Gap, where Yellow Creek Road intersects the trail.

At 22.5 miles, arrive at Cable Gap Shelter and begin a gradual ascent of Yellow Creek Mountain before dipping into Black Gum Gap and continuing along the ridgecrest. After reaching a high point near the summit, the trail begins a long, gradual 2,010-foot descent to Walker Gap and Fontana Lake.

At 28 miles, cross NC 28 and descend a set of stone steps to the Fontana Lake Marina parking area. Follow the white blazes past the restrooms, through a wooded stretch, and then along the banks of Fontana Lake.

At 29.3 miles, reach the junction for the Fontana Dam Shelter, often referred to as the "Fontana Hilton" for its amenities. From here, descend along the sidewalk to the dam and visitor center, where you'll find exhibits, restrooms, and public showers.

Note: Fontana Dam marks the southern boundary of Great Smoky Mountains National Park. If you plan to continue hiking north, you must obtain a permit before camping in the park.

TRAIL TOWN: FONTANA DAM, NORTH CAROLINA

Experience the charm of Fontana Dam, North Carolina, a designated Appalachian Trail Community where the majestic Smoky Mountains and outstanding hiker amenities meet. This remote town, named for the towering hydroelectric dam built in the 1940s, is home to the tallest dam in the eastern United States. The Appalachian Trail famously crosses the top, offering hikers both a unique experience and breathtaking views.

At Fontana Dam you'll find excellent accommodations at **Fontana Village Resort**, which offers cabins, campsites, a lodge, and a variety of dining options. Or choose **The Hike Inn** for a cozy retreat with private rooms, full breakfast, and shuttle services.

The town also provides essential services for hikers, including the **Fontana Village Store** for resupplies, the visitor center for trail maps and local history, and a post office for mail drops. Explore nearby trails for more hiking or mountain biking. Anglers will find great fishing opportunities on Fontana Lake, one of the deepest man-made lakes in the country. The lake supports thriving populations of bluegill, bass, and catfish, while trout abound in the numerous streams that flow into the lake on the Smokies side. Check out the **Fontana Village Marina** to rent pontoon boats, canoes, kayaks, and stand-up paddleboards.

For more information or to make a reservation, contact Fontana Village Resort at (828) 498-2211, The Hike Inn at (828) 479-3677, and the Fontana Dam Visitor Center at (828) 498-2155.

KEY POINTS

SECTION		ELEVATION (FEET)	MILES FROM SPRINGER MOUNTAIN	MILES FROM DAMASCUS
0.0	Nantahala Outdoor Center, US 19/74, Nantahala River	1,732	136.9	334.1
0.2	Side trail to bunkhouse	1,771	137.1	333.9
1.7	Wright Gap, Watia Road (closed during snow)	2,403	138.6	332.4
2.6	Wade Sutton memorial, spring	2,979	139.5	331.5
2.9	Grassy Gap, Grassy Gap Trail west to spring	3,012	139.8	331.2
4.3	Spring	3,575	141.2	329.8
4.9	The Jump-Up	3,814	141.8	329.2
6.2	Swim Bald	4,720	143.1	327.9
7.1	Sassafras Gap Shelter 0.1 mile west, spring	4,391	144.0	327.0
8.3	Cheoah Bald	5,062	145.2	325.8
8.5	Bartram Trail to the west	4,911	145.4	325.6
10.7	Locust Cove Gap, camping, water to west	3,640	147.6	323.4
11.8	Simp Gap	3,556	148.7	322.3
13.8	Stecoah Gap, NC 143, Sweetwater Circle Road, water on blue-blazed trail (parking)	3,165	150.7	320.3
14.8	Sweetwater Gap, start of Jacob's Ladder	3,270	151.7	319.3
16.2	Brown Fork Gap Shelter, spring	3,813	153.1	317.9
17.1	Bushnell Knob	3,928	154.0	317.0
18.5	Hogback Gap	3,500	155.4	315.6
19.3	Cody Gap, water 0.2 mile west	3,620	156.2	314.8
21.3	Stream	3,255	158.2	312.8
21.6	Yellow Creek Gap, CR 1242, Yellow Creek Road (parking)	2,954	158.6	312.4
22.5	Cable Gap Shelter, stream	2,878	159.4	311.6
23.9	Black Gum Gap	3,403	160.8	310.2
25.3	Walker Gap	3,403	162.2	308.8
25.6	Footbridge, stream	3,266	162.5	308.5
27.3	Spring	2,287	164.2	306.8
28.0	NC 28, Fontana 28 AT crossing (parking)	1,756	164.9	306.1
29.3	Fontana Dam Shelter, water spigot	1,853	166.2	304.8
29.7	Fontana Dam Visitor Center (parking)	1,700	166.6	304.4

13 FONTANA DAM VISITOR CENTER TO NEWFOUND GAP

View from Fontana Dam, Mile 166.5

The longest hike in this guidebook, this segment of the Appalachian Trail is renowned for its dramatic scenery, taking you through the wildest and most untouched part of the Great Smoky Mountains. It features the trail's longest continuous section without road crossings and runs along the North Carolina–Tennessee state line for much of its distance. As you trek, you'll summit **Kuwohi (formerly Clingmans Dome)**, the highest peak on the AT at 6,643 feet, and pass notable landmarks like **Fontana Dam** and **Rocky Top**, the inspiration behind Tennessee's state anthem. Other notable peaks include **Shuckstack Mountain**, **Thunderhead Mountain**, and **Silers Bald**. Be prepared for climbing, as there are many deep gaps and high peaks to traverse, completing this roller-coaster adventure at **Newfound Gap**.

Distance: 41.3 miles
Difficulty: Strenuous due to distance and a series of demanding climbs to high peaks
Nearest town: Fontana Village, North Carolina (2 miles west of trailhead at NC 28); Gatlinburg, Tennessee (15 miles west of Newfound Gap)
Water Availability: Many water sources in this section are unreliable. Fill up at visitor center and plan accordingly.
Trailhead GPS: 35.4414 / -83.7968

Good to know:

- The visitor center at Fontana Dam is open from early May to late October.
- No pets are allowed on the AT in Great Smoky Mountains National Park.
- Overnight permits are required.
- The road that leads to the parking lot at Kuwohi is closed in winter.
- Fontana Dam Shelter, often referred to as the "Fontana Hilton" for its impressive design and creature comforts, is 0.4 mile north of the visitor center. If you are getting a late start, enjoy staying the night here to start out refreshed in the morning.
- Consider hiking this section from north to south, as it entails less elevation gain compared to hiking in the opposite direction. Hiking north to south, you'll ascend approximately 5,200 feet, whereas hiking south to north involves a steeper ascent of about 6,800 feet.

View from Fontana Dam, Mile 166.5

THE HIKE

Start your hike at the trailhead near the Fontana Dam Visitor Center, heading north on the AT, following the shore of Fontana Lake. Walk briefly along a paved road before passing a bulletin board and beginning the 2,000-foot ascent of Shuckstack Mountain, crossing into Great Smoky Mountains National Park. At 3.2 miles, navigate the boulder fields as you climb toward Shuckstack.

Reaching the summit of Shuckstack at 4.7 miles, you can take a short 0.1-mile side trail to the east to visit the Shuckstack fire tower and enjoy impressive views of the surrounding landscape.

Continue hiking, passing through Sassafras Gap and reaching Birch Spring Gap, which features tent pads, bear cables, and a nearby spring just over a mile from Shuckstack. The AT continues to climb, reaching Doe Knob at 4,520 feet, and drops down to 3,842 feet at Ekaneetlee Gap.

At 11.4 miles reach Mollies Ridge Shelter. From here the trail turns into a roller coaster, traversing many ups and downs with minimal elevation gain or loss. Hike up to Devils Tater Patch before descending approximately 660 feet to Little Abrams Gap. At 14.5 miles the AT passes the Russell Field Shelter, which accommodates fourteen hikers with a spring nearby.

View from Shuckstack tower, Mile 171.2

Mollies Ridge Shelter, Mile 177.9

At 17.4 miles into the hike, the Eagle Creek Trail intersects from the east. This trail leads 0.2 mile to Spence Field Shelter and continues on to connect with the Lakeshore Trail at Fontana Lake. Shortly after this junction, the Bote Mountain Trail intersects from the west. A spring can be found approximately 0.2 mile down this trail as it extends farther to Laurel Creek Road.

Following a couple of steep climbs, the Appalachian Trail reaches the summit of Rocky Top, renowned for its breathtaking panoramic views and as the inspiration for Tennessee's official state song. Relish the vistas from Rocky Top before continuing to Thunderhead Mountain, which once offered outstanding views but is now obscured by dense rhododendron thickets. Be cautious in this area, as rattlesnakes are known to sunbathe on the warm rocks. Over the next 4.5 miles, you will navigate through several gaps before arriving at Derrick Knob Shelter. Water is available here from a nearby spring.

At 25.8 miles, cross over Cold Spring Knob at an elevation of 5,204 feet and descend rapidly to Buckeye Gap. From Buckeye Gap, hike approximately 3 miles to Silers Bald, a mountaintop meadow offering lovely views of the Smokies while gently gaining elevation. In the summer months you might be rewarded with delicious wild blackberries along the way. Beyond Silers Bald you will reach the Double Spring Gap Shelter at 30.9 miles, named for two nearby springs; the better of the two springs is located about 15 yards west of the shelter on the North Carolina side.

Hiker approaching Spence Field Shelter in the snow, Mile 183.9

Spence Field Shelter, Mile 183.9

View from Rocky Top, Mile 185.0

View from Thunderhead Mountain, Mile 185.6

Fireplace inside Siler Bald Shelter, Mile 195.7

From the shelter, you face a steady climb for roughly 3 miles, crossing over Mount Buckley and gaining more than 1,000 feet in elevation. At 33.4 miles, you will encounter a paved side trail leading to a small gift shop, restrooms, and a parking lot for Kuwohi (formerly Clingmans Dome) and Andrews Bald. Continue on the Appalachian Trail to reach Kuwohi, at 6,658 feet the highest peak on the Appalachian Trail. An observation tower (located east of the AT) sits at the summit, offering 360-degree views of the Smokies, although frequent cloud cover may obscure the view.

The trail then descends steeply and traverses the summit of Mount Love before plunging into Collins Gap at 35.3 miles. From Collins Gap, ascend to Mount Collins, reaching the 6,187-foot summit at 36.1 miles. Here you will pass the Sugarland Mountain Trail, which branches off 0.5 mile west to the Mount Collins Shelter and continues farther to Little River Road at Fighting Creek Gap.

Kuwohi observation tower, Mile 200.3

Views from Kuwohi observation tower, Mile 200.3

Kuwohi tower path and parking area, Mile 200.3

Sugarland Mountain Trail,
Mount Collins Shelter sign,
Mile 203.0

Mount Collins Shelter privy,
Mile 203.0

Mount Collins Shelter, Mile 203.0

View from Newfound Gap, Mile 207.9

At 36.8 miles a side trail intersects from the east. This trail leads to the Fork Mountain Trail, which extends 14.7 miles to a public road at the NPS Deep Creek Campground. Continuing on the AT, descend for 2.7 miles to reach the Road Prong Trail, where you will find parking for Kuwohi Road.

Next, traverse the crest of Mount Mingus, where you will see two wild hog exclosures, designed to protect fragile plant life. Shortly after, enjoy glimpses of Mount LeConte through the trees from the ridge before descending approximately 1.5 miles to Newfound Gap.

KEY POINTS

SECTION	LANDMARK	ELEVATION (FEET)	MILES FROM SPRINGER MOUNTAIN	MILES FROM DAMASCUS
0.0	Fontana Dam Visitor Center (parking)	1,700	166.6	304.4
4.6	Shuckstack fire tower, 0.1 mile east	3,889	171.2	299.8
5.9	Birch Spring Gap, campsite 100 yards west, unreliable spring	3,736	172.5	298.5
7.9	Side trail to Gregory Bald, 0.3 mile west	4,443	174.5	296.5
8.1	Doe Knob	4,520	174.7	296.3
9.6	Ekaneetlee Gap, spring	3,842	176.2	294.8
11.3	Mollies Ridge Shelter, unreliable spring	4,585	177.9	293.1
11.8	Devils Tater Patch	4,775	178.4	292.6

(continued)

SECTION	LANDMARK	ELEVATION (FEET)	MILES FROM SPRINGER MOUNTAIN	MILES FROM DAMASCUS
12.9	Little Abrams Gap	4,120	179.5	291.5
14.4	Russell Field Shelter, weak spring 0.1 mile west	4,247	181.0	290.0
17.3	Spence Field Shelter 0.2 mile east on Eagle Creek Trail, spring	4,914	183.9	287.1
18.4	Rocky Top	5,440	185.0	286.0
19.0	Thunderhead Mountain	5,527	185.6	285.4
19.7	Water to west	4,965	186.3	284.7
21.6	Starkey Gap	4,552	188.2	282.8
23.4	Derrick Knob Shelter, spring near shelter	4,884	190.0	281.0
23.7	Sams Gap, water 0.1 mile west on Greenbriar Ridge Trail	4,771	190.3	280.7
25.9	Miry Ridge Trail to west	4,944	192.5	278.5
26.1	Buckeye Gap	4,817	192.7	278.3
29.1	Silers Bald Shelter, spring	5,452	195.7	275.3
29.3	Silers Bald	5,607	195.9	275.1
30.8	Double Spring Gap Shelter, spring	5,509	197.4	273.6
31.4	Goshen Prong Trail to west	5,775	198.0	273.0
33.3	Trail to Kuwohi (formerly Clingmans Dome) parking area, 0.5 mile west	6,553	199.9	271.1
33.6	Kuwohi tower path, paved path from parking area to observation tower	6,643	200.2	273.1
33.7	Kuwohi, observation tower to east	6,658	200.3	270.7
34.1	Mount Love	6,446	200.7	270.3
35.2	Collins Gap	5,737	201.8	269.2
36.0	Mount Collins	6,187	202.6	268.4
36.4	Sugarland Mountain Trail, Mount Collins Shelter and spring 0.5 mile west	6,187	203.0	268.0
36.7	Fork Mountain Trail east to Kuwohi Road, water	5,889	203.3	267.7
39.4	Road Prong Trail (parking)	5,273	206.0	265.0
39.8	Mingus Ridge	5,436	206.4	264.6
41.3	Newfound Gap, US 441 (parking)	5,045	207.9	263.1

FONTANA DAM VISITOR CENTER TO NEWFOUND GAP

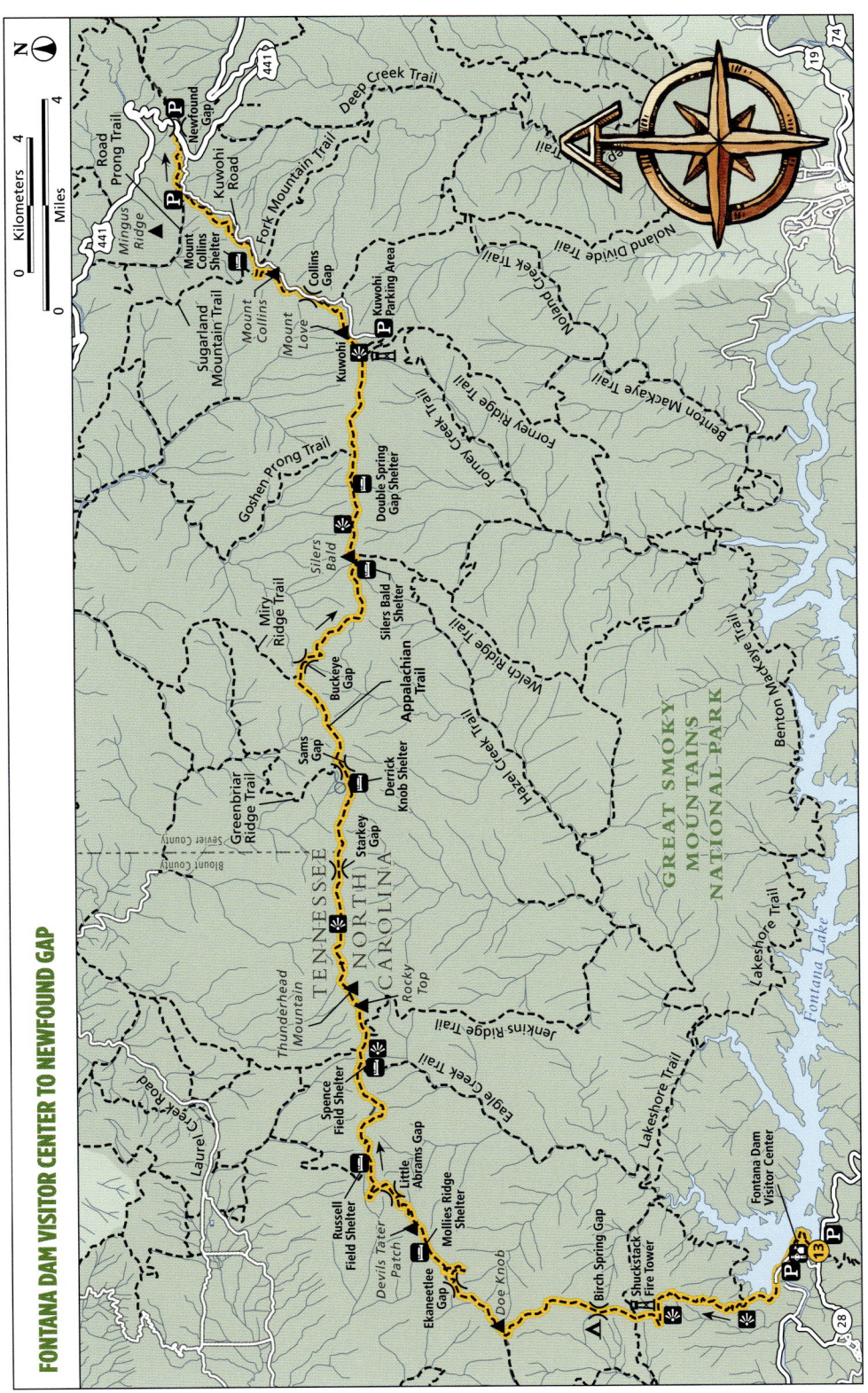

TRAIL TOWN: GATLINBURG, TENNESSEE

Gatlinburg, Tennessee, is a must-stop for hikers traveling the Appalachian Trail. Nestled in the heart of Great Smoky Mountains National Park, this vibrant town serves as the gateway to some of the most stunning natural beauty in the country. Once a remote mountain village, Gatlinburg has transformed into a popular tourist destination known for its walkability, rich Southern hospitality, and access to the park's 850 miles of hiking trails. Gatlinburg is the perfect base camp for adventurers seeking to explore cascading waterfalls, wildlife, and the remnants of old mountain settlements.

Start your adventure at the **Sugarlands Visitor Center**, where you can gather the latest trail information and learn about historical hiking routes that offer insights into the lives of early Smoky Mountains settlers. For all your gear and supply needs, visit the **Nantahala Outdoor Center (NOC)**, a one-stop shop for outdoor equipment and essentials. Indulge in a sweet treat at the **Donut Friar**, where you can enjoy a delicious French cruller and pick up a few snacks for the trail.

Explore the unique offerings of the **Great Smoky Arts and Crafts Community** with a relaxing ride on the **Gatlinburg Trolley**, and immerse yourself in the creativity of the acclaimed **Arrowmont School of Arts and Crafts**. For a taste of local tradition, visit **Ole Smoky Moonshine**, the first federally licensed distillery in east Tennessee, and sample some authentic mountain-made moonshine.

For shuttle services and guided adventures, check out **Smoky Mountain Guides** or **A Walk in the Woods**. The **Gatlinburg Welcome Center** and **Gatlinburg Post Office** are also available for visitor information and mailing needs.

Whether you're preparing for the trail or just exploring, Gatlinburg is the ideal base camp for your Great Smoky Mountains adventure.

14 NEWFOUND GAP TO DAVENPORT GAP

Historical AT sign and hikers entering the trail north at Newfound Gap, Mile 207.9

Journey through the heart of the **Great Smoky Mountains** along this challenging 31.4-mile stretch of the Appalachian Trail. There are numerous highlights along this hike, each offering its own unique charm. **Charlies Bunion**, a rocky outcrop, provides breathtaking vistas of the surrounding peaks and valleys, especially during vibrant fall colors. Take a moment to pay homage to **Cherokee heritage** along Hughes Ridge, adding depth to your journey. And don't miss the opportunity to ascend the **Mount Cammerer** fire tower for even more awe-inspiring views. From rugged rocky ledges to lush forests, this section traverses some of the wildest terrain in the Smokies, with ascents totaling roughly 4,600 feet and descents totaling more than 7,650 feet. Prepare accordingly with ample food and water, and allow extra time for climbs in and out of gaps and over peaks.

Distance: 31.4 miles
Difficulty: Strenuous due to distance and high-elevation exposure
Nearest town: Gatlinburg, Tennessee (15 miles west of Newfound Gap)

Water availability: Water is available at the trailhead. Some water sources are far apart throughout this hike; plan accordingly.
Trailhead GPS: 35.6112 / -83.4257

Good to know:

- Restrooms are located at the Newfound Gap trailhead.
- This is a very popular day-hike destination, as Charlies Bunion is only 4 miles from Newfound Gap. Expect crowds.
- Overnight permits are required to camp within Great Smoky Mountains National Park.
- There are considerable amounts of climbing in both directions; prepare accordingly.

View near Sweat Heifer Creek Trail

THE HIKE

From the large parking area, head toward the Rockefeller Memorial; follow the trail veering to the right of the memorial, winding its way into the spruce-fir forest. Approximately 1.5 miles along the trail, the terrain levels out as it intersects the Sweat Heifer Creek Trail at 1.8 miles.

Continue your ascent along the ridge until you reach the junction with the Boulevard Trail. This trail stretches westward for 5.3 miles, leading to Mount LeConte, the third-highest peak in the Smokies. Nestled just below the summit lies the Mount LeConte Lodge, providing rustic accommodations and hearty family-style meals. Remember to secure reservations in advance for this mountain retreat. About 100 yards from the AT, a spur trail off the Boulevard Trail leads to Mount Kephart and the Jumpoff.

At 3.1 miles, reach the Icewater Spring Shelter, a nice spot to take a break in the thick soft grass. Water for this shelter is available from a spring 25 yards north on the AT. The trail descends for about a mile, reaching the south end of the Charlies Bunion loop trail.

At the 4.0-mile mark, the trail diverges. The right fork follows the AT; the left fork guides you along a narrow, rocky ledge to Charlies Bunion before rejoining the AT in just 0.2 mile.

From Charlies Bunion, the panoramic vista encompasses Mount LeConte, the Jumpoff, Mount Kephart, the gorges on the headwaters of Porters Creek and beyond, Greenbrier Pinnacle, and the Sawteeth, a jagged knifelike section of the state line. Named by Horace

Accessible portion of Charlies Bunion, Mile 211.9

Mount Kephart from Charlies Bunion, Mile 211.9

View from Charlies Bunion, Mile 211.9

> **DID YOU KNOW?**
> Charlies Bunion was once blanketed by heath bald, but a logging fire in 1925 devastated the vegetation, and a 1929 cloudburst washed away the exposed soil. Today, lichens and mosses dot some of the crevices, while rhododendron, mountain laurel, and sand myrtle strive to establish themselves.

Kephart in homage to the sore foot of local mountaineer Charlie Conner, who aided Kephart and photographer George Masa in assessing fire and storm damage in 1929, Charlies Bunion holds historical significance. It's vital to exercise caution, particularly in foggy, wet, icy, or stormy conditions. Be aware that the terrain here can be quite treacherous due to the high iron content in the Anakeesta Formation slate, which breaks into slippery slabs that can be hazardous for hikers. Sadly, there have been fatal accidents in this area, so please take extra care, especially if you're with children.

Continuing along the AT, the trail skirts to the right of the ridgetop, passing through dense patches of spruce. At 4.5 miles a sign on the right marks the junction with the Dry Sluice Gap Trail. This trail provides access to Smokemont Campground, 8.5 miles downhill, and Kephart Shelter, 3.8 miles downhill via the Dry Sluice Gap and Kephart Prong Trails.

From the Dry Sluice Gap junction, the AT ascends along a rock ledge to the left of the ridgetop. You might notice the ledge sprinkled with vibrant, colorful lichens on the surface, with clumps of moss nestled in the cracks. As you continue, the ledge narrows, reaching its peak atop the section of jagged exposed rock known as the Sawteeth.

At 5.4 miles you reach Porters Gap. From this point, the trail undulates, offering panoramic views on both sides as it winds back and forth along the state line. At 9.2 miles you arrive at Bradleys View, an ideal spot to take a break and savor the breathtaking vista of a sea of mountains stretched out before you.

Cross Hughes Ridge, which originates in Qualla Boundary, the land encompassing Cherokee, North Carolina, where a handful of Cherokee families once resided. Continue hiking until the junction with the Hughes Ridge Trail at 10.5 miles. This trail leads eastward for 0.5 mile to Pecks Corner Shelter. Beyond this point and all the way to Davenport Gap, hikers will share the trail with horseback riders.

After a challenging rocky ascent, you reach Eagle Rocks at 11.4 miles, where you can bask in the stunning views of the valley and gorge below. Descend to Copper Gap and continue until you reach Mount Sequoyah at 12.9 miles. This peak is named for a Cherokee leader who developed the Cherokee written language; the giant sequoia trees of the American West also bear a form of his name. Mount Sequoyah rises slightly less than 6,000 feet. From here, descend to Chapman Gap and then ascend the side of Mount Chapman, reaching a high point of 6,218 feet at 14.9 miles.

Continue along the trail as it descends and eventually arrives at the junction with the Tricorner Knob Shelter at 15.7 miles. Three ridge crests and county lines meet here. Just north of the shelter junction, the AT intersects the Balsam Mountain Trail, which leads east.

The trail ascends gradually then skirts the summit of Mount Guyot, maintaining an elevation above 6,000 feet over the next 1.5 miles. Mount Guyot rises to 6,621 feet, making it the second-highest peak in the Smokies. It was named for Arnold Guyot, a Swiss-born geologist who meticulously measured many of the mountains along the AT before trails were even established. Water is available at Guyot Spring at the 17.1-mile mark.

The AT briefly levels out before embarking on a long descent into Camel Gap. At 18.6 miles you arrive at Deer Creek Gap, offering excellent vistas of Mount Guyot, Mount Sterling, and other prominent peaks. From here the AT does not rise above 6,000 feet again until Roan Mountain, Tennessee, a staggering 150 miles to the north.

As you pass Yellow Creek Gap and continue the descent, keep an eye out for the wreckage of the Air Force F-4 Phantom jet that crashed into Inadu Knob on January 4, 1984. (*Inadu* is Cherokee for "snake.") Upon reaching the junction with the Snake Den Ridge Trail at 19.5 miles, you'll find a side trail leading west for 5.3 miles to Cosby Campground. The next 2.3 miles involve a steep ascent to Camel Gap, where Camel Gap Trail intersects the AT.

Arrive at Cosby Knob Shelter, a great spot to camp for the night before tackling the remaining 8 miles of this section. From the shelter, descend 0.7 mile into Low Gap before beginning to ascend once more. Climb until you reach a high point on the ridge of Mount Cammerer. Here you have the option of taking a 0.6-mile side trail to the summit, where you'll find a lookout tower offering breathtaking panoramic views.

At 26.5 miles you'll find a spring to the west of the AT near a site where the Civilian Conservation Corps (CCC) camped while constructing the Mount Cammerer fire tower in the late 1930s. From here the trail is mostly downhill until you reach Davenport Gap, with the exception of a short climb before reaching the Davenport Gap Shelter. You'll arrive at the shelter at 30.3 miles. Take a moment to rest, replenish your water supply, and enjoy a snack before embarking on the final mile of this section, which concludes at Davenport Gap.

> ### DID YOU KNOW?
>
> On September 2, 1940, President Franklin D. Roosevelt formally dedicated Great Smoky Mountains National Park at Newfound Gap, straddling the border between North Carolina and Tennessee, "for the enjoyment of the people." Prior to its designation as a park, the land was owned by the Cherokee, local farmers, timber companies, and families. The Smokies was the first national park in America to necessitate fundraising and the acquisition of land from private owners. The Rockefeller Memorial, situated along the Appalachian Trail, serves as a tribute to the numerous individuals who generously donated their land and funds to establish the park, now cherished by many.

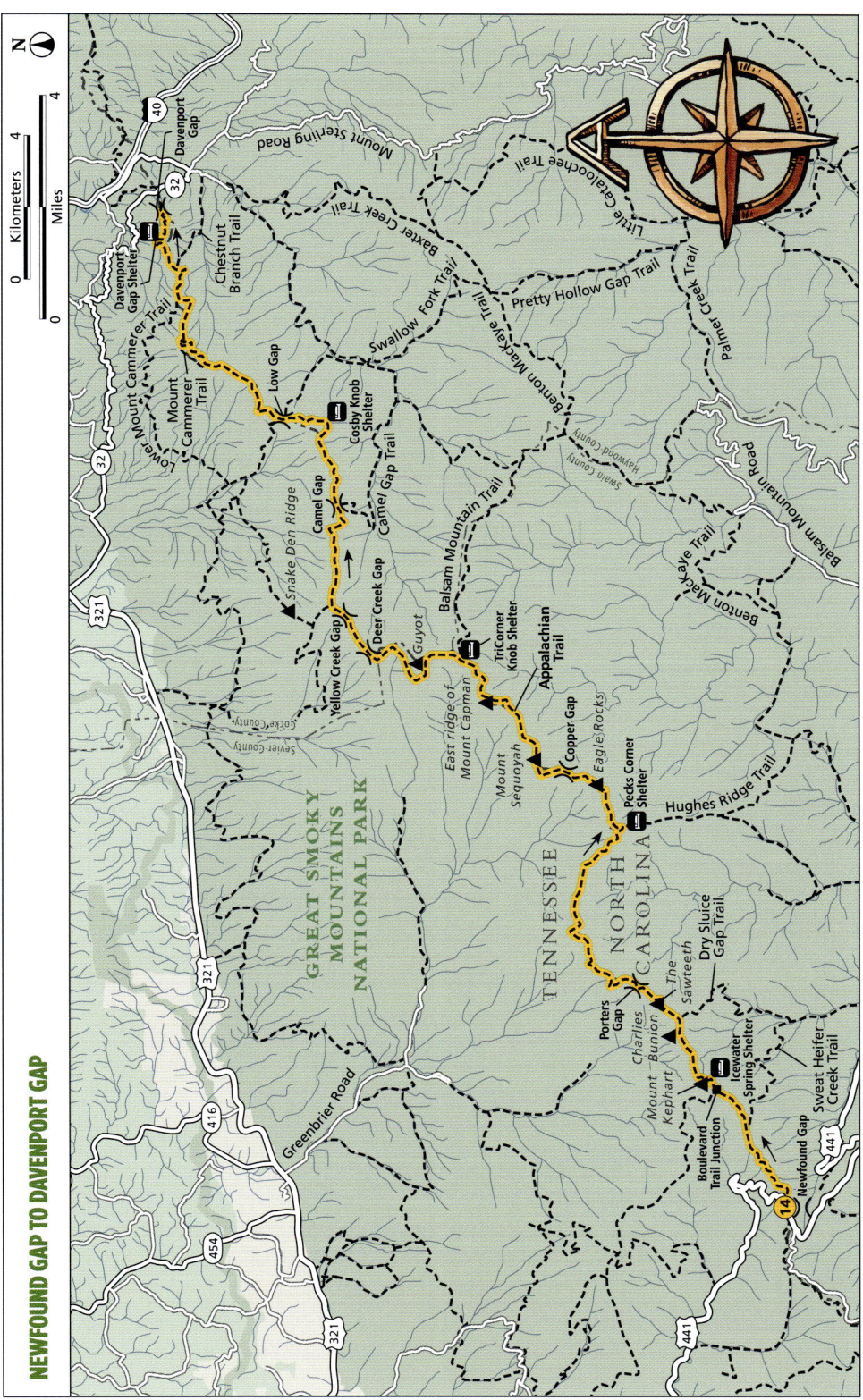

KEY POINTS

SECTION		ELEVATION	MILES FROM SPRINGER MOUNTAIN	MILES FROM DAMASCUS
0.0	Newfound Gap, US 441	5,045	207.9	263.1
1.8	Sweat Heifer Creek Trail to east	5,834	209.7	261.3
2.8	Boulevard Trail Junction	6,035	210.7	260.3
3.1	Icewater Spring Shelter, spring 50 yards north on AT	5,935	211.0	260.0
4.0	Charlies Bunion Trail, 0.1 mile west	5,521	211.9	259.1
4.5	Dry Sluice Gap Trail to east	5,399	212.4	258.6
5.1	The Sawteeth	5,396	213.0	258.0
5.4	Porters Gap	5,366	213.3	257.7
9.2	Bradleys View	5,481	217.1	253.9
10.5	Pecks Corner Shelter and spring 0.5 mile east	5,556	218.4	252.6
11.4	Eagle Rocks	5,847	219.3	251.7
12.2	Copper Gap	5,515	220.1	250.9
12.9	Mount Sequoyah	5,946	220.8	250.2
14.9	East ridge of Mount Capman	6,218	222.8	248.2
15.7	Tricorner Knob Shelter, spring	5,895	223.6	247.4
15.8	Balsam Mountain Trail to east	5,963	223.7	247.3
17.1	Guyot Spring	6,302	225.0	246.0
18.6	Deer Creek Gap	6,054	226.5	244.5
19.3	Yellow Creek Gap	5,900	227.2	243.8
19.5	Snake Den Ridge, Cosby Campground 5.3 miles west	5,790	227.4	243.6
21.8	Camel Gap, Camel Gap Trail to east	4,671	229.7	241.3
23.5	Cosby Knob Shelter, spring	4,788	231.4	239.6
24.1	Low Gap, Cosby Campground 2.5 miles west	4,240	232.0	239.0
26.2	Mount Cammerer Trail, 0.6 mile west to summit with lookout tower	4,948	234.1	236.9
28.4	Lower Mount Cammerer Trail, Cosby Campground 7.8 miles west	3,467	236.3	234.7
29.3	Chestnut Branch Trail, Big Creek Ranger Station 2.0 miles east	2,874	237.2	233.8
30.3	Davenport Gap Shelter, spring	2,592	238.2	232.8
31.4	Davenport Gap, TN 32, NC 284	1,975	239.3	231.7

15 DAVENPORT GAP TO MAX PATCH ROAD

View from Snowbird Mountain, Mile 246.4

The highlight of this hike is Snowbird Mountain, a grassy bald resting at 4,263 feet, and an FAA control tower at the summit offering excellent views. Although this section is rated strenuous for the long ups and downs into gaps, it is well graded with no particular rough spots. The gap is situated on both the North Carolina–Tennessee border and the Great Smoky Mountains National Park boundary.

Distance: 15.3 miles
Difficulty: Strenuous due to distance and long ascents and descents
Nearest town: Hot Springs, North Carolina
Water availability: Water is not available at the trailhead, so be sure to fill up before starting your hike. The first water source is just a mile into the trail, and water sources remain plentiful until the end of the section.
Trailhead GPS: 35.770 / -83.1115

Good to know:

- Overnight parking is not permitted at the Davenport Gap trailhead. Vandalism has been reported in this area. Park at the Big Creek Ranger Station, 1 mile east of the gap, and walk to the trailhead, or park your vehicle at the Max Patch parking area, the northern section of this hike, and arrange for a shuttle drop-off.
- Big Creek Campsite is roughly 2 miles east from Davenport Gap. Campsites with potable water are available but no showers. Open from early April to late October, reservations are required. Chestnut Branch Trail (2 miles) connects to the AT 0.1 mile south of Davenport Gap.
- Reservations and permits are required for all overnight stays. Camping is only allowed at designated campsites and shelters. Backpackers must stick to their reserved site, whether it's a campsite or a shelter. Only those with official AT hiker tags may camp outside a shelter if it is full. To obtain a permit or learn more about backcountry regulations, visit www.nps.gov/grsm/planyourvisit/backcountry-regs.

FAA control tower, Mile 246.4

THE HIKE

From Davenport Gap, follow the AT for about 20 yards, cross a gravel road, and ascend into the woods. Keep an eye out for orchids blooming orange July through August. Trek through pines, oaks, and mountain laurel during the brief uphill climb before descending steeply through rhododendron, crossing under power lines at 0.7 mile. After the power line clearing, the AT crosses the State Line Branch at 1.1 mile. Be sure to follow that familiar white blaze.

At 1.6 miles you arrive at the southern end of the bridge spanning the Pigeon River. Cross the bridge, hike under I-40, and proceed along Green Corner Road for 150 yards until you reach rock steps.

Arrive at Painter Branch and cross the creek to reach a small campsite. A blue-blazed trail leads to a spring nearby. Continue walking upstream along Painter Branch, then follow the ridgeline as the trail ascends, reaching Spanish Oak Gap at 5.7 miles.

At 7.1 miles, arrive at a grassy bald along the western ridge of Snowbird Mountain. A short side trail leads to a Federal Aviation Administration tower—take in the sweeping views from this open summit before continuing on. The trail dips through a sag between the mountain's peaks before beginning a steady descent.

Pass Wildcat Spring at 7.9 miles, located about 25 feet uphill from the AT, and continue to Turkey Gap at 8.6 miles. The descent continues, reaching another spring at 9.4 miles. Shortly after, arrive at Deep Gap, where Groundhog Creek Shelter is located 0.2 mile east of the trail—an ideal spot for a rest or an overnight stay.

From the shelter junction, begin the ascent toward the ridge of Harmon Den Mountain. Around mile 12, a spur trail leads 350 feet west to Hawks Roost, a rock formation offering a quiet place to camp or take in the surroundings. At 12.5 miles reach Brown Gap, where you'll be walking atop 1.1-billion-year-old granite gneiss—rock sometimes referred to as the "core" of the Appalachians.

Beyond the gap, the AT rolls along the ridge, passing the yellow-blazed Cherry Creek Trail at 15 miles and arriving at Max Patch Road at 15.3 miles.

Pisgah sign for Max Patch at Max Patch Road, Mile 254.6

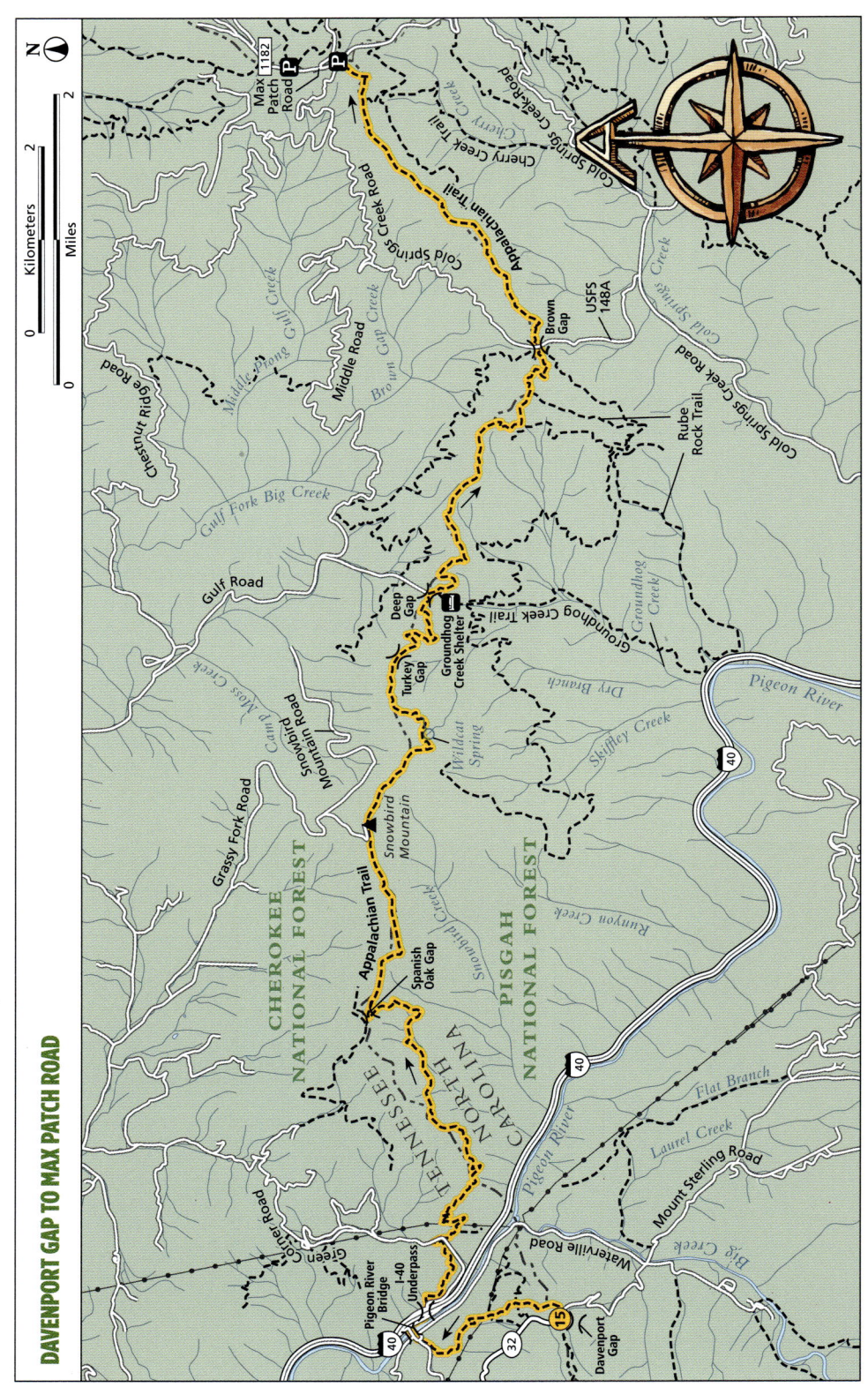

DAVENPORT GAP TO MAX PATCH ROAD

> **DID YOU KNOW?**
> "Painter Branch" is likely named for the panthers, or mountain lions, that once roamed the area before being hunted to extinction.

KEY POINTS

SECTION		ELEVATION (FEET)	MILES FROM SPRINGER MOUNTAIN	MILES FROM DAMASCUS
0.0	Davenport Gap, TN 32, NC 284	1,975	239.3	231.6
1.1	Stateline Branch, water	1,698	240.4	230.6
1.6	Pigeon River Bridge	1,371	240.9	230.1
1.9	I-40 underpass	1,435	241.2	229.8
2.1	Stream	1,568	241.4	229.6
2.7	Green Corner Road, water	1,761	242.0	229.0
4.8	Painter Branch, blue-blazed trail to east across Painter Creek to campsite and spring	2,845	244.1	226.9
5.7	Spanish Oak Gap	3,465	245.0	226.0
7.1	Snowbird Mountain, Grassy Fork Road	4,263	246.4	224.6
7.9	Wildcat Spring	4,083	247.2	223.8
8.6	Turkey Gap	3,630	247.9	223.1
9.4	Spring	3,022	248.7	222.3
9.6	Deep Gap, Groundhog Creek Shelter 0.2 mile east, spring to left of shelter	2,897	248.9	222.1
11.4	Spring 30 yards east	3,566	250.7	220.3
11.9	Rube Rock Trail to Hawks Roost	3,872	251.2	219.8
12.5	Brown Gap, USFS 148A, spring	3,500	251.8	219.2
15.0	Cherry Creek Trail, water 0.3 mile east	4,338	254.3	216.7
15.3	Max Patch Road, NC 1182, stream to north	4,254	254.6	216.4

16 MAX PATCH ROAD TO HOT SPRINGS

View from Max Patch with blaze facing south, Mile 255.1

The highlight of this section is the 4,629-foot summit of **Max Patch**, a large grassy bald with jaw-dropping views of many prominent mountains, including the **Great Smoky Mountains**, **Black Mountains**, and **Mount Mitchell**. Finish your hike in downtown **Hot Springs**, a historic, hiker-friendly trail town and designated Appalachian Trail Community.

Distance: 20.6 miles
Difficulty: Moderate but challenging due to a lengthy descent
Nearest town: Hot Springs, North Carolina
Water availability: Water is available at Roaring Fork and Walnut Mountain Shelters. The trail also crosses several streams where water can be treated for drinking.
Trailhead GPS: 35.796 / -82.9627

Good to know:

- There are shuttle services available in Hot Springs. Check in with Bluff Mountain Outfitters.
- If you are leaving a car at the Max Patch parking area, avoid driving without four-wheel drive following heavy rain or snow. The gravel road can become muddy and dangerous.

View from Max Patch with rainbow, Mile 255.4

THE HIKE

From Max Patch Road, begin hiking north on the AT, climbing modestly in elevation. Arrive at the summit of Max Patch at 0.8 mile. From here, the views are endless. You will most likely encounter others enjoying the far-reaching views, picnicking, tossing a Frisbee, and basking in the serenity.

Follow the white blazes painted on wooden posts through the meadow and downhill. Cross several streams and footbridges as you make your way through dense rhododendron and hemlocks. Arrive at Roaring Fork Shelter, a log shelter built by the Carolina Mountain Club in 2005. The shelter accommodates eight. Sleep here for the night, or, if it is still early and you have enough energy, continue hiking north for roughly 5 miles to the former Walnut Mountain Shelter, which now serves as a campsite. From the campsite the trail plunges for 0.7 mile to Kale Gap.

After a short stretch on an old roadbed, the trail reaches Catpen Gap, where a spur trail leads to views of Max Patch. Hike uphill 1 mile to the tree-covered summit of Bluff Mountain. From here it is a long, gradual descent into the town of Hot Springs, where this section concludes. The small mountain town offers lodging and plenty of places to eat and resupply. (See page 145.)

Approximately 2.5 miles from the summit of Bluff Mountain lies a brook with picturesque cascades, an excellent opportunity to refill your water bottle. After crossing the brook, you arrive at Garenflo Gap, where the USFS Shut-In Trail heads west. At 14.7 miles, pass through Taylor Hollow Gap, crossing over two footbridges. At 17.4 miles, reach the junction for Deer Park Mountain Shelter, located 0.2 mile east of the AT. Shortly after this junction, arrive at Gragg Gap, where the water source for the shelter is located. The trail then traverses over Deer Park Mountain and descends for roughly 2.5 miles, eventually leading you to downtown Hot Springs.

For an updated list of hiker resources, visit www.hotspringsnc.org/appalachian-trail-hikers-resource-guide-for-hot-springs.

DID YOU KNOW?

Max Patch was cleared in the 1800s to create a pasture for sheep and cattle. In the 1920s it served as a landing strip for planes offering sightseeing rides. Today, the Forest Service mows and performs prescribed burns to maintain the site, while the ATC actively removes non-native plants and plants native species to restore natural vegetation and attract pollinators.

Hikers on Max Patch summit, Mile 255.4

View of Bluff Mountain from Max Patch, Mile 255.4

Max Patch Road to Hot Springs

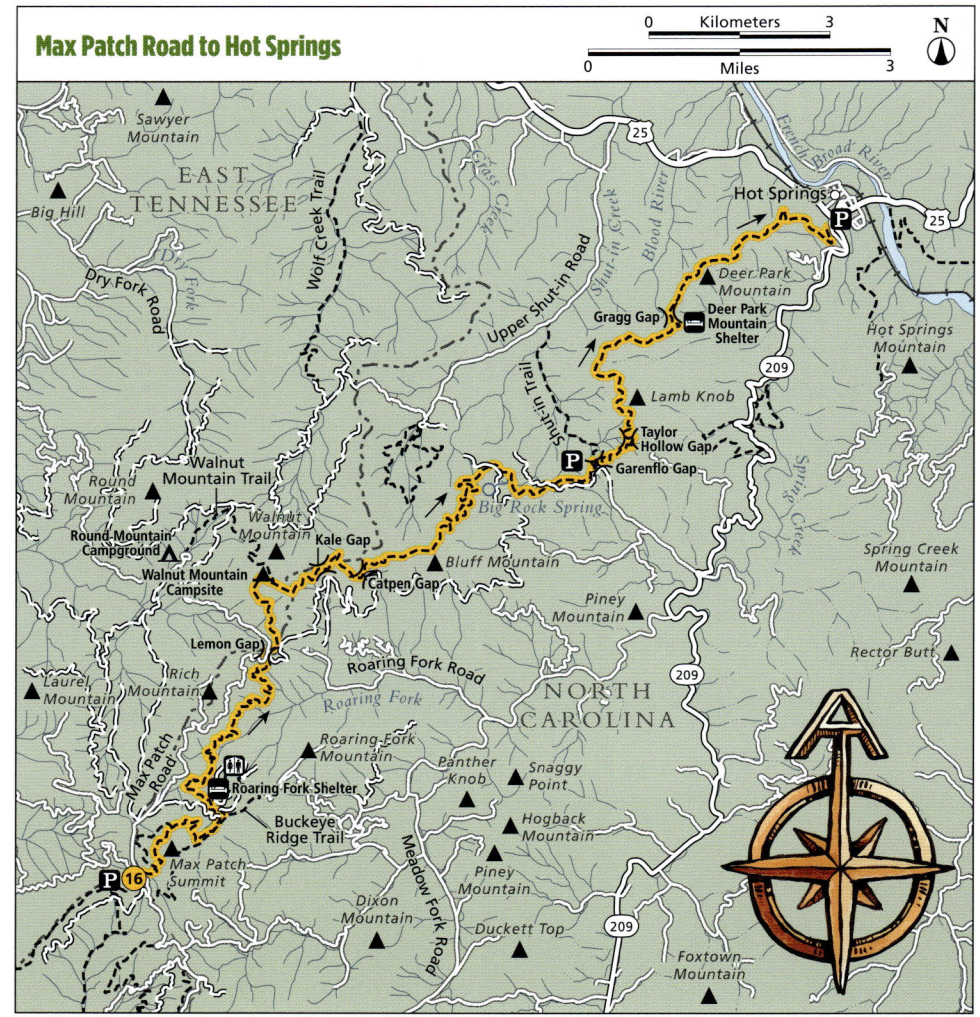

KEY POINTS

SECTION		ELEVATION (FEET)	MILES FROM SPRINGER MOUNTAIN	MILES FROM DAMASCUS
0.0	NC 1182, Max Patch Road	4,254	254.6	216.4
0.8	Max Patch summit	4,629	255.4	215.6
1.3	Stream	4,375	255.9	215.1
1.8	Roadbed, Buckeye Ridge Trail to east	4,209	256.4	214.6
2.7	Roaring Fork Shelter, water	4,025	257.3	213.7
6.2	Lemon Gap, NC 1182, TN 107	3,550	260.8	210.2
7.1	Walnut Mountain, grassy clearing	4,299	262.0	209.0
7.5	Campsite (former Walnut Mountain Shelter), Walnut Mountain Trail to west, water	4,252	262.1	208.96

SECTION		ELEVATION (FEET)	MILES FROM SPRINGER MOUNTAIN	MILES FROM DAMASCUS
8.2	Kale Gap, campsite 25 yards north on AT	3,725	262.8	208.2
8.9	Catpen Gap, campsite on small knoll 0.1 mile east	4,126	263.5	207.5
9.9	Bluff Mountain	4,686	264.5	206.5
10.6	Spring 50 yards west	4,195	265.2	205.8
11.2	Old roadbed, spring	3,921	265.8	205.2
11.5	Big Rock Spring	3,730	266.0	204.9
12.1	Dirt road	3,407	266.7	204.3
12.7	Brook with cascades	2,978	267.3	203.7
13.1	Old road	2,710	267.7	203.3
14.0	Garenflo Gap, Shut-in Trail to west (parking)	2,500	268.6	202.4
14.7	Taylor Hollow Gap, two footbridges, stream	2,639	269.3	201.7
17.4	Deer Park Mountain Shelter 0.1 mile east, spring on trail to shelter; treat all water due to slow flow	2,319	272.0	199.0
18.2	Deer Park Mountain	2,571	272.8	198.2
20.6	NC 209 & US 25/70, Hot Springs, North Carolina (parking)	1,326	275.2	195.8

TRAIL TOWN: HOT SPRINGS, NORTH CAROLINA

Hot Springs, North Carolina, is one of the few towns where the Appalachian Trail goes right through the center. Named an Appalachian Trail Community by the ATC in 2012, this charming town offers hikers a rich blend of natural and cultural experiences.

Located 39 miles northwest of Asheville on the banks of the French Broad River, Hot Springs has been a favorite retreat since the 1800s due to its natural hot springs, discovered by Native Americans and used for spiritual ceremonies at Paint Rock, where you can still see ancient pictographs.

After hiking, enjoy some food from **Smoky Mountain Diner**, relax in the historic **Hot Springs Resort & Spa**, or visit **Big Pillow Brewery** for local brews and live music on weekends. Explore **Artisun Gallery and Cafe** for local gifts, delicious ice cream, and coffee.

Bluff Mountain Outfitters is your go-to for resupply needs; the **welcome center** offers visitor info and Wi-Fi. The **Hot Springs Library**, a peaceful spot named "The Best Small Library in America" in 2018, offers computer use and educational programs.

For lodging, check out **Laughing Heart Lodge** or **Blue Ridge Hiking Company & Bunkhouse** for gear and a comfortable stay, or choose from historic **Sunnybank Inn** or **Iron Horse Station Inn** for a restful night and good food.

Visit the Appalachian Trail Hiker's Resource Guide at www.hotspringsnc.org for the latest updates.

17 HOT SPRINGS TO ALLEN GAP

View from Lovers Leap with views of Hot Springs, Mile 276.4

This section of the Appalachian Trail offers a diverse range of landscapes from meadows and wooded areas to stunning mountain vistas, all dotted with historic landmarks like **Lovers Leap**, a site steeped in Cherokee history. Beginning with a stroll from the welcoming town of Hot Springs, hikers trace the path alongside the picturesque **French Broad River**. Soon after, the trail embarks on a dramatic ascent from the river gorge, leading through gaps and across ridgetops, each turn offering breathtaking sites of beauty and wonder. Views from Rich Mountain fire tower (about halfway through this section) are superb.

Distance: 14.8 miles
Difficulty: Moderately challenging due to multiple ascents and descents
Nearest town: Hot Springs, North Carolina

Water availability: There are numerous water sources easily accessible throughout this hike.
Trailhead GPS: 35.8897 / -82.8327

Good to know:

- Parking is also available across the bridge at the Silvermine trailhead, at the southern end of this hike.
- There is limited parking at Allen Gap, the northern end of this hike.

Nearby accommodations:

Blue Ridge Hiking Company & Bunkhouse—also known as "The Trail-er"—offers affordable bunks with access to showers, laundry, and a shared kitchen. A small selection of backpacking gear is also available on-site. Located directly along the trail at 200 Lance Avenue, the bunkhouse provides shuttle services within a 2-hour range. For more information call (828) 622-3319.

Sunnybank Inn & Hostel, also known as "Elmer's." This historic home has been welcoming Appalachian Trail hikers since 1948. The inn offers affordable, comfortable rooms with linens provided, along with access to showers and laundry. A home-cooked organic breakfast is available for purchase. Conveniently located directly along the trail at 26 Walnut Street. For more information call (828) 622-7206.

View from Lovers Leap on the French Broad River, Mile 276.4

THE HIKE

From the parking area near US 25/70, follow the AT as it starts along the sidewalk adjacent to Bridge Street through the heart of Hot Springs. As you walk, you will pass the welcome center, local outfitters, the library, and various other hiker-friendly establishments.

As you approach the railroad tracks, note the Hot Springs Spa on your left. Continue across the railroad tracks and onto the US 25/70 bridge spanning the French Broad River, where you might catch sight of rafters and kayakers navigating the rapids below. On the right side, make your way around the guardrail and descend the stairs leading down to Silvermine Road. (Future plans will reroute the trail to go under the bridge, so take care to follow the white blazes.)

Reach the river's edge and follow the AT upstream, passing some rafting outfitters as the trail hugs the French Broad. After 0.9 mile, embark on the challenging 7.3-mile ascent to Rich Mountain, ascending roughly 2,200 feet in elevation. Within the first 0.5 mile of the climb, you'll encounter several rocky outcrops offering sweeping views of Hot Springs and the meandering French Broad River, with Lover's Leap rock the second prominent viewpoint. Exercise caution on the rocky ledge, as loose gravel may be present.

> **DID YOU KNOW?**
> Legend has it that Lovers Leap derived its name from the tragic tale of a Cherokee maiden known as "Mist-on-the-Mountain." The story recounts how she leaped to her death from the craggy outcrop following the demise of her lover, Magwa, who was killed by a jealous rival.

The AT intersects the Silvermine Trail and climbs uphill, eventually reaching Pump Gap at 3.3 miles, where a blue-blazed loop trail intersects the AT, leading westward to the Silvermine Creek Valley. Continue onward with a gradual ascent, passing the northern end of the Pump Gap Loop trail. Nearby, a campsite awaits in a grassy field, complete with an intermittent box spring.

At 5.1 miles, traverse through open meadows offering splendid views atop Mill Ridge. Here, the Mill Ridge Bike Trail intersects the AT. Hike uphill through the woods a little farther before descending into Tanyard Gap, where the trail crosses over US 25/70, leading 4 miles west to Hot Springs. Parking facilities are available at Tanyard Gap.

After crossing the highway on the concrete overpass, the AT veers into the woods and initiates the ascent to Rich Mountain. The climb is steady on a well-graded trail with switchbacks, offering occasional glimpses of the surrounding landscape through the trees. Mountain laurel blooms along the edges of the trail in late spring and early summer.

At mile 7.3, about 1 mile from the summit of Rich Mountain, you will encounter a piped spring. Continue on to reach the Roundtop Ridge Trail, a yellow-blazed side trail spanning 3.5 miles to River Road, which leads into the town of Hot Springs, tracing the former route of the AT.

Pond, Mile 279.9

Dam below pond, Mile 279.9

Rich Mountain lookout tower, Mile 283.4

View from Rich Mountain lookout tower, Mile 283.4

At 8.3 miles the AT elevates to 3,500 feet and intersects a side trail leading 0.1 mile to the summit of Rich Mountain, where the fire tower stands proudly. From this vantage point, breathtaking panoramic views of the Smokies to the southwest and the Black Mountains to the southeast unfold. There's another piped spring just north of here along the AT.

Continue along the ridgeline, passing another spring situated on the west side of the trail, until reaching Hurricane Gap. Here, a gravel road (USFS 467) intersects the AT, providing a route back to US 25/70.

The trail ascends for nearly 2 miles to Spring Mountain Shelter at an elevation of 3,536 feet and then descends to Deep Gap at 2,892 feet. At Deep Gap, you'll find the intersection with the Little Paint Creek Trail, which extends 2.5 miles west to USFS 31B and connects to other trails.

From Deep Gap, continue hiking for 2 miles downhill to Allen Gap at the North Carolina–Tennessee state line, the conclusion of this section.

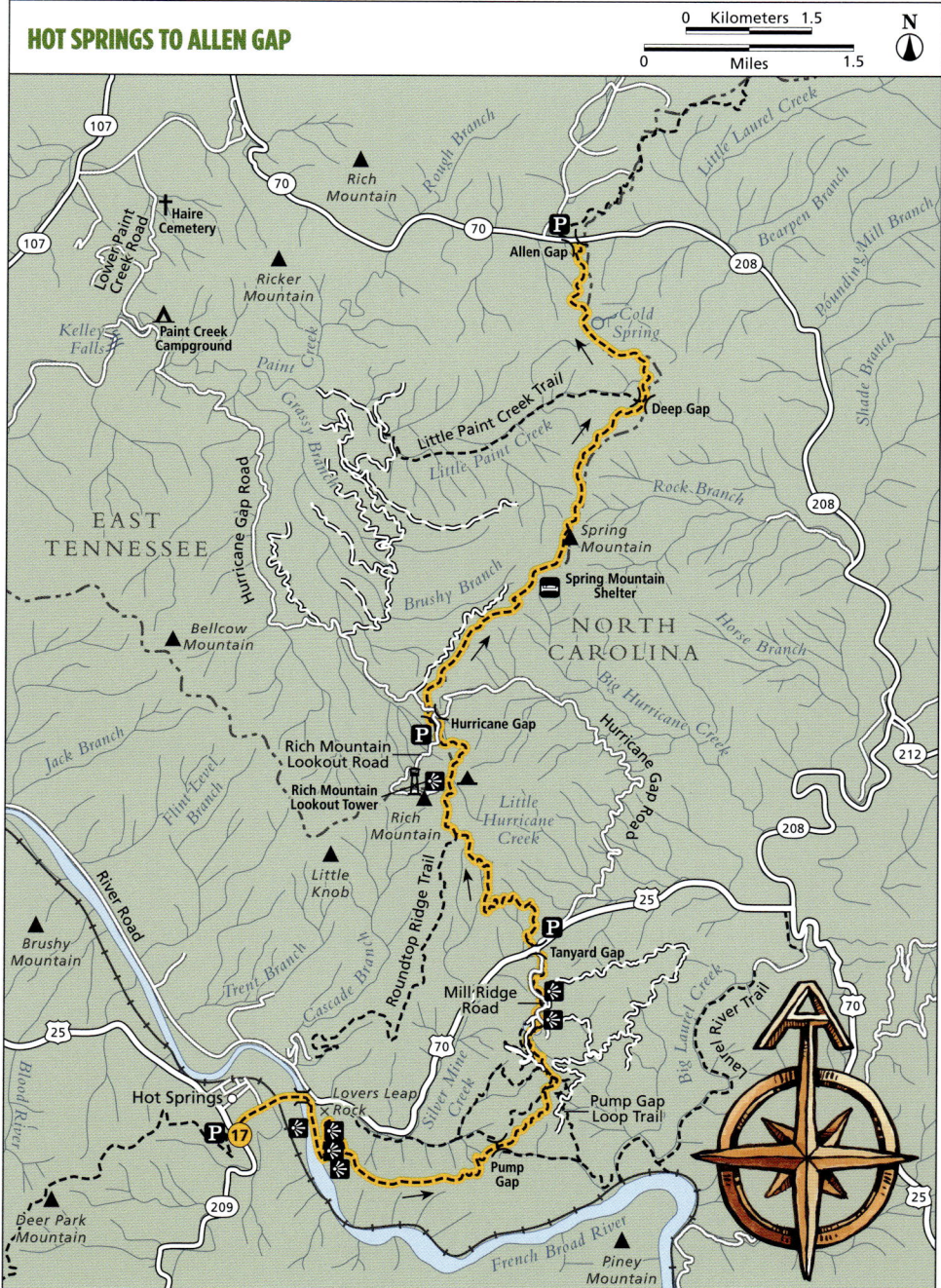

KEY POINTS

SECTION		ELEVATION (FEET)	MILES FROM SPRINGER MOUNTAIN	MILES FROM DAMASCUS
0.0	Hot Springs, NC (NC 209 & US 25/70)	1,326	275.2	195.8
0.4	US 25/70 bridge over French Broad River	1,339	275.6	195.4
1.3	Lovers Leap rock, Silvermine Trail to west, water	1,686	276.5	194.5
3.3	Pump Gap	2,130	278.5	192.5
3.7	Spring	2,299	278.9	192.1
4.2	North intersection with Pump Gap Loop Trail	2,410	279.4	191.6
4.8	Pond with boxed spring	2,467	280.0	191.0
5.1	Cross Mill Ridge to gravel road	2,604	280.3	190.7
5.6	Stream	2,429	280.8	190.2
5.9	Tanyard Gap, US 25/70 overpass	2,270	281.1	189.9
7.3	Piped spring	3,039	282.5	188.5
7.8	Roundtop Ridge Trail to west, 3.5 miles to Hot Springs (former route of AT)	3,194	283.0	188.0
8.3	Side trail 0.1 mile west to campsite, Rich Mountain lookout tower, piped spring north on the AT	3,506	283.5	187.5
8.8	Spring	3,195	284.0	187.0
9.2	Hurricane Gap	2,945	284.4	186.6
9.5	Gravestone	2,990	284.7	186.3
11.0	Spring Mountain Shelter, water on blue-blazed trail across from shelter	3,536	286.2	184.8
12.8	Deep Gap. Little Paint Creek Trail, spring 200 yards west	2,892	288.0	183.0
14.2	Spring 30 yards west in ravine	2,735	289.4	181.6
14.8	Allen Gap, NC 208, TN 70, Paint Creek 0.2 mile west	2,218	290.0	181.0

18 ALLEN GAP TO DEVIL FORK GAP

View of Blackstack Cliffs from Camp Creek Bald, Mile 296.5

The stretch of the Appalachian Trail from Allen Gap to Devil Fork Gap is just over 21 miles with nice, convenient shelters and campsites, making this section a great two- to three-day backpacking trip. Ascend through dense woods to **Camp Creek Bald**, home to North Carolina's oldest lookout tower. Explore **Jones Meadow**, adorned with wildflowers in spring and summer, and take in the vistas from **White Rock Cliffs**. Traverse the open ridge of **Firescald Knob** for breathtaking panoramic views. History enthusiasts can pay tribute at the **Shelton Graves**, a significant Civil War landmark along the trail.

Distance: 21.3 miles
Difficulty: Strenuous due to distance, rocky terrain, long ascent, and some steep sections
Nearest town: Hot Springs, North Carolina

Water availability: Carry plenty of water. You can refill at the shelter; otherwise water sources are scarce/unreliable.
Trailhead GPS: 35.9870 / -82.7846

Good to know: There is limited parking at Allen Gap.

Nearby accommodations:

Hemlock Hollow Inn offers a peaceful, wooded retreat just 0.7 mile off the AT. Accommodations include private cabins, a bunkhouse, and tenting spots, along with hot showers, laundry, resupply options, and mail drop services. Shuttle services are available upon request. Located at 645 Chandler Circle, Greeneville, Tennessee. Go west on Log Cabin Drive and follow the blue blazes. For more information call (423) 820-9228 or visit hemlockhollow.com.

Camp Creek Bald lookout tower and parking lot, Mile 296.5

THE HIKE

From Allen Gap, walk 0.1 mile on TN 70 before entering the woods and ascending the ridge. After a mile the AT skirts a gravel road and then crosses Log Cabin Drive in 0.5 mile. A private home is in view to the east. Please do not trespass.

The trail climbs diligently for the next 3 miles to reach Little Laurel River Shelter, sitting at 3,652 feet in elevation. A boxed spring is located 100 yards down a blue-blazed trail, and there are campsites north of the shelter near the bear box as well as south of the shelter on the west side of the AT.

From the shelter, continue the uphill climb until reaching a junction with Hickey Fork Trail (formerly Pounding Mill Trail) at an elevation of 4,695 feet. Nearby, Camp Creek Bald can be found on a side trail just 0.2 mile west of the AT. This bald features North Carolina's oldest remaining lookout tower, initially built in 1928 and later replaced with a proprietary circular live-in cab during the 1960s. The tower atop Camp Creek Bald is currently inaccessible, and due to dense vegetation, most views from the bald itself are obstructed by trees and shrubs. However, despite these limitations, the historical significance of the site remains noteworthy, particularly as a place that hosted Earl Shaffer during his first Appalachian Trail thru-hike in 1948.

The trail begins to gradually level out for a while as you walk along an old lumber road for a short distance before arriving at a blue-blazed trail that leads to Jones Meadow, a spacious grassy area adorned with beautiful views and wildflowers during the warmer months. A brief side trail leads to even more breathtaking vistas from White Rock Cliffs. Just north of here, another short side trail veers westward to the edge of Blackstack Cliffs, offering exceptional open views into Tennessee.

At 8.8 miles the trail arrives at Bearwallow Gap, enveloped by a dense rhododendron thicket. Here, a junction marks the path for the Jerry Miller Trail, which stretches eastward for 4.6 miles to Big Creek Road. Alternatively, the Firescald bad-weather route heads west, rejoining the AT after a 1.5-mile northern trek.

Firescald bad-weather trail sign, Mile 298.7

Summer view on Big Firescald Knob

Winter view on Big Firescald Knob looking north on the AT

Winter view on Big Firescald Knob looking south on the AT toward Jones Meadow

Upon reaching the southern end of Big Firescald Knob at 9.5 miles, continue along the narrow ridge for approximately 0.5 mile. Exercise extreme caution as you traverse this high, open ridge, particularly in wet conditions. In the presence of lightning, utilize the bad-weather route. Firescald experienced severe burning in this area, leaving it exposed and offering magnificent views of the surrounding mountains. Descend the steep, rocky knob, arriving at the northern end of the bypass trail at 10.4 miles.

Arrive at the Round Knob Trail intersection and continue following the AT as it parallels and merges with an old woods road for approximately 3 miles. Along the way you'll pass the Fork Ridge Trail, which descends steeply down a rugged path for 2 miles to a parking area at Big Creek Road in the valley of Shelton Laurel.

From the junction with the Fork Ridge Trail, descend for 0.2 mile into Chestnut Log Gap. Here you'll find the Jerry Cabin Shelter on the right, with water available on the opposite side of the shelter. This shelter is dedicated to Sam Waddle, who adopted it in 1972 and diligently maintained it for the next three decades. As Ed Garvey noted, Waddle transformed "the dirtiest shelter on the entire trail into one of the cleanest."

Arrive at Bald Ridge and traverse a cleared field, passing a massive boulder to the east of the AT. At 13.3 miles Sarvis Cove Trail intersects the AT. Eventually you'll reach a small grassy area with picturesque views and a small stone memorial dedicated to

Jerry Cabin Shelter, Mile 302.0

Shelton gravesite, Mile 305.7

Howard C. Bassett, an AT hiker who passed away in the late 1980s. The trail continues its ascent, leading to Big Butt Mountain at 4,815 feet.

From here the trail gradually falls in elevation until you reach the Shelton Graves, a significant historical landmark at the 15.8-mile mark. David Shelton and his nephew William were laid to rest here after leaving their mountain home to support the Union during the Civil War, only to be ambushed and killed by Confederate soldiers upon their return for a family gathering. In 1915 two graves were erected for them at this spot. After paying your respects at the gravesite, continue your descent for 2.3 miles to Flint Gap, site of an old logging railroad grade.

The AT ascends sharply from Flint Gap for approximately 0.5 mile before descending a south-facing slope to reach Flint Mountain Shelter. This shelter, constructed by the Carolina Mountain Club in 1988, is ideally positioned for your final night on the trail. Facing east with a spring nearby, it comfortably accommodates up to eight hikers. Continue hiking north from the shelter as the trail meanders across a series of ridges.

After 21.3 miles, arrive at Devil Fork Gap, nestled at 3,113 feet. Nearby is Lamar Alexander Rocky Fork State Park, 2,076 acres of scenic wilderness along the North Carolina–Tennessee border often referred to as "the little Smokies" for its natural beauty and diversity.

ALLEN GAP TO DEVIL FORK GAP

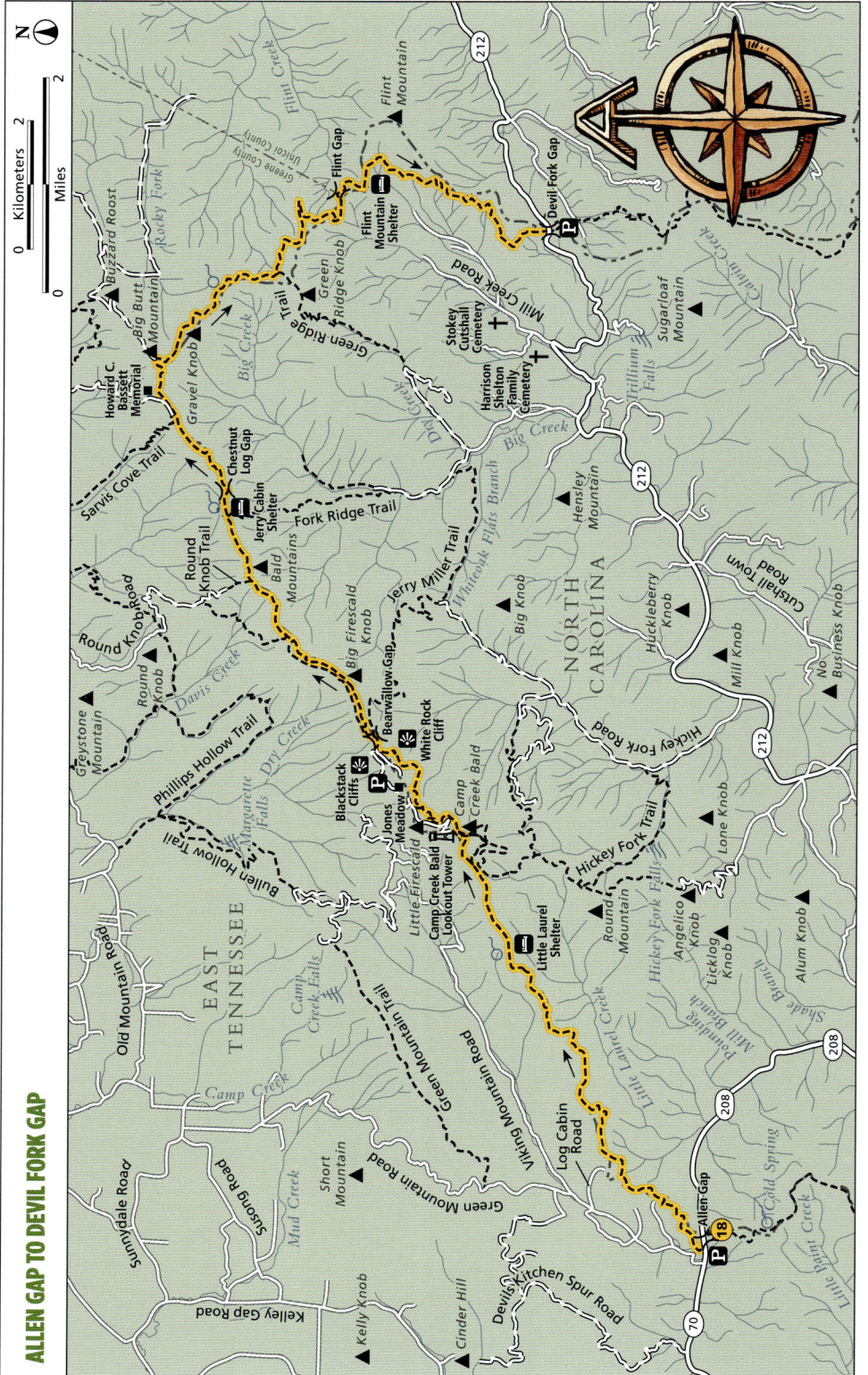

KEY POINTS

SECTION		ELEVATION (FEET)	MILES FROM SPRINGER MOUNTAIN	MILES FROM DAMASCUS
0.0	Allen Gap, NC 208, TN 70	2,218	290.0	181.0
1.5	Log Cabin Road	2,376	291.5	179.5
4.8	Little Laurel Shelter, boxed spring 100 yards down blue-blazed trail behind shelter	3,652	294.8	176.2
6.6	Camp Creek Bald lookout tower 0.2 mile west, Hickey Fork Trail to east	4,695	294.8	174.4
7.4	Jones Meadow, spring 100 yards south	4,413	296.6	173.6
8.4	Side trail to Jones Meadow to west, White Rock Cliff 30 yards east	4,443	297.4	173.6
8.6	Side trail 200 feet west to view from Blackstack Cliffs.	4,466	298.6	172.4
8.8	Bearwallow Gap, Firescald bad-weather trail to west (reconnects with AT 1.5 miles north), Jerry Miller Trail to east	4,388	298.8	172.2
9.5	Big Firescald Knob	4,540	299.5	171.5
10.4	Bad-weather trail to west (reconnects with AT 1.5 miles south)	4,190	300.4	170.6
11.1	Round Knob Trail to west	4,274	301.1	169.9
11.9	Fork Ridge Trail to east	4,252	301.9	169.1
12.1	Chestnut Log Gap, Jerry Cabin Shelter, spring	4,146	302.1	168.9
12.9	Bald Ridge	4,535	302.9	168.1
13.3	Sarvis Cove Trail to west	4,565	303.3	167.7
13.7	Howard C. Bassett Memorial	4,705	303.7	167.3
14.0	Big Butt Mountain (summit to west), short bypass trail	4,815	304.0	167.0
14.4	Seasonal water source	4,670	304.4	166.6
15.8	Shelton gravesite 80 yards east	4,441	305.8	165.2
18.1	Flint Gap	3,438	308.1	162.9
18.8	Flint Mountain Shelter, water 50 yards north of shelter on the AT	3,555	308.8	162.2
21.3	Devil Fork Gap, NC 212	3,113	311.3	159.7

19 DEVIL FORK GAP TO SAMS GAP

Devil Fork Gap, Mile 311.2

The highlight of this section is **High Rock**, a stunning vista perched at 4,460 feet offering panoramic views of the surrounding mountains and valleys. For optimal viewing, consider tackling this hike in winter, when dense tree foliage is less likely to obstruct the scenery. Remnants of former homes and farms scattered throughout the southern part of this hike offer glimpses into the area's rich history. Whether you opt for a single-day adventure or a leisurely overnight trip, camping options include Hogback Ridge Shelter or the Big Flat Campsite.

Distance: 8.7 miles
Difficulty: Strenuous due to a lengthy ascent and descent, as well as several steep sections along the way
Nearest town: Erwin, Tennessee (17 miles from Devil Fork Gap and 18 miles from Sams Gap)
Water availability: Water is available at several sources for the first mile and then again at Hogback Ridge Shelter at the northern end of this section; although the spring is 0.3 mile off the AT. If you plan on camping at Big Flat, be sure to fill up your water containers before you arrive.
Trailhead GPS: 36.0105 / -82.6086

Good to know:

- For the majority of this hike, you are actually hiking compass-south. (See page viii for how this guidebook refers to directions.)
- Asheville, a vibrant creative hub and adventurous haven 28 miles south of Sams Gap, boasts a full range of services and exciting sightseeing opportunities.

Nearby accommodations:

Laurel Hostel, 0.2 mile east of the AT from the Rector Laurel Road crossing. The hostel is open year-round and offers basic bunks, showers, laundry, and shuttles to Erwin, Sams Gap, and Spivey Gap. Call (423) 270-0909 for reservations.

View from High Rock, Mile 318.1

THE HIKE

From the North Carolina side of Devil Fork Gap, cross the stile and ascend through the pasture. Shortly after, enter the woods and reach a high point on the ridge at about 0.2 mile. Next, descend via switchbacks and cross Laurel Rector Road. The following mile brings creek crossings, forest roads, and a picturesque cascade. A small fenced cemetery and remnants of old homes and farms along the way are a testament to the rich history and human connection to these lands, enriching your experience of journeying through nature and time.

Reach Sugarloaf Gap, situated at about 4,000 feet, at 2 miles. From here, continue climbing until you reach Lick Rock at 3.4 miles, standing tall at 4,562 feet. Keep an eye out for blackberries and old apple trees along the way. Descend from Lick Rock and arrive at Big Flat just over 0.5 mile later. Big Flat is a level area and serves as a pleasant camping spot; however, it's important to note that there is no water available here.

At 5.1 miles the AT crosses Rice Gap at 3,851 feet and begins the ascent to High Rock. Climb out of the gap and note a blue-blazed side trail on your right that leads 0.1 mile to Hogback Ridge Shelter at 6.3 miles. There's a spring 0.2 mile beyond the shelter.

From the shelter junction, the 4,460-foot summit of High Rock awaits just over 0.5 mile away, offering breathtaking views of the valley. The viewpoint is slightly off the AT down a blue-blazed path. While summer foliage may obstruct part of the view, in winter the vistas are spectacular.

From High Rock, the AT descends for nearly 2 miles to Sams Gap, where this hike concludes at the parking area.

KEY POINTS

SECTION		ELEVATION (FEET)	MILES FROM SPRINGER MOUNTAIN	MILES FROM DAMASCUS
0.0	Devil Fork Gap, NC 212	3,113	311.3	159.7
0.5	Rector Laurel Road, spring to north	2,948	311.8	159.2
0.9	Stream	3,229	312.2	158.8
1.2	Cascade	3,411	312.5	158.5
1.4	Stream	3,602	312.7	158.3
2.0	Sugarloaf Gap	4,046	313.3	157.7
3.4	Lick Rock	4,562	314.7	156.3
4.1	Big Flat, campsite to east	4,309	315.4	155.6
5.1	Rice Gap	3,851	316.4	154.6
6.3	Hogback Ridge Shelter 0.1 mile east, spring 0.2 mile down side trail near the shelter	4,324	317.6	153.4
6.9	High Rock (blue-blazed trail to view)	4,460	318.2	152.8
8.7	Sams Gap, US 23, I-26	3,724	320.0	151.0

DEVIL FORK GAP TO SAMS GAP

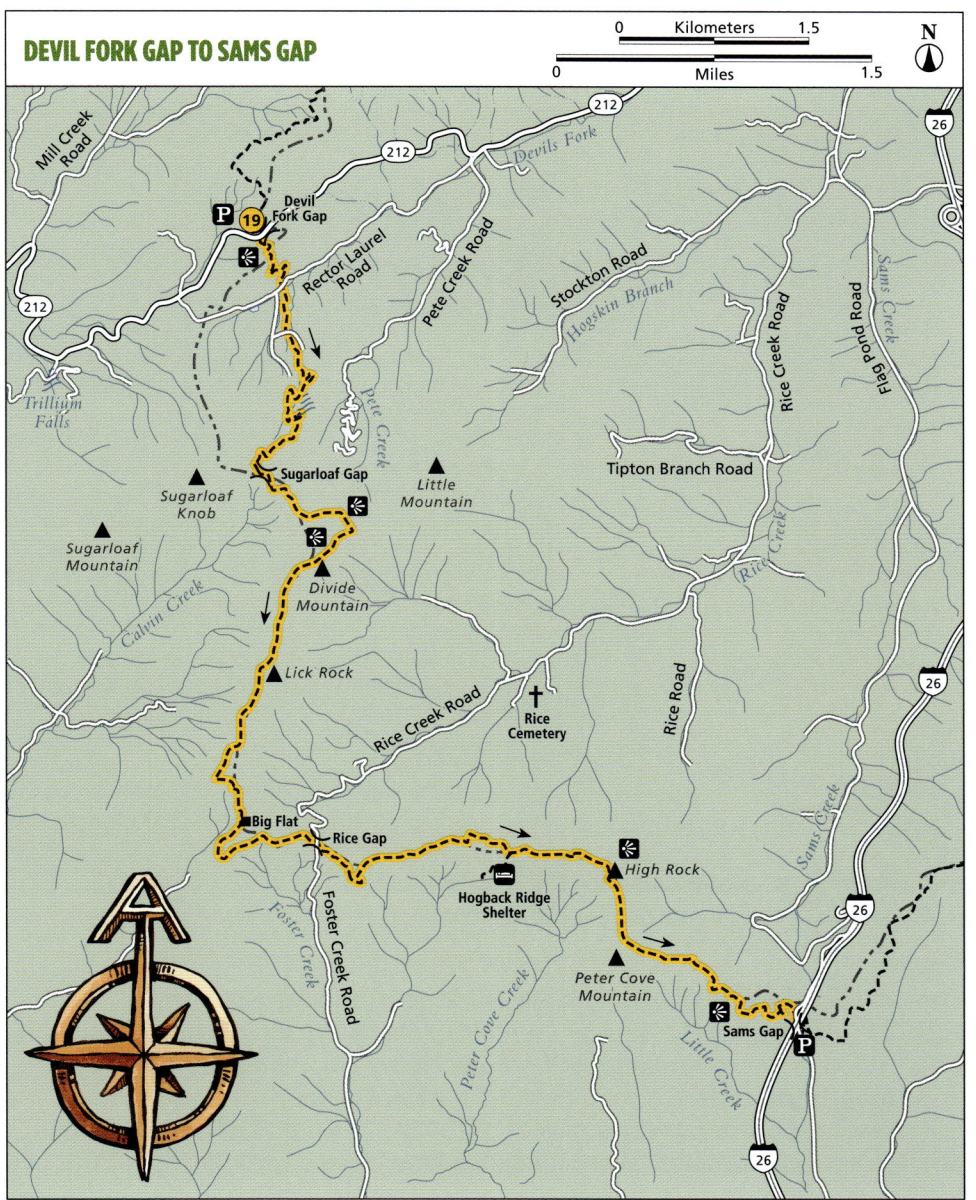

20 SAMS GAP TO SPIVEY GAP

Meadow with view of Big Bald in the distance, Mile 321.7

The trail ascends from Sams Gap, offering stunning vistas from the scenic high point of the grassy summit of **Big Bald**, where panoramic views encompass **Mount Mitchell**, **Unaka Mountain**, the **Great Smokies**, and **Roan Highlands**. Continuing north, **High Rocks** presents another epic vista. Be prepared for steep ascents and descents, rocky terrain, and potential weather challenges, but be rewarded with glimpses into the area's rich history, including the tale of David Greer, legendary hermit of **Greer Rock**. Total climbing amounts to around 2,900 feet northbound and about 3,500 feet southbound, providing a challenging yet fulfilling hiking experience.

Blaze and trail on Big Bald, Mile 326.4

Distance: 13.4 miles
Difficulty: Strenuous due to steep terrain
Nearest towns: Erwin, Tennessee (8 miles north of Spivey Gap and 18 miles north of Sams Gap); Asheville, North Carolina (28 miles south of Sams Gap)
Water availability: No water source at Sams Gap; however, numerous springs and other sources are available throughout this hike.
Trailhead GPS: 35.9529 / -82.5606

THE HIKE

From the parking area at Sams Gap, proceed through the aluminum gate and follow the white blaze as the AT runs parallel to I-26 for a couple hundred yards. Take one last look down to Sams Gap before the AT veers into the woods.

The trail cuts around the right side of the ridge and crosses two springs 660 feet apart. After about 1.5 miles, you'll come to the remains of an abandoned talc mine. Talc, a soft soapy mineral, is formed when two types of metamorphic rocks are crushed against each other over extended periods. Prehistoric Native Americans, or Paleo-Indians, utilized talc to craft bowls and other implements, highlighting its historical significance in the region.

A potential campsite near the old talc mine offers a convenient resting spot for weary hikers before climbing to an open field. At 1.8 miles you reach a picturesque meadow providing an excellent view of Big Bald rising prominently to the northeast. Traverse this open field for 0.4 mile, where wildflowers bloom abundantly in the spring and delicious wild berries await in late summer.

View from Big Bald summit, Mile 326.4

Reach Street Gap, where an abandoned Christmas tree farm is close to the north. From Street Gap, the AT descends steeply before embarking on the long ascent to Big Bald, the final mile becoming progressively steeper, lush, and rugged. At 3.7 miles you'll encounter a dirt-track crossing near Low Gap, where a nice campsite and spring await to the west of the AT.

Continue climbing for about a mile until you reach another spring. Keep an eye out for trout lilies and spring beauty in the first wave of wildflowers, typically in March, followed by trillium, jack-in-the-pulpit, and blue cohosh in April. As the trail ascends, it passes under power lines and briefly levels out before intersecting a blue-blazed bypass trail junction. Utilize this bypass trail during poor visibility or in the presence of lightning, as it leads around the southeastern side of Big Bald before reconnecting with the AT at Big Stamp.

Arrive at the 5,516-foot summit of Big Bald, the highest point on the AT since the Smokies, at the 6.5-mile-mark. Traverse the expansive summit while soaking in the breathtaking vistas, with Mount Mitchell gracing the eastern horizon and the Smokies dominating the western panorama. To the northeast, catch a glimpse of Unaka Mountain while Camp Creek Bald beckons from the northwest, offering a truly magnificent vista of the surrounding landscape.

Descend to Big Stamp, a treeless saddle at the northern base of Big Bald, and take note of the blue-blazed bypass trail on your right. At 7.7 miles the AT intersects a side trail leading west for 0.1 mile to Bald Mountain Shelter. Water can be found 50 feet down a side trail starting halfway between the shelter and the AT. Please refrain from camping near the shelter or spring due to the fragile alpine soil. For camping, tent on the east side near the bear box or continue a little farther north.

At 8.1 miles a short blue-blazed trail veers left to Big Bald Creek, offering excellent camping spots on the ridge crest. Farther along the trail you'll encounter a piped spring. After some gentle ups and downs, reach the now tree-covered summit of Little Bald, at 5,220 feet. These balds were once cleared and maintained by Native Americans, early settlers, and farmers. However, since becoming part of Forest Service lands,

> **DID YOU KNOW?**
> Greer Rock, located near the summit of Big Bald, was once home to David Greer, a notorious hermit who settled in the area during the 1800s after being spurned by a woman he loved. He constructed a log cabin and eventually took up residence in a cave beneath it, spending his days writing about religion and government, akin to a Southern Henry David Thoreau. Surviving through hunting, fishing, and hog farming, he earned the nickname "Old Hog Greer" and was dubbed the "King of the Bald" by locals. Faced with attempts to tax his land, he famously appeared in court armed with a shotgun, challenging authority. Despite his notoriety, he met a tragic end when he was killed by a blacksmith whose tools he had borrowed without permission. He resided at Greer Rock from 1802 to 1834, leaving behind a legacy both colorful and cautionary.

grazing cattle and other practices have ceased, resulting in many of the balds becoming tree-covered over time.

From Little Bald, navigate a steep descent and continue northward toward Whistling Gap, where a small clearing and nice campsite await. From Whistling Gap, brace yourself for a steep ascent to High Rocks, reaching a sag in the ridge at 11.8 miles. Take a short side trail to enjoy a splendid view from the rocky promontory, ideal for enjoying lunch while soaking in the scenery before the long descent to Spivey Gap.

As you journey from High Rocks, prepare for a downhill trek, although some sections may be rocky and rugged, especially in wet conditions. Cross several small streams and descend stone steps, all while keeping an eye out for potential campsites along the trail's edge. At 13.2 miles pass a field maintained by the Forest Service, providing food for deer and other wildlife. Arrive at Spivey Gap at 13.4 miles, where you'll cross US 19W to reach the parking area and conclude your adventure.

Rock with AT symbol

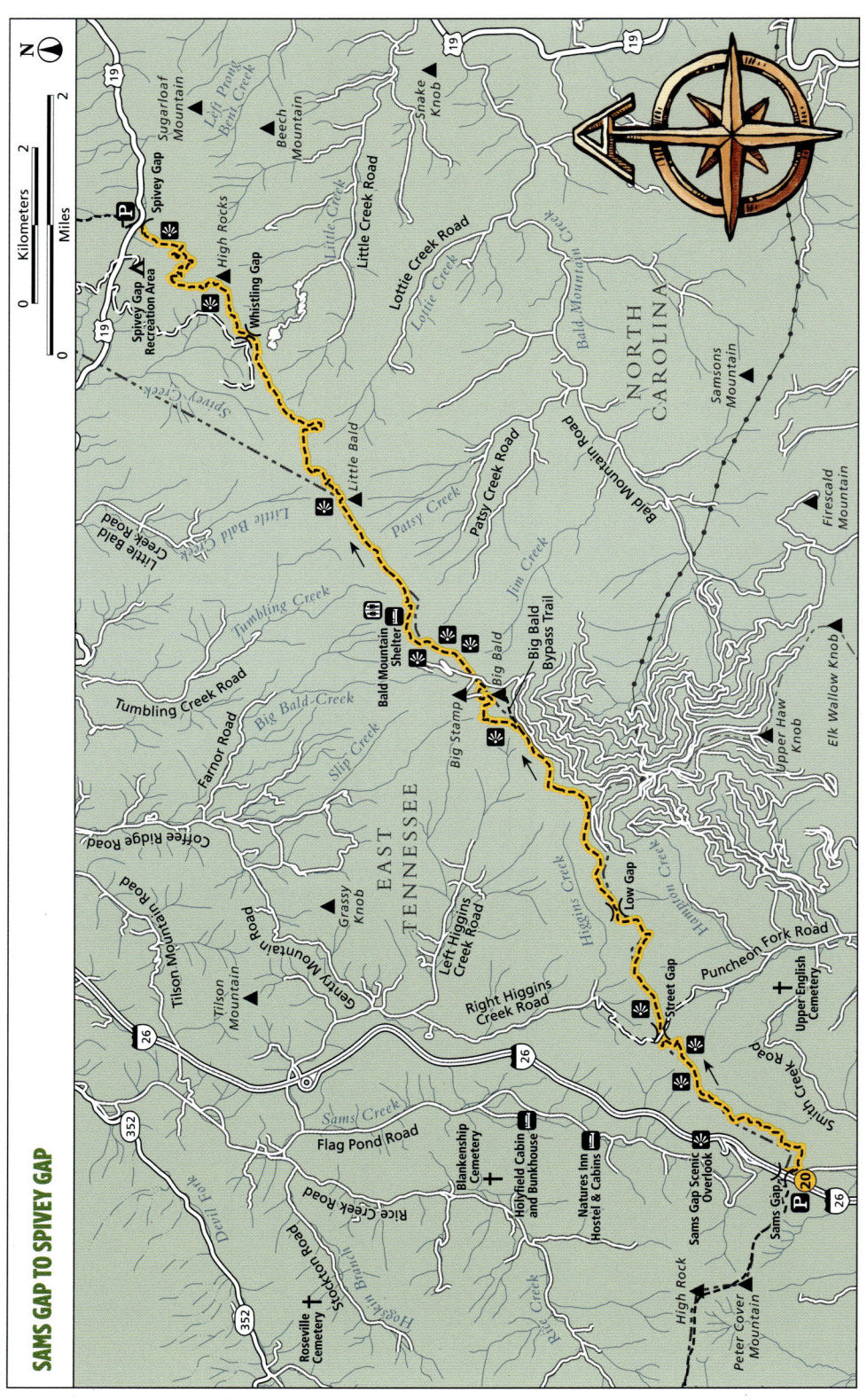

KEY POINTS

SECTION		ELEVATION (FEET)	MILES FROM SPRINGER MOUNTAIN	MILES FROM DAMASCUS
0.0	Sams Gap, US 23, I-26 (parking)	3,724	320.0	151.0
1.8	Meadow	4,436	321.8	149.2
2.3	Street Gap, gravel road	4,100	322.3	148.7
2.5	Power line	4,183	322.5	148.5
3.7	Low Gap, campsite and piped spring to west	4,300	323.7	147.3
4.5	Spring	4,670	324.5	146.5
4.9	Power line	4,842	324.9	146.1
6.0	Blue-blazed trail to water, bypass trail to east	5,059	326.0	145.0
6.1	Spring	5,210	326.1	144.9
6.3	Yellow-blazed trail to west	5,365	326.3	144.7
6.5	Big Bald, survey marker	5,516	326.5	144.5
7.1	Big Stamp, treeless saddle on ridge, bypass trail to east, spring	5,379	327.1	143.9
7.4	Dirt road	5,262	327.4	143.6
7.7	Bald Mountain Shelter 0.1 mile west, spring on trail to shelter	5,262	327.7	143.3
7.9	Blue-blazed trail to piped spring 0.2 mile west	4,982	327.9	143.1
9.1	Little Bald (tree covered)	5,220	329.1	141.9
10.2	Spring	4,406	330.2	140.8
11.2	Whistling Gap, campsite, unreliable water	3,889	331.2	139.8
11.8	Trail to High Rocks 0.1 mile east	4,241	331.8	139.2
12.9	Stream, footbridges	3,570	332.9	138.1
13.4	Spivey Gap, US 19W, stream south of gap (parking 0.5 mile west)	3,200	333.4	137.6

21 SPIVEY GAP TO INDIAN GRAVE GAP

Oglesby Branch, Mile 326.4

The standout feature of this hike is undoubtedly the 2-mile descent into the **Nolichucky River** gorge. Along the nearly 20-mile stretch, you'll encounter two shelters and be treated to stunning vistas of the gorge, Unaka Springs, and the **town of Erwin** from various points along the ridge. Abundant wildflowers dot the landscape in spring and summer, but be prepared for challenging terrain with rough, rocky sections and potential water sources that dry up in summer adding to the strenuousness of the hike. This section lies entirely within Cherokee and Pisgah National Forests, where camping is permitted unless otherwise noted.

Distance: 19.5 miles
Difficulty: Strenuous due to several climbs, a long descent, and some rocky terrain
Nearest town: Erwin, Tennessee (8 miles north of Spivey Gap parking area)
Water availability: Water is available at the trailhead; other sources are evenly spread for most of the hike with the exception of a dry stretch starting at No Business Knob Shelter. Sources may be dry in summer, so carry plenty of water.
Trailhead GPS: 36.0319 / -82.4202

Good to know: The parking area at Spivey Gap is very limited.

Nearby accommodations:

Uncle Johnny's Nolichucky Hostel, just steps off the AT near mile marker 344, offers lodging, shuttles, resupply items, and mail services. For reservations call (423) 707-4013. If you call late in the evening, please text or leave a voicemail with your information.

USA Raft Adventure Resort and Red Banks Campground, on the banks of the Nolichucky River, offer cabins, campsites, and an on-site tavern. For reservations call (800) USA-RAFT (800-872-7238) or visit usaraft.com.

Nolichucky Gorge Campground, approximately 1 mile off the AT at mile marker 345.7, provides tent sites, cabin rooms, a bathhouse, and day passes. To make reservations, call (423) 743-8876 and leave a voice message.

Devils Creek Gap, Mile 334.8

THE HIKE

Starting at Spivey Gap, ascend the stone steps alongside US 19W, weaving through rhododendron, hemlock, and white pine trees. At 0.4 mile cross a footbridge rising over Oglesby Branch, named for Frank Oglesby, founder of the Tennessee Eastman Hiking and Canoeing Club. Legend has it that the stream earned its name after Frank took an unplanned plunge into its waters. As the AT continues its ascent, expect rocky terrain and a second crossing of Oglesby Branch via another plank bridge. Follow the white blazes as the trail climbs, briefly leveling out after about a mile of hiking.

At 1.3 miles you'll reach a small stream, which tends to dry up in the summer months, followed by a crossing of an old logging road at Devils Creek Gap. Occasional views of Flattop Mountain and the Nolichucky River valley are present along the various ridges the AT meanders over.

From Devils Creek Gap, the AT descends on stone steps to a rocky creek at around 3.7 miles, crossing another footbridge. It then begins the ascent to No Business Knob, reportedly named by a traveler who struggled through tangled mountain laurel and rhododendron and concluded that he had "no business" being up there.

Although the trail's elevation change is minimal in this area, it becomes notably rocky. Look for a blue-blazed tree on the left at around 4.7 miles, indicating a short side trail to a piped spring in a hemlock grove. While the spring typically flows well throughout much of the year, it may run dry during the summer months. Ascend from the creek, navigating two switchbacks up to a ridgetop and an open area. At 4.9 miles you'll find the No Business Knob Shelter, a three-sided building of concrete blocks, to the left at an elevation of 3,181 feet.

Arrive at Temple Hill Gap, 7.3 miles from Spivey Gap, where you will walk a short distance on an old logging road. Continue climbing along the ridge crest as the trail drops into a saddle and climbs again, reaching the north end of Temple Ridge at 8.6 miles. From there the trail begins its long descent to the Nolichucky River.

At 9.4 miles the trail treats you to breathtaking vistas of Unaka Springs and the town of Erwin. You might spot what resembles a miniature toy train traversing the tracks, hauling coal. Note the stretch between I-26 and a profound river cut flanked by clay cliffs; this was the scene of the Civil War Battle of Red Banks, where 73 Confederate soldiers perished in a surprise assault by a contingent of 400 Union soldiers.

Follow the white blaze as the trail descends via several long switchbacks to the Nolichucky River. Keep an eye out for the showy pink lady's slipper orchid, which blooms in May or June.

Once you've reached the banks of the Nolichucky River, cross over it on the Chestoa Bridge (visit appalachiantrail.org/helene for updated information on this crossing). On

> ### DID YOU KNOW?
> *Pink lady's slipper orchids require specific soil conditions to thrive; like many orchid species, they rely on particular fungi for survival and reproduction. Often growing in colonies, if you encounter one, search for more nearby. Remember to practice Leave No Trace principles and refrain from picking or disturbing these delicate flowers—capture their beauty with photographs instead.*

View of Erwin, Mile 342.7

the far side awaits a war memorial and a small parking lot, offering an early exit or a chance to restock supplies if necessary. Downtown Erwin lies approximately 2 miles from this point, providing access to food, resupply items, shuttles, and lodging.

At 11.4 miles proceed with caution while crossing the CSX railroad tracks, as trains can be especially quiet when traveling from the east. By 12.4 miles you'll come to a side trail on the right leading to the Nolichucky Gorge and USA Raft campgrounds, 0.1 mile away.

The trail meanders through hemlock trees, crossing Jones Branch four times within the next 1.5 miles before ascending to Curley Maple Gap Shelter. This shelter, originally constructed by the USFS in 1961 and renovated by the TEHCC in 2010, is spacious, accommodating up to fourteen hikers and featuring a covered eating area. Water is available at a small nearby stream, which can have low flow in drier times.

From the shelter the trail winds along the ridge, maintaining a consistent elevation for approximately 2 miles. Along this stretch it crosses a spring at mile 15.9, followed by two streams, at 16.5 miles and again shortly thereafter.

The AT descends into a gap, climbs once more, and finally reaches Indian Grave Gap at mile 19.5.

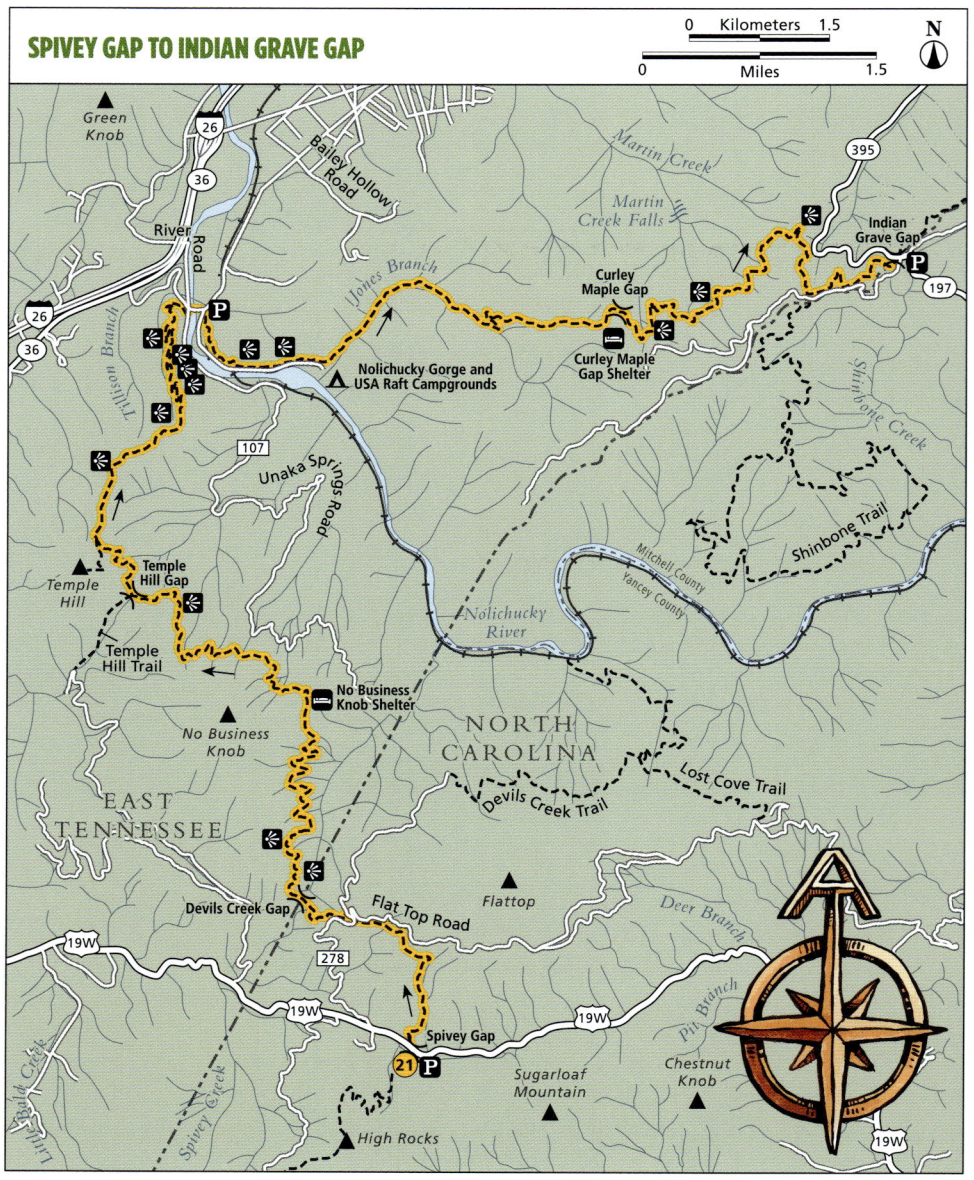

KEY POINTS

SECTION		ELEVATION (FEET)	MILES FROM SPRINGER MOUNTAIN	MILES FROM DAMASCUS
0.0	Spivey Gap, US 19W, stream south of gap (parking 0.5 mile west)	3,200	333.4	137.6
0.4	Oglesby Branch, water	3,555	333.8	137.2
1.3	Stream	3,820	334.7	136.3
1.5	Devils Creek Gap	3,754	334.9	136.1
3.7	Stream	2,984	337.1	133.9
4.9	No Business Knob Shelter, water 0.2 mile south on AT	3,181	338.3	132.7
7.3	Temple Hill Gap, Temple Hill Trail	2,850	340.7	130.3
9.4	Views of Erwin	2,694	342.8	128.2
11.1	River Road, Unaka Springs Road (parking)	1,662	344.5	126.5
11.4	Railroad tracks	1,707	344.8	126.2
12.4	Side trail east to Nolichucky Gorge and USA Raft campgrounds, water	1,744	345.8	125.2
12.8	Four footbridges over Jones Branch	1,797	346.2	124.8
15.4	Curley Maple Gap Shelter, water south of shelter	3,039	348.8	122.2
15.9	Spring	3,193	349.3	121.7
16.5	Stream	3,272	349.9	121.1
16.7	Stream	3,308	350.1	120.9
19.5	Indian Grave Gap, TN 395 (parking), water 0.1 mile east	3,350	352.9	118.1

Stream crossing while ascending toward Curley Maple Gap Shelter

TRAIL TOWN: ERWIN, TENNESSEE

Nestled in Unicoi County, Erwin, Tennessee, is a charming Appalachian Trail Community that offers hikers a warm welcome and a range of amenities. This historic railroad town, just 15 miles from Johnson City, is a hub for trail enthusiasts and history buffs alike.

Erwin is steeped in history and natural beauty. Once home to the Cherokee, residents still occasionally unearth arrowheads in their gardens, a testament to the area's rich past. In spring the town comes alive with the Tennessee Trails and Tunes Festival (formerly the Erwin Great Outdoors Festival), celebrating the great outdoors and Tennessee's vibrant music heritage with food, vendors, live music, and outdoor demos.

For hikers making their way from the Appalachian Trail, the quickest route to Erwin is via the Chestoa Bridge, which you cross in Hike 21. The town is well-equipped with a variety of services and amenities: a large grocery store, a hospital, and a post office. You'll also find several motels and eateries to make your stay comfortable. The YMCA, located at the corner of Ohio and Love Streets, roughly 3.5 miles from the AT, provides hot showers for a small fee.

For overnight accommodations, consider staying at **Uncle Johnny's Nolichucky Hostel**, which offers lodging, shuttles, resupply items, and mail services. Outdoor adventurers will appreciate **USA Raft Adventure Resort**, a sprawling property along the Nolichucky River offering unique lodging options, from tiny houses and vintage Airstreams to riverside geodomes with stunning views. Hikers can choose to stay at the main resort property, which offers an on-site sauna, tavern, and camp store, or at the Red Banks Campground, just 2.5 river miles downstream, known for its excellent swimming hole. The campground is situated at the historic site of the Civil War Battle of Red Banks.

For those interested in local history, a visit to the **Clinchfield Railroad Museum** is a must. Modeled after an old-fashioned train depot, this museum pays homage to Erwin's rich railroad heritage and offers a glimpse into the town's past.

If you have time for a short trip, head to David Crockett Birthplace State Park in Limestone, Tennessee, to explore the life of this legendary frontiersman.

22 INDIAN GRAVE GAP TO IRON MOUNTAIN GAP

Jarred Douglas on Unaka Mountain, Mile 358.3

Hike along a rolling ridge crest as the AT roams across **Beauty Spot** and traverses the dramatic red spruce forest atop **Unaka Mountain**. Although there is considerable climbing in the stretch, the rewards are well worth it.

Distance: 11.9 miles
Difficulty: Strenuous due to steep terrain and elevation changes
Nearest town: Erwin, Tennessee (roughly 7 miles west of Indian Grave Gap)

Water availability: Water is available at the trailhead (0.1 mile east outside curve in the road) and Cherry Gap Shelter, as well as at several springs along the way.
Trailhead GPS: 36.1107 / -82.3609

Nearby accommodations:

Rock Creek Recreation Area (USFS), roughly 3 miles west from Indian Grave Gap in Cherokee National Forest, offers electric hookups, RV sites, double sites, walk-in tent sites, and multiple bathhouses. Open May to October. Leashed pets are welcome. For reservations and inquiries, call (423) 638-4109

Campsite on Unaka Mountain, Mile 358.3

THE HIKE

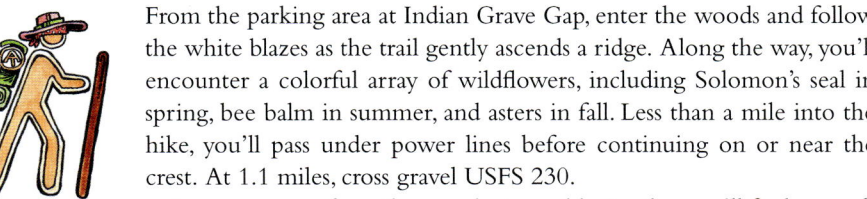

From the parking area at Indian Grave Gap, enter the woods and follow the white blazes as the trail gently ascends a ridge. Along the way, you'll encounter a colorful array of wildflowers, including Solomon's seal in spring, bee balm in summer, and asters in fall. Less than a mile into the hike, you'll pass under power lines before continuing on or near the crest. At 1.1 miles, cross gravel USFS 230.

As you emerge from the woods at roughly 2 miles, you'll find yourself in an open meadow known as Beauty Spot. Traverse the summit, surrounded by tall grass and meadow flowers like yarrow and goldenrod. Beauty Spot offers breathtaking 360-degree views, with Roan Mountain towering to the compass-east and the Black Mountains to the compass-south. From this vantage point you can also admire Big Bald, Flattop Mountain, and the upper Toe River Valley.

At the northern end of Beauty Spot, a blue-blazed trail leads west to a spring and USFS 230, accessible by vehicle. Descending for 0.5 mile from Beauty Spot, the AT arrives at Beauty Spot Gap at 4,100 feet (formerly referenced as Deep Gap), where a campsite and piped spring await across USFS 230. From here the trail embarks on a steep climb of 1.5 miles, navigating switchbacks to reach the 5,180-foot summit of Unaka Mountain.

Unaka Mountain's dense red spruce coverage obscures any view from the top but doesn't diminish its majesty and wonder. The name "Unaka" is believed to be of Indian

Forest portrait on Unaka Mountain, Mile 358.3

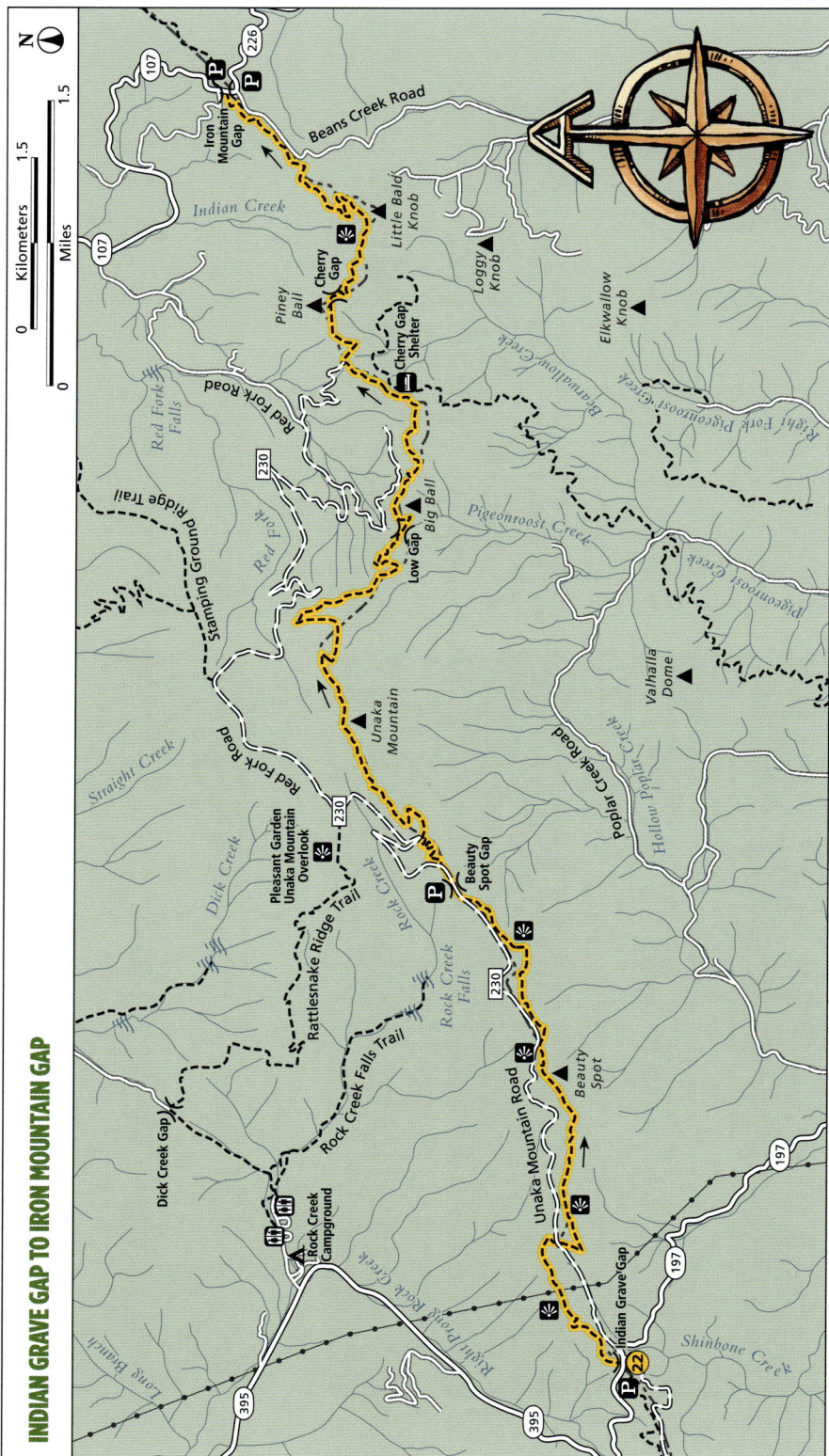

origin, meaning "fog draped," fitting for the low-lying clouds and fog that often cloak the southern Appalachian Mountains, especially in the early morning or on humid days.

From Unaka, the AT descends on switchbacks and steep terrain for over 2 miles to Low Gap and then traverses a series of steep knobs. At 8.6 miles, cross a footbridge before reaching Cherry Gap Shelter, an ideal spot to camp after a challenging day of hiking. A spring can be found via a blue-blazed trail behind the shelter. Descend 0.4 mile to Cherry Gap, then continue hiking as the trail ascends to Little Bald Knob, now densely tree-covered, and skirts the summit.

From Little Bald Knob, descend 1.7 miles to Iron Mountain Gap at TN 107/NC 206, where you'll find a small parking lot.

KEY POINTS

SECTION		ELEVATION (FEET)	MILES FROM SPRINGER MOUNTAIN	MILES FROM DAMASCUS
0.0	Indian Grave Gap, TN 395 (parking), water 0.1 mile east	3,350	352.9	118.1
0.6	Survey marker (USFS 381-28)	3,696	353.5	117.5
0.7	Power line	3,740	353.6	117.4
1.1	USFS 230, Red Fork Road (gravel)	3,770	354.0	117.0
2.3	Beauty Spot	4,437	355.2	115.8
3.5	Beauty Spot Gap (parking)	4,321	356.4	114.6
4.0	Piped spring and campsite to west across USFS 230	4,141	356.9	114.1
5.5	Unaka Mountain	5,180	358.4	112.6
7.7	Low Gap, campsite and unreliable spring 0.1 mile west	3,900	360.6	110.4
8.6	Footbridge over stream	4,129	361.5	109.5
8.8	Cherry Gap Shelter, spring on blue-blazed trail behind shelter	3,963	361.7	109.3
9.2	Unmarked trail crossing	3,906	362.1	108.9
10.2	Little Bald Knob (AT skirts summit)	4,367	363.1	107.9
10.4	Stream	4,291	363.3	107.7
11.9	Iron Mountain Gap, TN 107, NC 226 (parking)	3,723	364.8	106.2

23 IRON MOUNTAIN GAP TO HUGHES GAP

View north from Little Rock Knob, Mile 371.9

This hike offers spectacular views after just 0.5 mile, including distant sights of Buffalo Mountain, site of the Pinnacle Mountain fire tower. Enjoy the scenic uphill trek, passing through an old apple orchard, crossing gaps and knobs, and encountering stunning vistas framed by mountain laurel. The hike reaches its highest point at **Little Rock Knob** before descending into **Hughes Gap**, covering a mix of steep and undulating terrain along the way.

Looking northwest at Little Rock Knob, Mile 371.9

Distance: 9.4 miles
Difficulty: Moderate
Nearest town: Unicoi, Tennessee (10 miles from Iron Mountain Gap)

Water availability: Water is available at two campsites you pass and at Clyde Smith Shelter.
Trailhead GPS: 36.1433 / -82.2332

THE HIKE

From the parking lot at Iron Mountain Gap, cross the highway and turn left to begin walking uphill. Spectacular views await after 0.5 mile of hiking. In the distance you'll spot Buffalo Mountain, where the Pinnacle Mountain fire tower, restored in 2011, stands at 3,520 feet—one of only four remaining fire towers in the Cherokee National Forest. This tower now serves as a popular destination for hikers, offering panoramic views of the region's highest peaks, including Unaka Mountain, Roan Mountain, and Mount Mitchell in North Carolina, as well as vistas of Johnson City, Unicoi, and Erwin.

Continue your uphill trek, enjoying more views from an open field at the 0.8-mile mark. About a mile into the hike, you'll reach an old apple orchard. At the northern end of the orchard, down a blue-blazed trail, you'll find a nice campsite and a piped spring.

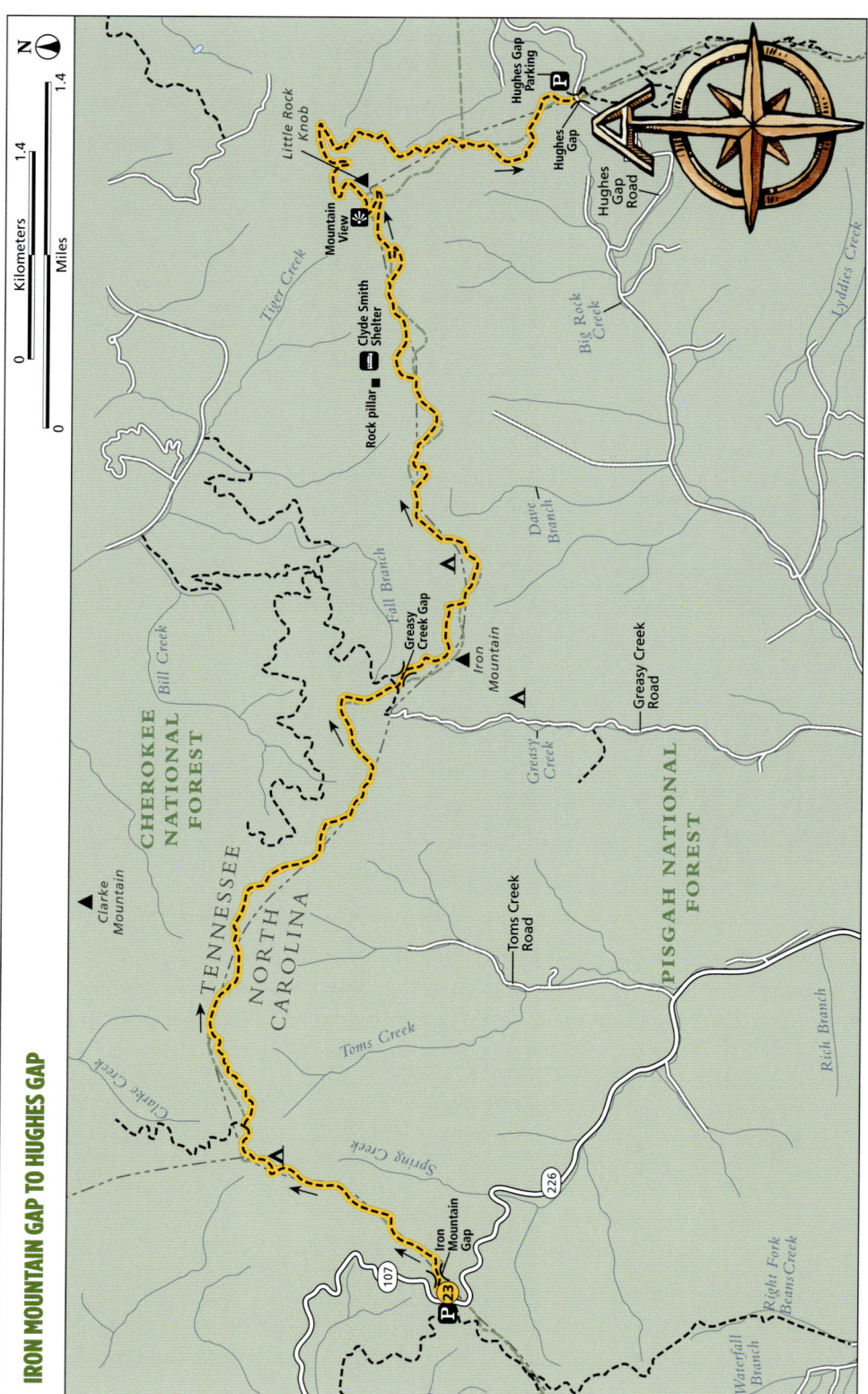

AT blaze just after Little Rock Knob

From the old apple orchard, descend steeply but briefly and begin a 5-mile stretch of undulating ridgetop hiking. Pass a large rock formation at the high point (4,429 feet) around 2.4 miles. Continue traversing gaps and knobs, eventually reaching Greasy Creek Gap at 4.1 miles. A possible campsite is available at the gap, and water can be found 0.2 mile west of the AT. At 4.9 miles arrive at another campsite nestled among gnarled maple trees. The AT intersects a blue-blazed trail at 6 miles, leading left 120 yards to the Clyde Smith Shelter.

From the shelter junction, 4,918-foot Little Rock Knob is 1.2 miles away, mostly uphill along a rocky ridge crest. Little Rock Knob is the highest point of the hike, offering wonderful views into North Carolina just south of the summit from its rocky promontory. In late spring and early summer, mountain laurel beautifully frames the view.

Descend Little Rock Knob for a little more than 2 miles into Hughes Gap, where this hike concludes.

KEY POINTS

SECTION		ELEVATION (FEET)	MILES FROM SPRINGER MOUNTAIN	MILES FROM DAMASCUS
0.0	Iron Mountain Gap, TN 107, NC 226 (parking)	3,723	364.8	106.2
1.3	Campsite and piped spring 0.1 mile west	4,015	366.1	104.9
2.4	Rock pillar	4,429	367.2	103.8
4.1	Greasy Creek Gap, campsite, water 0.2 mile west	4,034	368.9	102.1
4.9	Campsite	4,118	369.7	101.3
6.0	Clyde Smith Shelter 0.1 mile west; tent sites and spring 100 yards behind shelter	4,486	370.8	100.2
7.2	Little Rock Knob	4,918	372.0	99.0
7.5	Stream	4,767	372.3	98.7
9.4	Hughes Gap, TN 1330, Hughes Gap Road (parking)	4,040	374.2	96.8

24 HUGHES GAP TO CARVER'S GAP

Chimney remnant, Mile 378.6

Explore the southern side of **Roan Mountain** as you weave through a blend of deciduous trees transitioning to evergreens and rhododendron. Take a moment to explore the historic **Cloudland Hotel site** nestled within an open grassy area and pass **Roan High Knob Shelter**, the highest shelter on the Appalachian Trail. Despite its short length, this hike presents a moderate challenge, with an elevation gain of 2,380 feet up many switchbacks.

Distance: 6.6 miles
Difficulty: Strenuous due to long ascent and descent
Nearest town: Roan Mountain, Tennessee (13 miles south of Carver's Gap)
Water availability: There is a reliable spring at the beginning of the hike, another at the north end, and one at the shelter. Be sure to purify any water sourced from streams along this hike, which may be polluted.
Trailhead GPS: 36.1368 / -82.141

Good to know:

- Dress in layers and bring rain gear. Even if it's sunny in the valley, the summit may be covered in rain, fog, or ice. Conditions at high elevations can change abruptly.
- Vandalism has been reported at Carver's Gap. Consider arranging a shuttle if you plan on staying in the woods overnight.

Facade of Roan High Knob Shelter, Mile 379.2

THE HIKE

From Hughes Gap, the AT climbs steadily with some relief on switchbacks for nearly 2.5 miles to the summit of Beartown Mountain. A small piped spring is located down a short side trail about 0.5 mile from Hughes Gap.

From Beartown Mountain, follow the ridge crest as it descends to Ash Gap and then climbs again to 6,190 feet, the highest point on this hike. Ash Gap, located about two-thirds the way up the southern (compass north-western) side of Roan Mountain, has a nice level spot ideal for setting up camp with water available 0.1 mile down a blue-blazed trail.

> **DID YOU KNOW?**
> Roan Mountain isn't a singular peak; it stretches across a considerable ridge extending approximately 5 miles. Renowned for its breathtaking natural displays of Catawba rhododendron, Roan Mountain harbors a wealth of biodiversity, ranging from dense spruce-fir forests to expansive grassy balds. Its elevation ranges from 6,285 feet at Roan High Knob to 5,512 feet at Carver's Gap. The mountain's name has an elusive origin, with some speculating a connection to Daniel Boone's roan horse, given his frequent visits to the region.

Reach Toll House Gap at 4.4 miles. A short trail leads to the Roan High Knob parking area, where there are restrooms and picnic tables open from Memorial Day to the last Friday in September. Nearby is the site of the old Cloudland Hotel, open from the 1800s until 1910 and founded by General John Wilder. Its ruins lie at the summit, nestled within a grassy area with interpretive signs set on the crest a few yards east.

While traversing mostly level terrain, you'll encounter remnants of an old chimney before merging onto an old roadbed. At 5.1 miles the AT intersects a blue-blazed trail leading 0.1 mile to the Roan High Knob Shelter. The shelter, at 6,285 feet the highest on the AT, is situated in a wooded area with no views. It was formerly a fire warden's cabin before being converted into a shelter by the Forest Service in the 1980s. Water is available at a piped spring 50 yards from the shelter.

From the shelter the AT descends steeply for 1.5 miles to Carver's Gap, marking the conclusion of this hike. During your descent you'll traverse several board bridges spanning small streams that drain from the recreation areas. Please be aware that these streams may be polluted. A small parking lot and a pit toilet are available at Carver's Gap. Considering reports of vandalism on cars parked overnight here, it might be wise to arrange for a shuttle from this point.

Fire tower remnant behind Roan High Knob Shelter, Mile 379.2

Fire tower remnant behind Roan High Knob Shelter, Mile 379.2

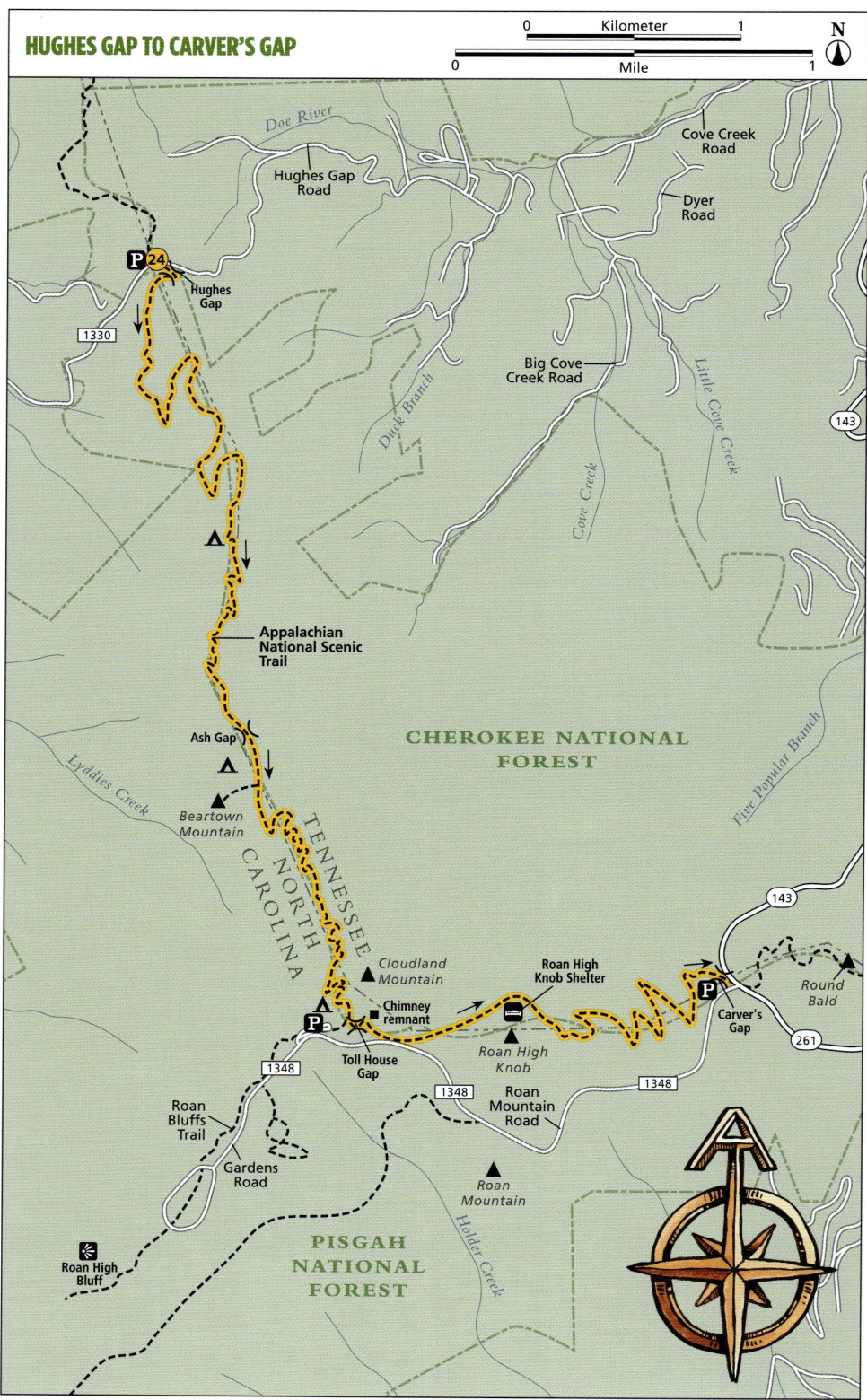

Carver's Gap National Forest sign and North Carolina welcome sign, Mile 380.7

KEY POINTS

SECTION		ELEVATION (FEET)	MILES FROM SPRINGER MOUNTAIN	MILES FROM DAMASCUS
0.0	Hughes Gap, TN 1330, Hughes Gap Road (parking)	4,040	374.2	96.8
0.4	Piped spring 50 yards east	4,234	374.6	96.4
3.0	Ash Gap, campsite, water 0.1 mile east	5,350	377.2	93.8
4.4	Toll House Gap (parking), water	6,190	378.6	92.4
4.5	Chimney remnant	6,132	378.7	92.3
5.1	Roan High Knob Shelter 0.1 mile east, spring on blue-blazed trail near shelter	6,285	379.3	91.7
6.5	Multiple footbridges over streams	5,508	380.7	90.3
6.6	Carver's Gap, TN 143, NC 261 (parking)	5,512	380.8	90.2

25 CARVER'S GAP TO US 19E

Carver's Gap parking lot with Roan Mountain in the distance, Mile 380.7

This section offers an exhilarating trek over five summits rising more than 5,400 feet, each boasting incredible views. Begin at scenic Carver's Gap, where lush rhododendron tunnels greet you, and continue through **Round Bald** and **Jane Bald**, with panoramic vistas of the surrounding mountains. Skirt the shoulder of **Grassy Ridge** and descend into tranquil valleys, passing landmarks like the former **Overmountain Shelter** site and a memorial honoring a dedicated AT enthusiast. The total elevation gain is approximately 2,500 feet northbound and 5,000 feet southbound.

Distance: 14.8 miles
Difficulty: Moderately strenuous due to numerous climbs
Nearest town: Roan Mountain, Tennessee (12 miles); Bakersville, North Carolina (13 miles)
Water availability: There are several water sources spread throughout the hike.
Trailhead GPS: 36.1068 / -82.1106

Good to know:

- In June and July Catawba rhododendron and flame azalea cover the balds, attracting hundreds of visitors each year. Peak bloom times usually fall around mid-June.
- This hike is extremely popular in summer. To avoid crowds, consider hiking this section on weekdays in summer or at other times of year.
- Much of this hike is at high elevations, so be prepared for all types of weather. Typically, the temperature is 10 to 15 degrees cooler than the forecast for the towns below. It can still snow in the early spring.
- Due to local vandalism, overnight parking at US 19E or Bear Branch Road is not recommended. Arrange to leave your vehicle at either nearby hostel.

Azalea in bloom just past Round Bald

THE HIKE

From the parking lot at Carver's Gap, the allure of the upcoming hike is immediately apparent. The balds you'll soon ascend loom in the distance, offering a tantalizing glimpse of the journey ahead. As you step onto the trail, you're greeted by rows of Catawba rhododendron and tall pine trees, setting the stage for your ascent to the ridge.

As you climb, intermittent views of the bald ridgeline reward you, alternating with passages through groves of rhododendron and pine tree tunnels. During certain times of the year, this lush covering provides a haven for myriad mushroom species, creating a captivating contrast to the landscape you'll soon encounter for the remainder of your hike.

At the 0.7-mile mark you reach Round Bald, where panoramic vistas of rolling mountains unfold in every direction. Grassy fields and rocky slabs offer endless points of interest to admire, making this a memorable stop along your journey. These peaks provide some of the most dynamic views that Tennessee and North Carolina have to offer. Over the next 1.3 miles, you will cross the ridgeline, encountering a diverse selection of plant life.

The terrain is a bit of a rocky roller coaster; however, the elevation changes remain slight and manageable for most hikers. At 1.5 miles from Carver's Gap, you pass Jane Bald, a perfect spot to perch and take a break, enjoying an excellent view of Grassy Ridge Bald across the landscape. Half a mile beyond Jane Bald, you reach the intersection of the Grassy Ridge Bald Trail, marked by a blue blaze. This side trail offers outstanding views. Continuing on the AT, the trail begins to descend, passing a stream and eventually leading to a pleasant campsite at the 3.0-mile mark before reaching the Stan Murray Shelter at 3.7 miles. The shelter was built in 1977 and renamed in 1994 in memory of Stanley A. Murray, former ATC chairman and longtime member of the TEHCC.

Meadow with deer on Grassy Ridge, Grandfather Mountain in the distance

Bryan Anderson ascending Jane Bald, Mile 382.2

The AT approaching Grassy Ridge Bald Trail, with Roan Round Bald and Roan Mountain in the distance

> **DID YOU KNOW?**
> The original route of the AT did not include the Roan Highlands. We have Stan Murray to thank for his leadership alongside the USDA Forest Service in rerouting the AT across the balds. Murray, who served as the ATC chairman from 1961 to 1975, later founded and served as the director of the Southern Appalachian Highlands Conservancy. A plaque honors him on Hump Mountain, where his ashes were scattered.

From the Stan Murray Shelter, continue hiking as the AT briefly ascends before descending to reach Yellow Mountain Gap at 4,662 feet, one of the lower points along this stretch. The former Overmountain Shelter site, now a nice campsite, is located 0.3 mile east on a blue-blazed trail. Water can be sourced from a spring on the way to the shelter.

> **DID YOU KNOW?**
> The Overmountain Victory Trail crosses the AT at Yellow Mountain Gap. This historic route was once traveled by frontiersmen from the backcountry regions of present-day Tennessee, Virginia, and North Carolina who marched eastward during the American Revolutionary War to join Patriot forces for the decisive Battle of Kings Mountain in 1780. This battle marked a pivotal turning point in the Southern Campaign of the Revolutionary War. Today, marked with brown plastic posts and white triangles, the trail follows the approximate path taken by the "overmountain settlers" from their homes over the Appalachian Mountains to Kings Mountain in South Carolina.

Yellow Mountain Gap and former Overmountain Shelter from the AT

AT blaze and view from Little Hump Mountain, Mile 387.9

    The trail then begins to climb out of Yellow Mountain Gap, passing an old roadbed at 6.6 miles. Soon after, watch for a side trail heading east for 0.1 mile to Big Yellow Mountain. From there the AT ascends steeply to the top of Little Hump Mountain, offering outstanding views from its grassy 5,459-foot summit. Camping is permitted here, but be aware of exposure to wind, which can be strong.

Hump Mountain from Little Hump Mountain, Mile 387.9

Little Hump Mountain from Hump Mountain with summit sign, Mile 390.1

Follow the AT as it descends for 1.3 miles to Bradley Gap, passing a piped spring and additional campsites about halfway down Little Hump Mountain. Bradley Gap also offers nice campsites and several water sources, though they are sometimes trampled by cattle. Take special care to follow the white blazes in this grassy area during foggy conditions. From Bradley Gap, begin the ascent to Hump Mountain, which you reach after about a mile of hiking.

Hump Mountain offers incredible views of the Doe River Valley, Beech and Grandfather Mountains, and Grassy Ridge. You may also see cattle grazing, helping to maintain the balds. Continuing hiking as the trail leads down the crest and into the woods, passing the Stan Murray memorial.

Stan Murray plaque with ridgeline leading north, Mile 390.1

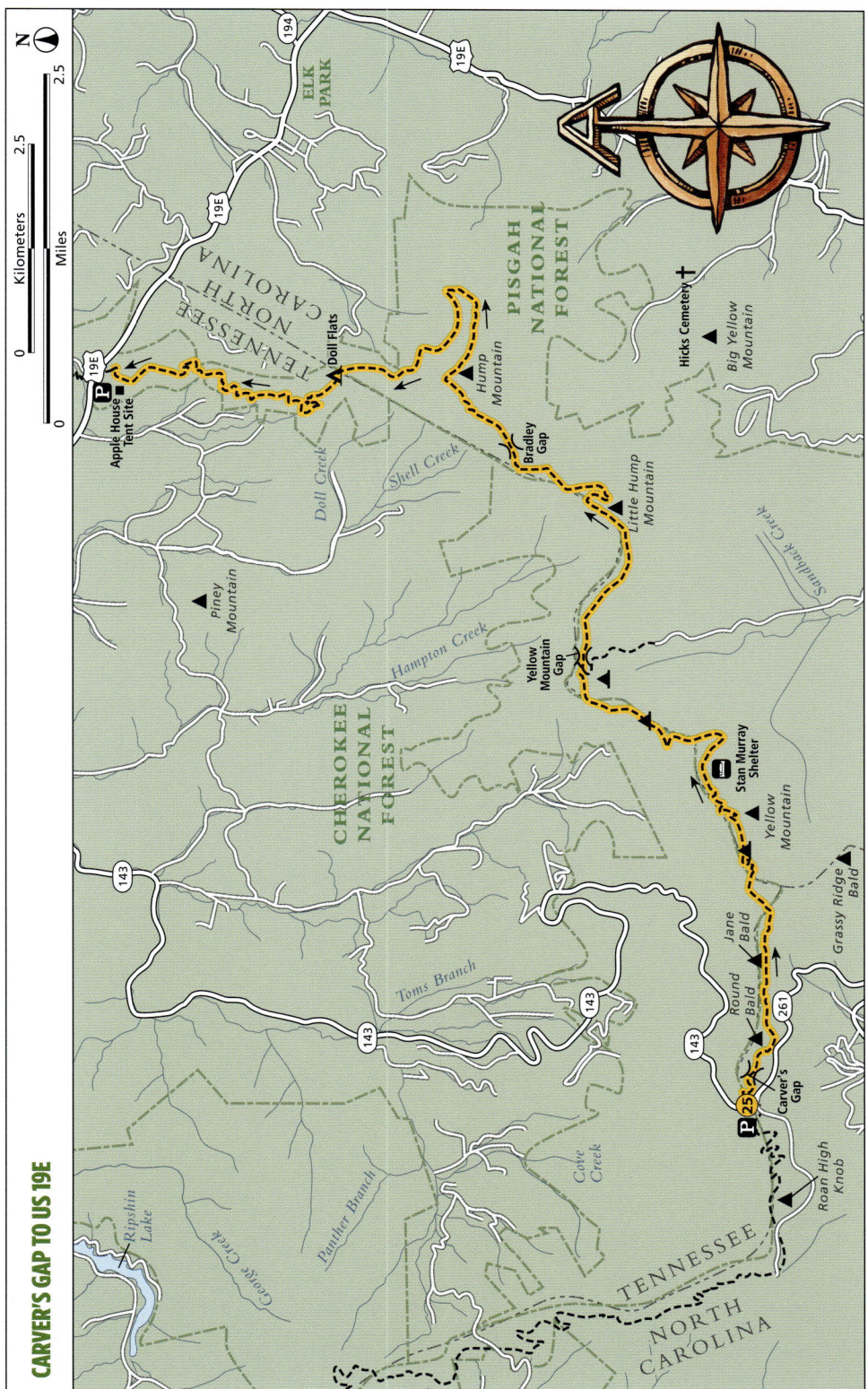

After several switchbacks, the AT reaches an open field at Doll Flats at 11.8 miles. This grassy area provides excellent campsites with views across North Carolina. In spring the forest floor transforms into a blanket of wildflowers. From here the trail leaves the North Carolina–Tennessee border and remains mostly in Tennessee all the way to Virginia. The AT continues its long descent on switchbacks and stone steps, passing a massive stone wall at 12.4 miles.

Reach Wilder Mountain Hollow at 14.2 miles, where good campsites and a spring are located. An abandoned iron mine, which operated from 1880 to 1912, lies east of the trail. Please exercise caution and do not enter underground mines—their roofs often collapse.

Shortly after, pass the Apple House tent site, a small camping area nestled in a dark hollow. From Apple House, hike 0.5 mile to arrive at US 19E. Elk Park, North Carolina, is approximately 2.5 miles east from here; Roan Mountain, Tennessee, is 3.5 miles to the west.

KEY POINTS

SECTION		ELEVATION (FEET)	MILES FROM SPRINGER MOUNTAIN	MILES FROM DAMASCUS
0.0	Carver's Gap, TN 143, NC 261 (parking)	5,512	380.8	90.2
0.7	Round Bald, summit 30 yards east, views	5,827	381.5	89.5
1.5	Jane Bald, big rock slab, views back to Roan Mountain	5,808	382.3	88.7
2.1	Side trail to Grassy Ridge Bald 0.5 mile east	5,899	382.9	88.1
2.3	Springs	5,860	383.1	87.9
3.0	Campsite to west	5,391	383.8	87.2
3.7	Stan Murray Shelter, spring on blue-blazed trail	5,059	384.5	86.5
5.6	Yellow Mountain Gap, camping 0.3 mile east (former Overmountain Shelter site), spring on blue-blazed trail on the way to campsite	4,662	386.4	84.6
6.6	Two intersections with old roadbed	5,189	387.4	83.6
6.8	Side trail to Big Yellow Mountain 0.1 mile east	5,260	387.6	83.4
7.2	Little Hump Mountain	5,459	388.0	83.0
7.9	Piped spring, campsites	5,147	388.7	82.3
8.5	Bradley Gap, spring 100 yards east	4,950	389.3	81.7
9.1	Fence	5,406	389.9	81.1
9.4	Hump Mountain, Stan Murray plaque	5,587	390.2	80.8
10.2	Fence	5,230	391.0	80.0
10.9	Spring	4,941	391.7	79.3
11.8	Doll Flats, North Carolina–Tennessee border	4,600	392.6	78.4
12.4	Spring, large stone wall	4,102	393.2	77.8
14.0	Stream	3,203	394.8	76.2
14.2	Wilder Mine group campsite, spring 150 yards north on AT	3,092	395.0	76.0
14.3	Apple House tent site	3,037	395.1	75.9
14.8	US 19E (limited parking for day use only)	2,895	395.6	75.4

TRAIL TOWN: ROAN MOUNTAIN, TENNESSEE

Known for its rich history and stunning natural beauty, Roan Mountain is a perfect place for a break from the trail. Just 5 miles from the AT, Roan Mountain, Tennessee, is a designated Appalachian Trail Community that offers hikers a variety of accommodations, dining options, and resupply services. Roan Mountain is steeped in history. In 1780 the Overmountain Men, Revolutionary War soldiers, traveled through Roan Mountain and camped at Shelving Rock. This historic site, located between Roan Mountain and Roan Mountain State Park, is part of the **Overmountain Victory National Historic Trail** and is listed on the National Register of Historic Places. In the early 1880s, John T. Wilder developed the Roan Mountain community as a key stop on the "Tweetsie" Railroad. Today you can enjoy the **Tweetsie Trail**, a scenic rail-to-trail route that offers walking and cycling opportunities while honoring the area's railroad legacy.

To refuel after hiking, stop by The Appalachian Station at 19E, a cozy pub and hostel located less than 0.5 mile from the US 19E trailhead. Enjoy delicious food, craft beer, and live music while you relax. The Roan Mountain Shuttle service also operates from this convenient spot.

For accommodations, you have options ranging from the **Roan Mountain State Park Campground** to several charming bed-and-breakfasts. Among them, **Mountain Harbour B&B and Hiker Hostel** stands out for its incredible breakfast, a highlight for hikers for more than a decade.

If you're visiting in June, don't miss the **Roan Mountain Rhododendron Festival**, which celebrates the blooming of the Catawba rhododendrons with local food, crafts, and music. Another highlight is the **Roan Mountain Appalachian Folk Festival** in August, featuring arts, crafts, and folk music.

For more information, Wi-Fi, and local insights, stop by the Roan Mountain Visitor Center at 1015 TN 143, Roan Mountain, TN 37687.

26 US 19E TO DENNIS COVE ROAD

View from the ridgeline approaching Buck Mountain Road

This is a well-graded section of the AT with few rocky or muddy areas and many camping spots to choose from. Hike along the **Elk River**, enjoy a break at **Jones Falls** or one of the tranquil cascades, take in views from rock outcrops at **White Rock Mountain**, and traverse old farmlands.

Distance: 24.7 miles
Difficulty: Moderately challenging due to distance
Nearest town: Elk Park, North Carolina; Roan Mountain, Tennessee
Water availability: Many water sources are available, including piped springs at the Mountaineer Falls and Moreland Gap Shelters. Remember to treat all water sourced from streams.
Trailhead GPS: 36.17752 / -82.01112

Good to know:

- This section crosses many minor channels, several of which drain from farms and pastureland upstream. They should be considered polluted and used only in emergencies. Depending on rainfall, they may or may not be dry.
- Due to local vandalism, overnight parking at US 19E or Bear Branch Road is not recommended. Arrange to leave your vehicle at either nearby hostel.

Nearby accommodations:

Mountain Harbour B&B and Hiker Hostel, located less than 0.5 mile west of US 19E, has been welcoming hikers since 2003. This well-regarded establishment offers a range of services, including comfortable lodging, a "world-famous" breakfast, and both slackpacking and shuttle services. They also have a general store for all your resupply needs. For more details and to make a reservation, call (866) 772-9494.

View from Jones Falls, Jarred Douglas and Bryan Anderson, Mile 400.9

THE HIKE

Cross US 19E, hiking 0.2 mile to reach Bear Branch Road, where there is a small parking area. From Bear Branch Road, the AT ascends for a mile, crossing a jeep path twice and reaching an open grassy area called Bishop Hollow. Many amazing views are available to the east and west as you traverse the ridge. Descending from the summit, the AT passes Isaacs Cemetery at 2.9 miles and reaches paved Buck Mountain Road at 3.3 miles. Water is available at High Point Memorial Baptist Church, which sits slightly off-trail.

Cross a small stream before reaching Campbell Hollow Road at 3.6 miles and enter a former Christmas tree farm. Continue hiking as the trail roams with gentle ups and downs, crossing two footbridges and eventually reaching a side trail to beautiful Jones Falls. From the Jones Falls intersection, the AT descends farther, reaching a brief side trail at 6.1 miles that leads to a pleasant campsite near the Elk River, named in homage to the area's historical prominence of these large beasts.

Continue hiking on gentle terrain with minimal elevation change for nearly 2 miles, crossing several small streams. At mile 8.7 the trail reaches Mountaineer Falls, a picturesque cascade offering a tent camping area. Just beyond the falls is the Mountaineer Falls Shelter, which can accommodate fourteen hikers on its two main sleeping platforms and loft.

From the shelter the AT gradually ascends, passing another campsite located down a blue-blazed trail to the east. Shortly after you will reach Slide Hollow Stream, named for a historic log slide used for timber harvesting in Appalachia. At mile 10.4, cross gravel Walnut Mountain Road, where the trail briefly levels out before undulating for several miles, crossing streams and passing lovely cascades. The AT intersects gravel USFS 293 at mile 13.6, just before a small waterfall. Two springs are located a mile from here, your

Jones Falls, Mile 400.9

The Elk River

best option for refilling water. Hike another 2 miles to reach a campsite near several streams before ascending roughly 3,900 feet to this section's highest point.

Moreland Gap Shelter is located shortly after the viewpoint. The water source is down a steep hill across from the shelter. Note that the open side of the shelter faces northwest and tends to get wet inside during storms. From the shelter the AT carries along, passing through a field that's maintained by the Forest Service for white-tailed deer to graze. The trail passes another Forest Service road and continues its undulating pattern, passing under power lines before reaching a blue-blazed trail leading 0.8 mile downhill to Coon Den Falls. From the Coon Den Falls side trail at mile 23, the AT descends for 1.7 miles to Dennis Cove Road, passing an old farm and other scenic views along the way.

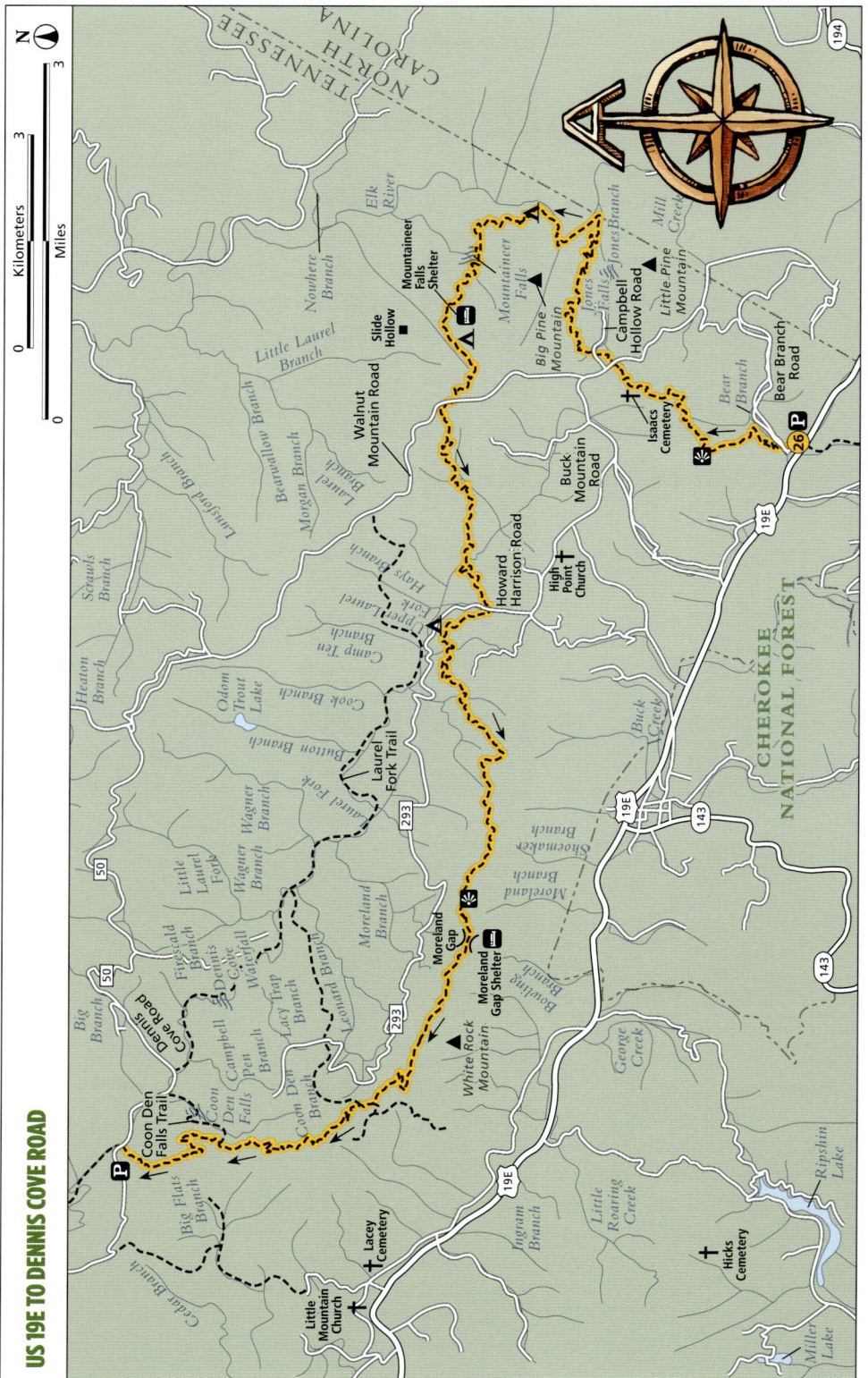

KEY POINTS

SECTION		ELEVATION (FEET)	MILES FROM SPRINGER MOUNTAIN	MILES FROM DAMASCUS
0.0	US 19E (limited parking for day use only)	2,895	395.6	75.4
0.2	Bear Branch Road, streams	2,900	395.8	75.2
1.0	South end of jeep path, stream	3,188	396.6	74.4
1.4	North end of peep path	3,441	397.0	74.0
2.4	Views from open ridge	3,758	398.0	73.0
2.9	Isaacs Cemetery	3,581	398.5	72.5
3.3	Buck Mountain Road, water at church	3,487	398.9	72.1
3.6	Campbell Hollow Road, streams	3,380	399.2	71.8
3.9	Footbridge over stream	3,399	399.5	71.5
4.3	Stream	3,370	399.9	71.1
5.4	Side trail 0.1 mile east to Jones Falls	3,018	401.0	70.0
6.1	Campsite, Elk River 0.1 mile east	2,730	401.7	69.3
8.3	Stream	2,988	403.9	67.1
8.7	Mountaineer Falls to west	3,054	404.3	66.7
8.8	Mountaineer Falls Shelter, water 200 feet down blue-blazed trail	3,183	404.4	66.6
9.6	Campsite to east, water	3,229	405.2	65.8
10.0	Slide Hollow Stream	3,347	405.6	65.4
10.4	Walnut Mountain Road	3,604	406.0	65.0
11.3	Footbridge over stream	3,444	406.9	64.1
12.1	Bench, easement trail	3,514	407.7	63.3
12.7	Upper Laurel Fork	3,247	408.3	62.7
13.6	USFS 293 (gravel), waterfall south on AT	3,421	409.2	61.8
15.0	Stream	3,438	410.6	60.4
15.4	Hardcore Cascades	3,378	411.0	60.0
16.7	Campsite, several streams and footbridges	3,560	412.3	58.7
18.3	View from rock outcroppings	3,908	413.9	57.1
18.4	Moreland Gap Shelter, water 0.2 mile down steep hill across from shelter	3,815	414.0	57.0
20.6	Piped spring	3,815	416.2	54.8
21.0	Forest Service road	3,778	416.6	54.4
23.0	Coon Den Falls Trail 0.8 mile east	3,411	418.6	52.4
24.7	Dennis Cove Road, USFS 50	2,508	420.3	50.7

27 DENNIS COVE ROAD TO WILBUR DAM ROAD

Laurel Falls, Mile 421.5

Experience one of the most picturesque stretches on the entire AT, showcasing the natural beauty of sheer rock walls, rapids, falls, and an ever-changing landscape within the **Cherokee National Forest**. Traverse the untamed and rugged gorge of Laurel Fork to view impressive **Laurel Falls**. Geologists can spend hours analyzing the thrust faults and quartz veins in this area. Abundant wildflowers adorn the trail in spring and summer, while numerous spots along the river offer opportunities for hammock camping and tent pitching. Enjoy walking along the shore of **Watauga Lake** at the **Shook Branch Recreation Area**, a popular picnic destination. Finish your hike with a stroll atop **Watauga Dam**, where you'll be treated to outstanding views of the lake and surrounding mountains.

Distance: 13.0 miles
Difficulty: Moderate but challenging due to rugged, rocky terrain
Nearest town: Hampton, Tennessee

Water availability: Water is available at Laurel Fork Shelter as well as other natural places along this stretch.
Trailhead GPS: 36.264150 / -82.123260

Good to know:

- USDA Forest Service lands between US 321 (Mile 422.9) and Wilbur Dam Road (Mile 433.2) are closed to recreation. Hiking through this area is permitted, but stopping, preparing or consuming food, or overnight stays are not allowed. This closure is in effect indefinitely.
- Laurel Falls is a popular destination for hikers due to its immense size and picturesque setting. Expect company on the weekends. The hike to the falls can be challenging and requires good footwear and physical ability. Bring trekking poles or a walking stick to help with balance on the rocky terrain.
- Bob Peoples, an Appalachian Trail Hall of Famer and renowned trail angel, provides shuttles from Dennis Cove Road. For shuttle services, please contact him at (423) 725-4409. His hostel, the Kincora Hiking Hostel, warmly welcomes old friends.

Nearby Accommodations:

Black Bear Resort, 0.5 mile east of Dennis Cove Road (USFS 50), offers a range of lodging options including creek-side cabins, campsites, and RV sites, along with shuttle service, resupply items, and laundry and shower facilities. Well-behaved pets are welcome. For reservations call (321) 271-5188.

Boots Off Hostel and Campground, 142 Shook Branch Road, Hampton, Tennessee (accessible via a short side trail at Mile 428.7), provides various lodging options, including private cabins and campsites, along with shuttle service, resupply items, and laundry and shower facilities. All stays include a light breakfast, and well-behaved pets are welcome. For reservations call (239) 218-3904.

THE HIKE

Begin your hike from the parking area at Dennis Cove Road, following an old railroad grade down Laurel Fork Valley. At 0.2 mile you'll pass a sign marking the southern boundary of the Pond Mountain Wilderness, with the trail remaining relatively level. Look across the creek to the right to spot high rocky cliffs signaling the start of the gorge.

Cross the Koonford Bridge at 0.8 mile, an award-winning bridge crafted by maintainers using only local materials and hand tools. Just beyond the bridge the AT intersects an unmarked trail leading to Potato Top, a sharp peak offering exceptional views of the gorge; however, be prepared for a rough and steep 0.2-mile side trail along a narrow rocky ridge.

At 1.1 miles you'll reach a blue-blazed high-water bypass trail that reconnects with the AT after about 0.5 mile. It should be used if Laurel Fork is flooded.

Laurel Falls and blaze from the AT

Follow the AT, descending on rocky stairs to reach Laurel Falls. A spacious flat area near the base provides an excellent viewing spot. Laurel Falls is a remarkable sight—a river-wide drop of approximately 40 feet in the form of a block waterfall, surrounded by cliffs on both sides. During springtime and after heavy rain, the steep 50-foot-wide rock wall is completely cloaked in water; in winter the falls transform into icy cascades. Exercise extreme caution near the falls; many accidents have occurred due to the strong undertow. In 2012 a father and his teenage son tragically lost their lives here.

From here the terrain becomes extremely rocky. Follow the trail downstream through the gorge, and at 1.4 miles skirt the base of the cliff on a built-up rock wall shelf. If this section of the trail is icy or underwater, it's safer to turn around and use the high-water route. Ascend steeply to reach the junction for the Laurel Fork Shelter and the southern end of the high-water bypass. The shelter is located uphill about 300 feet from the AT. Water is available at the shelter.

At the junction the AT veers left, leading along a narrow rocky ridge. Take in the beauty of Catawba rhododendron and mountain laurel lining the ridge that offers views of the gorge below. Descend through pine woods to creek level, passing Waycaster Spring on your left at the 2.3-mile mark. If you plan to continue to Pond Mountain, be sure to refill your water here.

Hike along a nearly level valley floor on a wide trail, crossing two well-crafted wooden footbridges spanning Laurel Fork. Upon reaching the trail junction for the Hampton Blueline Trail, a popular route from Hampton, Tennessee, to the falls, turn right to follow the white blaze, departing from Laurel Fork and marking the beginning of the 1,700-foot ascent up Pond Mountain.

Approaching tight rock path around Laurel Fork, Mile 421.5

Crossing tight rock path around Laurel Fork, Mile 421.5

> **DID YOU KNOW?**
> Amid the white-quartz boulders in this area, you'll find evidence of ancient life forms. Approximately 550 million years ago, animals, possibly worms, burrowed into the tidal sands, which have since solidified into hard quartzite. These formations consist of 3-inch lines of filled holes.

Reach the relatively level area known as the "Pond Flats" at 5.4 miles. Toward the northern end of Pond Flats lies a high-elevation "pond" nestled in a depression. While it often dries up in summer, it still sustains a habitat for frogs, toads, and mosquitoes. Nearby you'll find a camping spot. Continue along the level ridgetop, passing a spring as the AT continues.

Descend Pond Mountain via switchbacks on a well-graded trail, covering a descent of 1,680 feet, and cross the northern boundary of the Pond Mountain Wilderness at the 8.1-mile mark. Half a mile later, the AT intersects Shook Branch Road. Follow the white blaze to the right, carefully cross bustling US 321, and turn left along the shoreline of Watauga Lake. A paved road leads to the Shook Branch Recreation Area, offering picnic tables and a sandy beach with a swimming spot. At 9.3 miles pass through a gate on an old roadbed.

Watauga Lake

View from Watauga Dam, Mile 431.9

View from Watauga Dam, Mile 431.9

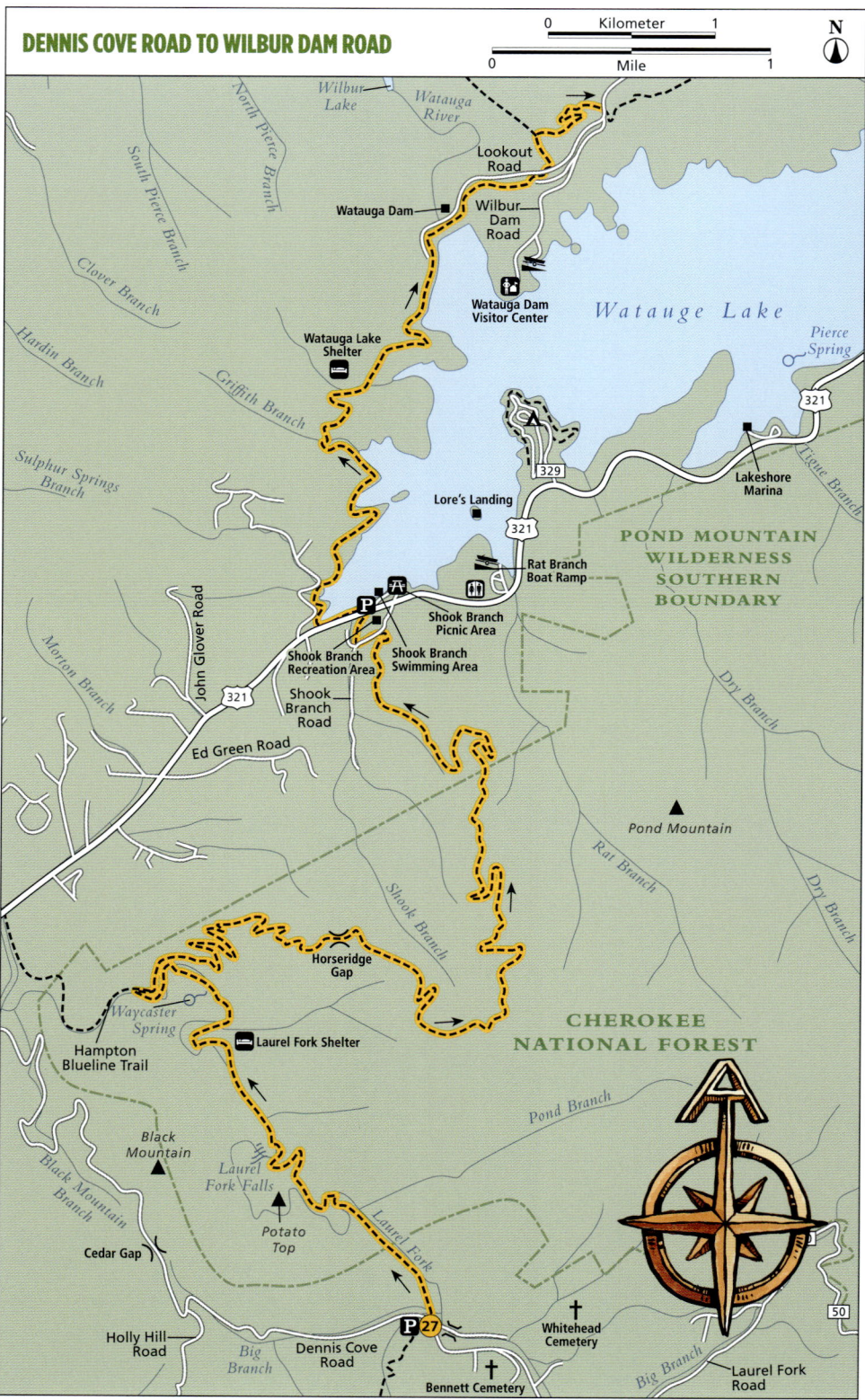

At 10.1 miles reach the small Griffith Branch. Note that water reliability may be uncertain here. Proceed toward the Watauga Dam as the trail undulates for the next 1.5 miles. Upon reaching the dam, cross the top, walking along a road for 0.4 mile while soaking in the breathtaking views of the river and surrounding mountains. After departing from the Watauga Dam, the AT ascends briefly before descending and ultimately arriving at Wilbur Dam Road at 13.0 miles.

KEY POINTS

SECTION		ELEVATION (FEET)	MILES FROM SPRINGER MOUNTAIN	MILES FROM DAMASCUS
0.0	Dennis Cove Road, USFS 50	2,508	420.3	50.7
0.2	Pond Mountain Wilderness southern boundary	2,440	420.5	50.5
0.8	Koonford footbridge over Laurel Fork	2,452	421.1	49.9
1.1	High-water bypass trail	2,375	421.4	49.6
1.2	Laurel Falls	2,105	421.6	49.4
1.9	Laurel Fork Shelter, stream 50 yards downhill from shelter on blue-blazed trail	2,161	422.2	48.8
2.3	Waycaster Spring	1,992	422.6	48.4
2.7	Hampton Blueline Trail	1,948	423.0	48.0
5.4	Pond Flats, weak spring 0.1 mile north on AT	3,689	425.7	45.3
8.5	Shook Branch Road	2,020	428.8	42.2
8.6	US 321, Shook Branch Recreation Area, water	1,990	428.9	42.1
10.1	Griffith Branch	2,053	430.4	40.6
11.7	Watauga Dam	2,014	432.0	39.0
13.0	Wilbur Dam Road	2,250	433.3	37.7

28 WILBUR DAM ROAD TO TN 91

View from campsite approaching Vandeventer Shelter

This section begins at the Wilbur Dam Road parking area and traverses the rugged crest of **Iron Mountain** on a well-graded trail, with the first 6 miles traveling through the Big Laurel Branch Wilderness Area. Highlights include ridgetop hiking, stunning views from **Vandeventer Shelter**, the historical **Nick Grindstaff monument**, and a scenic descent to TN 91, with opportunities for camping and water along the way.

Distance: 16.2 miles
Difficulty: Moderate
Nearest town: Hampton, Tennessee (10 miles west of Wilbur Dam Road); Shady Valley, Tennessee (3.6 miles east of TN 91)
Water availability: Water is available from springs and streams along this stretch, but some sources may be unreliable or difficult to access. Your best option for refilling is the spring located south of Iron Mountain Shelter, so be sure to bring adequate water.
Trailhead GPS: 36.328560 / -82.111610

Good to know:

- Long pants are recommended in midsummer, as nettles and briars grow thick in the southern half of this section.
- Traversing from north to south presents less of a challenge, with a climb of 2,600 feet compared to hiking south to north, where the climbs total 3,900 feet.
- Spectacular views are best in winter and fall, while summer offers vibrant blooms of rhododendron and flame azaleas.

View from back side of Vandeventer Shelter, Mile 437.9

THE HIKE

From the small parking area at Wilbur Dam Road, pass the wooden bulletin board and begin ascending as the AT travels north through the Big Laurel Branch Wilderness Area. After a mile of hiking you will start the 14-mile traverse along the narrow crest of Iron Mountain. The trail meets a spring at 3.0 miles and climbs briefly before leveling out, reaching Vandeventer Shelter at 4.7 miles. Enjoy outstanding views of Watauga Lake and the surrounding mountains from the concrete block shelter. The water source is located 0.3 mile down a very steep blue-blazed trail 0.1 mile south of the shelter. Consider getting water from the spring at mile 3.0 for the sake of convenience.

From the shelter continue along the ridge crest, crossing the northern boundary and exiting the Big Laurel Branch Wilderness Area at 6.1 miles.

At 8.5 miles there are good tent sites with a spring, although unreliable in dry seasons. Just beyond the campsite, the trail passes through dead pine trees in a boggy sag.

Enjoy a level grassy area abundant with blackberries in summer before reaching Turkey Pen Gap, named for a traditional method of turkey hunting, at 9.8 miles. The trail continues with minimal elevation change for 1.5 miles, passing beneath power lines and past a spring before a brief climb to Iron Mountain Shelter. If staying overnight, be sure to refill water at the spring located south of the shelter, the nearest water source.

Arrive at the Nick Grindstaff monument, located 12.8 miles along the trail, positioned 15 yards west of the AT. From the stone monument, continue following the white blazes as the trail descends over the next several miles.

At 15.3 miles the AT crosses a footbridge and a series of log bridges over a stream. Continue on this gentle terrain, passing an old road and reaching TN 91 at 16.2 miles.

DID YOU KNOW?

Nick Grindstaff (December 26, 1851–July 22, 1923) lived a reclusive life on Iron Mountain. Orphaned at age 3, he moved west at 26 but returned to his native mountains after the death of his wife, having been robbed and beaten. For the remaining 45 years of his life, he lived in isolation in the mountains. The chimneylike monument, built from the remains of his cabin, honors "Uncle Nick Grindstaff," who was buried here before the Appalachian Trail came into existence. Its inscription reads: "Born alone, suffered alone, died alone," a testament to his solitary life. Local legend tells that when residents tried to move Nick's body, his devoted dog resisted so intensely that they had to tie the dog to a tree. Both were eventually laid to rest together. Hikers camping at the site have reported hearing the mournful howls of the dog in the still of the night.

Vandeventer Shelter, Mile 437.9

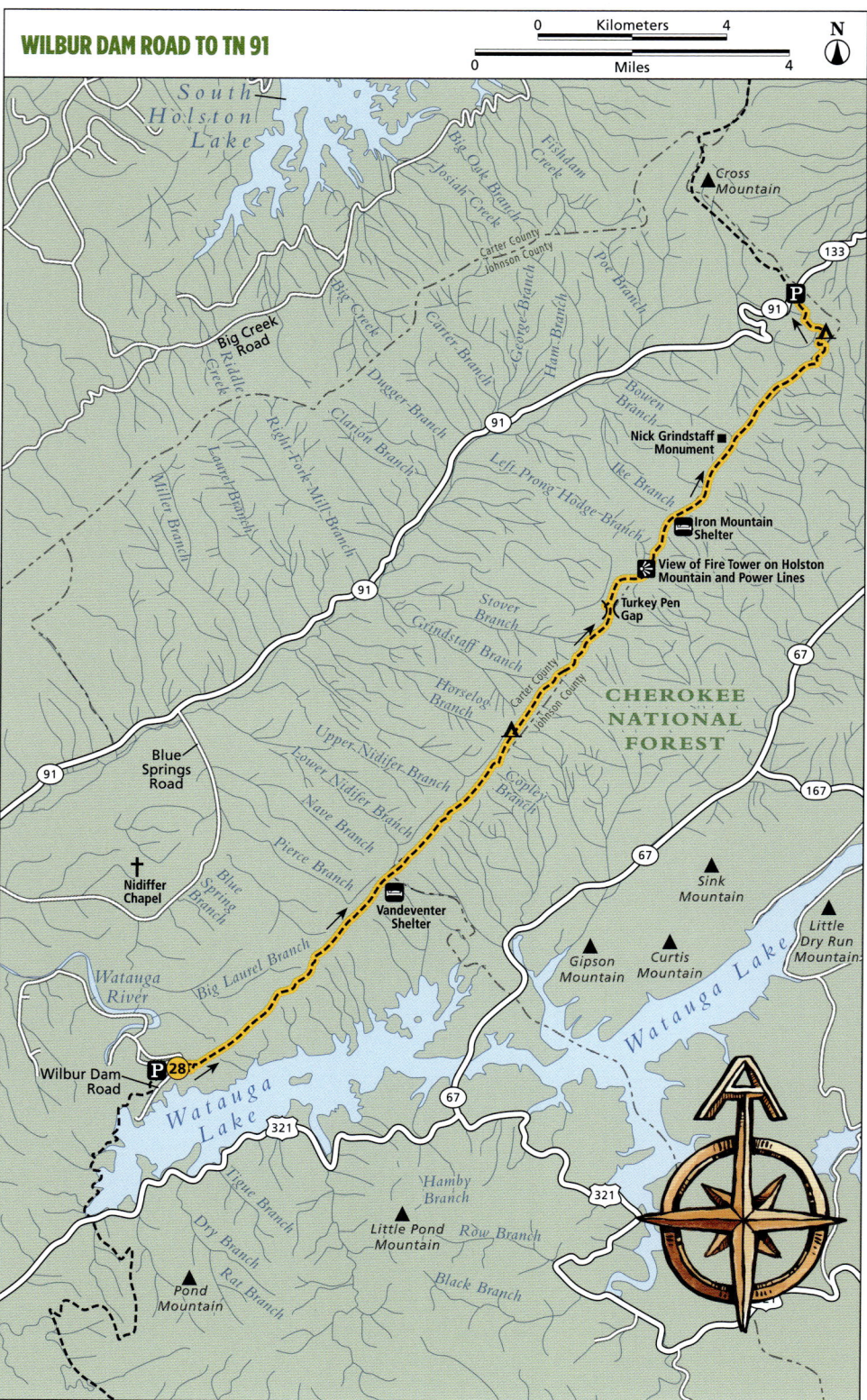

KEY POINTS

SECTION		ELEVATION (FEET)	MILES FROM SPRINGER MOUNTAIN	MILES FROM DAMASCUS
0.0	Wilbur Dam Road	2,250	433.3	37.7
3.0	Spring	3,316	436.3	34.7
4.7	Vandeventer Shelter, water 0.4 mile down difficult blue-blazed trail south of shelter on AT	3,558	438.0	33.0
8.5	Campsite, stream 100 yards east	3,857	441.8	29.2
9.8	Turkey Pen Gap	3,979	443.1	27.9
10.7	Power line	4,126	444.0	27.0
11.3	Spring	4,000	444.6	26.4
11.5	Iron Mountain Shelter (no water)	4,096	444.8	26.2
12.8	Nick Grindstaff Monument	4,090	446.1	24.9
15.3	Footbridge over stream	3,554	448.6	22.4
15.7	Roadbed	3,584	449.0	22.0
16.2	TN 91, south end of wheelchair-accessible trail	3,509	449.5	21.5

29 TN 91 TO LOW GAP

Legendary trail magic box approaching TN 91

Experience a moderate stretch of the AT in the scenic **Cherokee National Forest**, where well-graded trails offer occasional breathtaking views of **Shady Valley**. Highlights include walking through historic farmland once owned by the Osborne family, exploring the **"old berry fields"** of a former thriving cranberry bog, and traversing a unique **wheelchair-accessible section** across a lovely open grassy field.

Distance: 6.5 miles
Difficulty: Moderate
Nearest town: Shady Valley, Tennessee (4 miles east of TN 91)

Water availability: Water is available via springs at Double Springs Shelter and Low Gap.
Trailhead GPS: 36.4814 / -81.9603

THE HIKE

From the Cross Mountain trailhead parking area, cross TN 91 and use the special wheelchair-accessible stile to a 0.5-mile path through a grassy field. After this, the AT reaches the edge of the woods near an old farm once owned by the Osborne family, who sold it to the ATC in 2001 after they became too old to work it. Be sure to leave the gates as you find them, whether closed or open.

At 2.7 miles you reach a high point on Cross Mountain, where the trail then descends slightly before passing Double Springs Shelter at around 3 miles. A spring is located 100 yards west of the shelter. About 200 feet north of the shelter, the blue-blazed Holston Mountain Trail intersects, following the crest of Holston Mountain for 9.5 miles to a USFS road at Holston High Knob.

Hiker Jared Sims after lightning strike in 2010, Double Springs Shelter, Mile 452.4

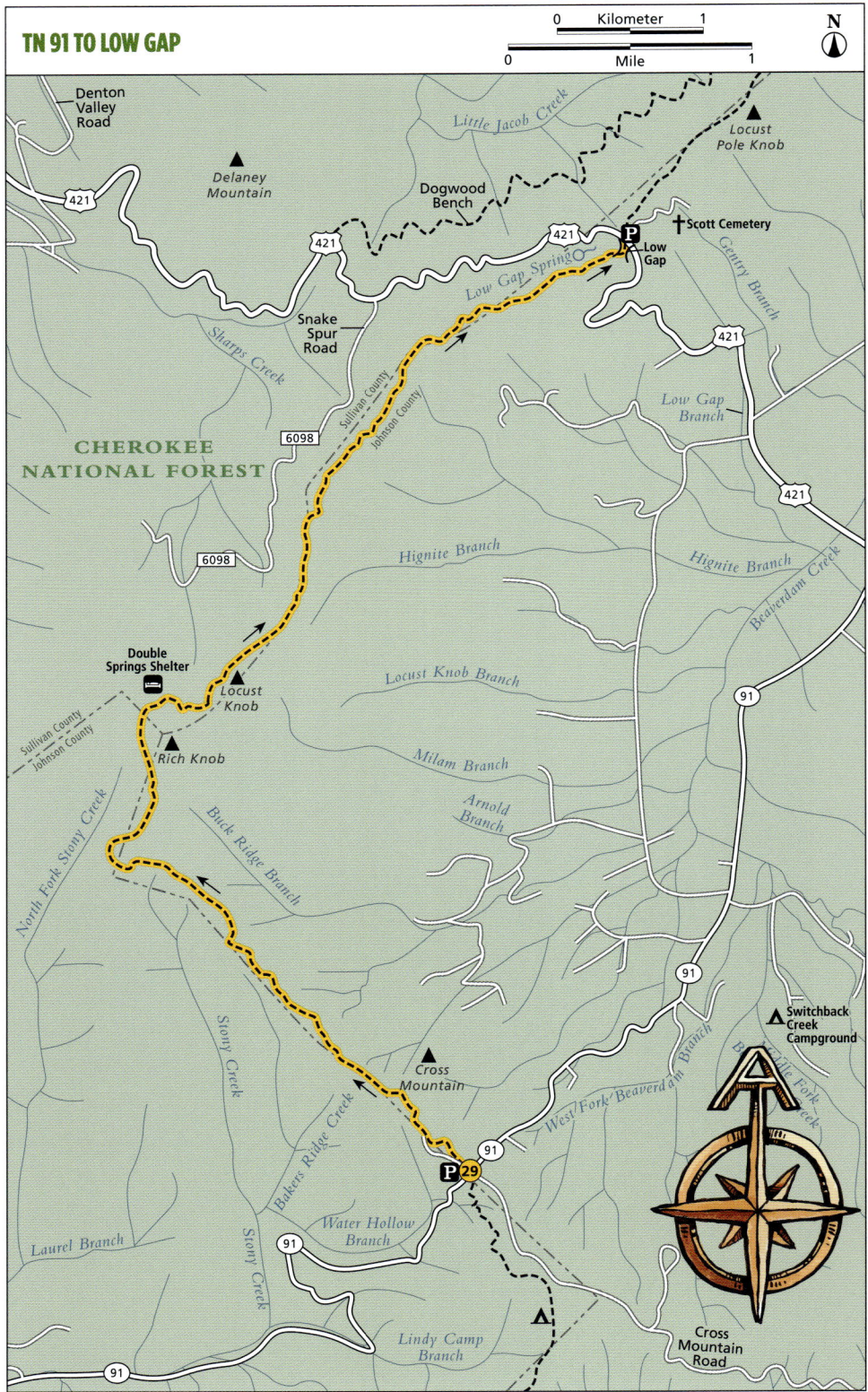

Campsite near Locust Knob

Starting from the shelter, the trail plunges down for about a mile and reaches Locust Knob at mile 4.7. You then traverse through the partly open "old berry fields," where you can see the farmlands of Shady Valley. This land, once spongy cranberry bogs, was drained and cleared for timber and agriculture, causing the bogs to dry up.

At 6.4 miles the trail passes a small campsite at a former homesite. From this point, descend steeply but briefly to Low Gap at US 421, where the hike concludes. A parking area and piped spring are located at Low Gap.

KEY POINTS

SECTION		ELEVATION (FEET)	MILES FROM SPRINGER MOUNTAIN	MILES FROM DAMASCUS
0.0	TN 91, south end of wheelchair-accessible trail	3,509	449.5	21.5
0.9	North end of wheelchair-accessible trail	3,615	450.3	20.7
3.1	Double Springs Shelter, spring near shelter	4,078	452.5	18.5
4.7	Locust Knob	3,636	454.1	16.9
6.5	Low Gap, USFS 421, piped spring	3,384	456.0	15.0

30 LOW GAP TO DAMASCUS

Out-of-commission shelter at McQueens Knob, Mile 459.2

On this section of the AT starting at **Low Gap**, you'll trek along a smooth, well-graded ridgetop path through lush woodlands and scenic fields, visiting historic landmarks along the way. The hike concludes with a long, gentle descent into the quaint town of **Damascus, Virginia**, where you can unwind after your journey.

Distance: 15.0 miles
Difficulty: Moderate
Nearest town: Shady Valley, Tennessee (2.7 miles east of Low Gap); Damascus, Virginia
Water availability: Water is available via a piped spring at Low Gap, Abingdon Gap Shelter, and on a blue-blazed trail at the northern end of this section.
Trailhead GPS: 36.5388 / -81.9482

THE HIKE

From Low Gap, enter the woods and begin hiking north. Your first landmark is an old stone wall that parallels the AT for a short distance, a testament to the many families who once farmed these lands.

Descend steeply to Double Spring Gap, arriving at 1.9 miles. Roughly half a mile from here is a weak, often muddy spring. Continue your hike with a gradual ascent to McQueens Knob, the site of a former fire tower.

At mile 3.7 you cross USFS 69 at McQueens Gap and then follow the undulating crest of Holston Mountain along an old woods road.

Arriving at Abingdon Gap Shelter at 4.8 miles, you will find a piped spring for water 0.2 mile behind the shelter, accessible via a blue-blazed trail. Continuing north, the AT descends and passes through a sag with a bowl-like depression to the right. A mile later, walk through a grove of hemlock trees near a shallow gap. Shortly after, pass a large ledge of white quartzite near a high point of the ridge.

At 9.9 miles you'll arrive at the Backbone Rock Trail junction. This trail offers a 3-mile route to a USFS recreation area complete with picnic tables, toilet facilities, and trails to the scenic features of Backbone Rock.

From the junction, the AT descends steadily under a lush canopy of mountain laurel and rhododendron. At 11.3 miles you'll cross from Tennessee into Virginia, leaving the Cherokee National Forest and entering the Jefferson National Forest and Mount Rogers National Recreation Area.

At 12.3 miles you'll pass a campsite that offers a perfect spot for one last night on the trail before heading into town.

At mile 12.9 a blue-blazed trail intersects, leading east to a spring at an abandoned homestead. Continue your descent for 1.8 miles to the friendly town of Damascus, Virginia, where the iconic wooden welcome sign marks the end of your hike

Tennessee–Virginia border, Mile 467.2

DID YOU KNOW?

Backbone Rock is named for a rugged spur ridge on Holston Mountain that abruptly ends at a sharp bend in Beaverdam Creek. A tunnel was carved through the rock in 1901 to create a railroad connection between Shady Valley and Damascus, Virginia, to transport chestnut extract and timber. This tunnel, known as "The Shortest Tunnel in the World," still allows motorists to pass through while traveling on TN 133. In the 1930s, the Civilian Conservation Corps developed the area for day use, building two picnic shelters and hiking trails with scenic native stonework. The campground was added in the 1960s and was rehabilitated in the mid-1990s.

Entrance/exit of the AT at Water Street in Damascus, Virginia, Mile 470.6

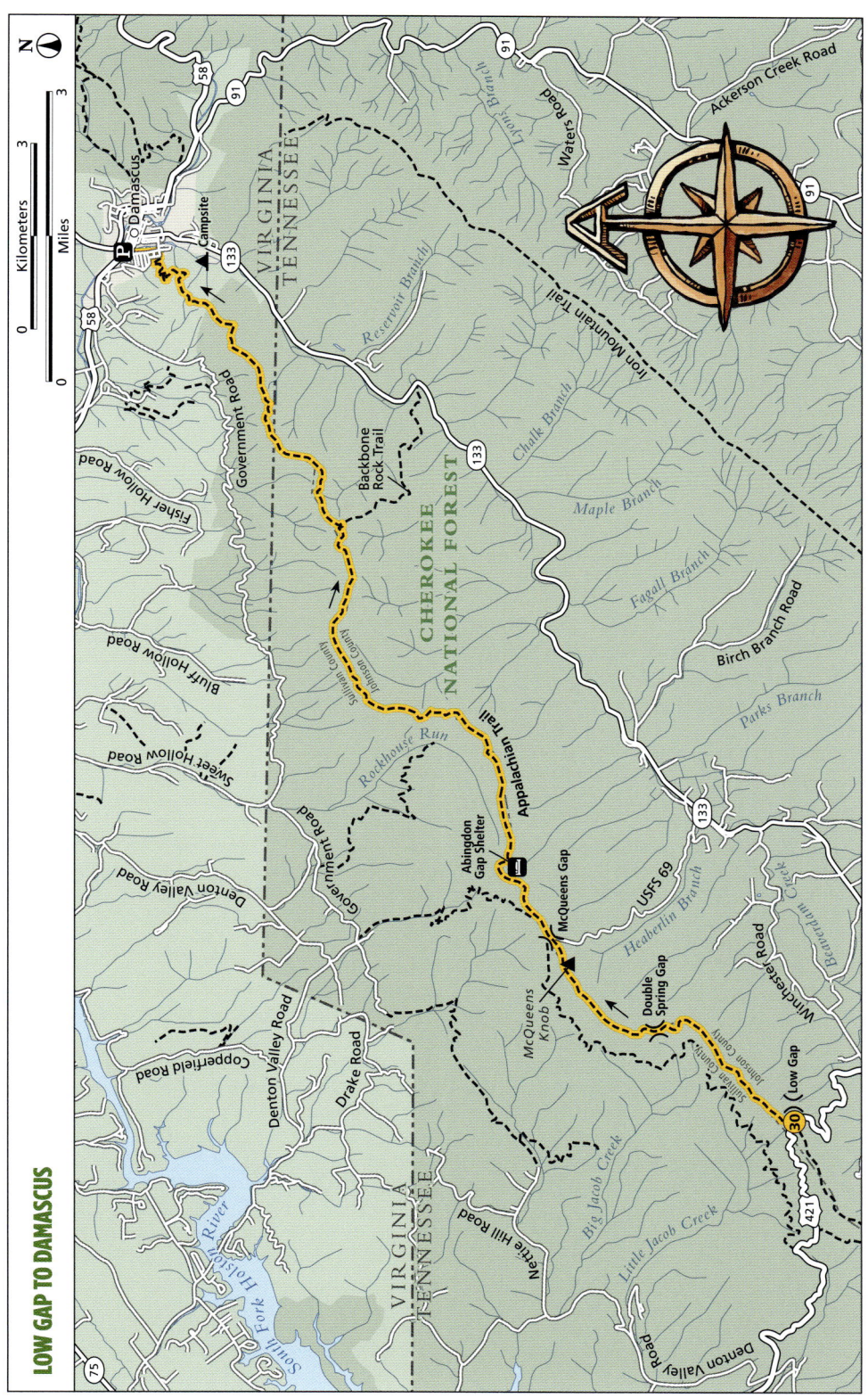

KEY POINTS

SECTION		ELEVATION (FEET)	MILES FROM SPRINGER MOUNTAIN	MILES FROM DAMASCUS
0.0	Low Gap, US 421, piped spring	3,384	456.0	15.0
1.4	Stone wall parallels AT	3,565	457.4	13.6
2.9	Double Spring Gap	3,538	458.8	13.1
2.3	Weak spring	3,638	457.9	13.1
3.3	McQueens Knob	3,900	459.3	11.7
3.7	McQueens Gap, USFS 69	3,680	459.7	11.3
4.8	Abingdon Gap Shelter, piped spring 0.2 mile behind shelter	3,786	460.8	10.2
9.9	Backbone Rock Trail, 2.3 miles east to USFS recreation area	3,481	465.9	5.1
11.3	Tennessee–Virginia border	3,234	467.3	3.7
12.3	Campsite	2,782	468.3	2.7
12.9	Spring 0.1 mile east on blue-blazed trail	2,758	468.9	2.1
15.0	Water Street, Damascus, Virginia; welcome sign arch	1,925	471.0	0.0

TRAIL TOWN: DAMASCUS, VIRGINIA

Damascus, Virginia, stands out as a quintessential Appalachian Trail town where the AT weaves right through the heart of the community. Designated an Appalachian Trail Community by the ATC in 2010, this welcoming town offers hikers a rich blend of outdoor adventure, history, and hospitality. Known as the "Friendliest Town on the Appalachian Trail," Damascus lives up to its reputation with a supportive trail community and a host of amenities and events for hikers. Each spring, the town hosts the **Damascus Trail Days** celebration, a lively festival featuring trail-oriented vendors, live music, and opportunities to connect with fellow hikers and outdoor enthusiasts.

Located 20 miles south of Abingdon, Virginia, Damascus was a major railroad hub in the early 1900s, playing a vital role in connecting the region with larger cities. Today it is known for its friendly community and vibrant outdoor culture, offering a perfect retreat for hikers and adventurers.

After a long hike, you can relax at the **Damascus Trail Center**, the hub for trail enthusiasts, where you can find up-to-date trail conditions, pick up AT hangtags, and attend various training workshops. For all your hiking needs, **Damascus Outfitters** offers a selection of gear, supplies, and hiker-friendly foods, while **The Place Hostel** provides accommodations, resupply options, and shuttle services. You can also find essentials at **Mt. Rogers Outfitters** and take care of mailing needs at the **Damascus Post Office**.

If you're looking for a place to stay, consider **Brinkwaters** for modern, comfortable accommodations, or choose from one of the area's many charming bed-and-breakfasts. Explore the natural beauty of the **Virginia Creeper Trail**, a 34.3-mile scenic trail starting right in town, perfect for biking or hiking. Visit **Backbone Rock Recreation Area** to see a historic railroad tunnel and stunning rock formations, or check out the nearby **Appalachian Folk School**, run by Warren Doyle, ALDHA founder and AT Hall of Fame inductee, offering educational programs and workshops about the Appalachian Trail and outdoor skills.

For the latest information on resources, events, and trail conditions, visit www.damascus.org.

RESOURCES

The Appalachian Trail Conservancy
www.appalachiantrail.org

   The ATC collaborates closely with the National Park Service, thirty-one volunteer maintaining clubs, and various other partners to actively involve the public in conserving this vital American resource. Their website offers a wealth of information on trail history, conservation efforts, hike planning, volunteer opportunities, and current trail conditions. Consider joining or donating to support the ATC in their important mission.

Contact your local club for volunteer opportunities:

Georgia
Georgia Appalachian Trail Club: georgia-atclub.org

North Carolina
Carolina Mountain Club: carolinamountainclub.org
Nantahala Hiking Club: nantahalahikingclub.org

Tennessee
Smoky Mountains Hiking Club: smhclub.org
Tennessee Eastman Hiking & Canoeing Club: tehcc.org

APPALACHIAN TRAIL COMMUNITIES: CONNECTING TRAIL AND TOWN

For hikers, trail towns offer more than just pit stops; they are lifelines providing essential services such as resupply, medical care, and opportunities to rest and connect with fellow travelers. These communities form a vital support network that aids hikers in completing their journeys, whether for a few days, weeks, or months, and enables them to experience the full potential of the Appalachian Trail.

The A.T. Community program is an initiative by the Appalachian Trail Conservancy aimed at building mutually beneficial relationships with towns and counties along the AT. This program focuses on boosting local economies, enhancing trail protection, and inspiring a new generation of volunteers. The program's focus on building these connections ensures that trail towns continue to serve as key hubs for the hiking community, enriching the trail experience for all. Listed below are the towns along the southern region of the AT that have been designated by the ATC as an official A.T. Community.

Southern Appalachian Trail

- Ellijay, Georgia
- Dahlonega, Georgia
- Blairsville, Georgia
- Suches, Georgia
- Helen, Georgia
- Clayton, Georgia
- Hiawassee, Georgia
- Franklin, North Carolina
- Fontana Dam, North Carolina
- Hot Springs, North Carolina
- Erwin, Tennessee
- Roan Mountain, Tennessee

Virginia

- Damascus, Virginia

GLOSSARY OF TRAIL TERMS

Thru-hiker language is interesting and, like all aspects of culture, is always evolving. Sooner or later, you may find yourself platinum-blazing a flip-flop with an aqua-blaze in the middle.
—Liz "Snorkel" Thomas, *Backpacker* magazine

"The Trail Provides": A phrase meaning that in emergencies or difficult situations, a hiker's needs will somehow be met.

aqua-blaze: To bypass a section of the AT by watercraft (e.g., canoe, kayak, raft).

AT: Appalachian National Scenic Trail.

ATC: Appalachian Trail Conservancy, the organization that oversees the maintenance of, conservation on, and advocacy for the preservation of the AT. Their headquarters is in Harpers Ferry, West Virginia.

CCC: Civilian Conservation Corps, a public work relief program that operated from 1933 to 1942. The CCC helped build the AT and many shelters.

chostle: A hostel housed in a church

flip-flop: To thru-hike the entire AT but in a noncontiguous manner.

GAME: An acronym used by northbound thru-hikers meaning "Georgia to Maine," often written as "GA→ME."

gorp: Nickname for "trail mix."

hiker legs: Strong legs capable of climbing mountains and taking long walks.

HYOH: "Hike Your Own Hike."

Nero: A day where a few miles are hiked during a long-distance hike. Short for "Nearly Zero."

NOBO: "Northbound." Often used to describe someone traveling north on the AT.

platinum-blazing: Elevating the traditional AT journey by indulging in premium experiences, such as luxury lodging, gourmet meals, and curated side trips.

purist: Someone who hikes every tiny inch of the AT, careful not to miss a single blaze.

section-hiker: Someone who hikes the Appalachian Trail in pieces, often over the course of several years.

shakedown: The act of combing through your gear, determining what is absolutely necessary for your hike. Often done by an expert hiker.

slackpacking: Hiking without a full pack during a multiday trip. Generally "slackpackers" hand off their pack to someone while they complete a section of the trail unencumbered by their backpack.

SOBO: "Southbound." Often used to describe someone traveling south on the AT.

the bubble: A large group of hikers traveling in the same direction. Commonly used when talking about the "NOBO and SOBO thru-hiker bubbles."

thru-hiker: Someone who hikes the entire AT in one season.

trail angel: Someone who shows kindness to hikers, often by giving rides into town or gifting food or cold drinks without asking anything in return. (See *trail magic*.)

trail magic: Any act of kindness or gift bestowed on hikers, including water, meals, transportation, lodging, or even money.

trail maintainer: Someone, usually a volunteer, who cares for a section of the AT.

trail name: A special nickname adopted by long-distance backpackers, a tradition on the AT and many other trails.

trailblazer: Someone who hikes. Someone who sets his/her own path or makes way for others.

tramily: "Trail family," those you spend a significant amount of time hiking with.

Triple Crown: Achievement of thru-hiking the Appalachian Trail (AT), Pacific Crest Trail (PCT), and Continental Divide Trail (CDT).

yellow-blazing: Using the highway to bypass a section of the AT, either by walking, hitchhiking, or driving. "Yellow blaze" is a reference to yellow dashes on the road.

zero day: A day when 0 miles are hiked. Generally spoken of when thru-hikers take a "day off" in town.

SOURCES

Adkins, Leonard M. *Nature of the Appalachian Trail: Your Guide to Wildlife, Plants, and Geology*, second edition. Menasha Ridge Press, 1998.

Anderson, Larry. *Peculiar Work: Writing about Benton MacKaye, Conservation, Community*. Quicksand Chronicles, 2012; revised 2013.

Appalachian Trail Conservancy. "ATC History." Appalachian Trail Conservancy, 2021. appalachiantrail.org/our-work/about-us/atc-history/. Accessed February 20, 2024.

Bartram, William. *Travels*. 1791. Documenting the American South, University of North Carolina at Chapel Hill. https://docsouth.unc.edu/nc/bartram/summary.html. Accessed July 17, 2024.

"BearWise: A Program of the Southeastern Association of Fish and Wildlife Agencies." *BearWise*, Southeastern Association of Fish and Wildlife Agencies. https://bearwise.org. Accessed March 7, 2024.

Birchard, William, Jr., and Robert Proudman. *Appalachian Design, Construction, and Maintenance*, second edition. Appalachian Trail Conference, 2000.

Chazin, Daniel D., ed. *Appalachian Trail Data Book*, forty-sixth edition. Appalachian Trail Conservancy, 2024.

Clark, Sandra H. B. *Birth of the Mountains: The Geological Story of the Southern Appalachian Mountains*. CreateSpace Independent Publishing Platform, 2014.

Earl Shaffer Foundation. *Walking with Spring*. Appalachian Trail Conference, 2004.

Foster, Steven, and James A. Duke. *Peterson Field Guide to Medicinal Plants and Herbs of Eastern Central North America*, third edition. Houghton Mifflin Harcourt, 2014.

Gove, Doris. *Exploring the Appalachian Trail: Hikes in the Southern Appalachians*. Stackpole Books, 1998.

Hasler, Vic, ed. A*ppalachian Trail Guide to Tennessee–North Carolina*, fifteenth edition. Appalachian Trail Conservancy, 2016.

Johnson, Thomas R. *From Dream to Reality: History of the Appalachian Trail*. Appalachian Trail Conservancy, 2021.

Jones Decker, Sarah. *The Appalachian Trail Backcountry Shelters, Lean-tos, and Huts*. Rizzoli, 2020.

MacKaye, Benton. "An Appalachian Trail: A Project in Regional Planning." *Journal of the American Institute of Architects*, 1921.

McDaniel, Lynda. *Highroad Guide to the North Carolina Mountains*. Longstreet Press, Inc, 1998.

Miller, David. *The A.T. Guide*. Wilmington, NC: AntiGravityGear, LLC, 2024.

National Geographic Society. *The Appalachian Trail*. The National Geographic Society, 1972.

National Park Service. "Black Bears." *National Park Service*, US Department of the Interior, 2 August 2022. https://www.nps.gov/grsm/learn/nature/black-bears.htm. Accessed July 16, 2024.

Opler, Paul A. *Peterson First Guide to Butterflies and Moths of North America*. Houghton Mifflin Harcourt Publishing Company, 1994.

Roosevelt, Franklin D. *The Public Papers and Addresses of Franklin D. Roosevelt. 1940 Volume: War and Aid to Democracies: With a Special Introduction and Explanatory Notes By President Roosevelt*. Macmillan, 1941.

Sylvester, Robert, ed. *Appalachian Trail Thru-Hiker's Companion*. The Appalachian Long Distance Hikers Association, Inc., 2022.

"Wayah Bald," Blue Ridge National Heritage Area. www.blueridgeheritage.com/destinations/wayah-bald/. Accessed July 16, 2024.

Weidensaul, Scott. *Mountains of the Heart: A Natural History of the Appalachians*, twentieth anniversary edition. Fulcrum Publishing, 2016.

Whisnant, Anne Mitchell. "The Blue Ridge Parkway: About the Parkway." *Documenting the American South*. University of North Carolina at Chapel Hill, n.d.. https://docsouth.unc.edu/blueridgeparkway/about/about_parkway/parkway/. Accessed July 17, 2024.

Williams, Lisa, Don O'Neal, William Van Horn, and Richard J Ketelle, eds. *Appalachian Trail Guide to North Carolina–Georgia*, fifteenth edition. Appalachian Trail Conservancy, 2016.

ABOUT THE AUTHORS

Amber, Josh, Indie, and River Niven at Amicalola Falls

Amber and Joshua Niven are coauthors of *Discovering the Appalachian Trail: A Guide to the Trail's Greatest Hikes*. They reside in Madison County, North Carolina, with a view of the Appalachian Trail in the distance. They can often be spotted in Hot Springs, having a beer at the local brewery, or hiking with their two children, River Axel and Indie Oaks.

Amber Adams Niven grew up in the heart of the Great Smoky Mountains, where she developed a deep love for nature and hiking at an early age. She has backpacked more than 1,400 miles of the Appalachian Trail from Maine to Virginia, as well as many other miles in the surrounding region. In addition to writing and hiking, Amber enjoys teaching yoga and facilitating creative workshops. Visit her at amberadamsniven.com.

Joshua Niven was born in Germany and raised in the hills surrounding Charlotte, North Carolina. Joshua graduated from the Savannah College of Art and Design with a degree in photography in 2012. He completed the entire Appalachian Trail on foot in 2013 and self-published a photography book with more than 150 images he made during his thru-hike. In addition to making artwork, Joshua owns and operates Asheville Fine Art Printing, where he helps reproduce and facilitate other artists' work. Visit him at www.joshuaniven.com.

FALCONGUIDES®

MAKE ADVENTURE YOUR STORY™

Since 1979, FalconGuides has been a trailblazer in defining outdoor exploration. Elevate your journey with contributions by top outdoor experts and enthusiasts as you immerse yourself in a world where adventure knows no bounds.

Our expansive collection spans the world of outdoor pursuits, from hiking and foraging guides to books on environmental preservation and rockhounding. Unleash your potential as we outfit your mind with unparalleled insights on destinations, routes, and the wonders that await your arrival.

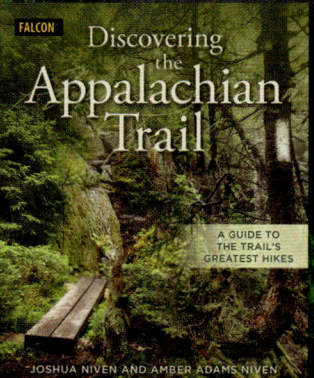
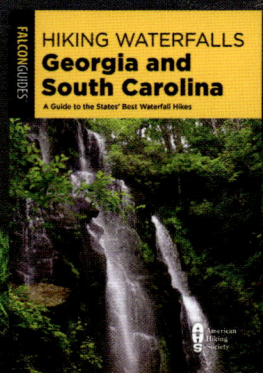
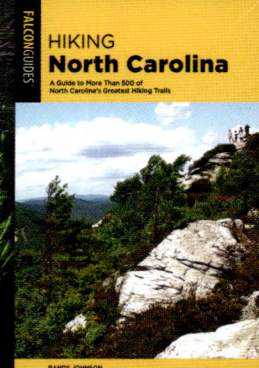

LET FALCON BE YOUR GUIDE

Available wherever books are sold.
Orders can also be placed at www.globepequot.com,
by phone at (800) 223-2336,
or by email at Purchaseorders@simonandschuster.com.